PUBLIC RELATIONS
PROMOTIONS,
AND FUND-RAISIN
FOR ATHLETIC AN
PHYSICAL EDUCAT
PROGRAMS

PUBLIC RELATIONS, PROMOTIONS, AND FUND-RAISING FOR ATHLETIC AND PHYSICAL EDUCATION PROGRAMS

ROBERT T. BRONZAN
San Jose State University
San Jose, California

JOHN WILEY & SONS

New York   Santa Barbara   London   Sydney   Toronto

To my wife,
Jo Ann

GV
714
.B76

Library of Congress Cataloging in Publication Data:

Bronzan, Robert T.
    Public relations, promotions, and fund-raising for athletic and physical education programs.

    Bibliography: p.
    Includes index.
    1. Public relations—Sports. 2. Fund raising.
3. School sports—Finance. 4. College sports—Finance.
I. Title.

GV714.B76   659.2′9′7960973   76-10950
ISBN 0-471-01540-7

Printed in the United States of America

10 9 8 7 6 5 4 3 2 1

PREFACE

Intercollegiate and interscholastic athletic programs in the United States are unique phenomena. Nowhere else in the world do educational institution-sponsored competitive sports exist in an identical manner or to the same magnitude.

The long and exciting history of intercollegiate athletic programs is testimony that this facet of our culture satisfies both psychological and sociological needs of both youths and adults. Numerous attempts have been made to either eliminate or diminish competitive sports in our colleges and schools. Most of these attempts have never succeeded; others have had minimal or temporary success.

Fortunately or unfortunately, intercollegiate athletics started without

v

the sanction or financial support of educational institutions. The notion that intercollegiate athletics should be totally or substantially self-supporting has persisted from the earliest informal athletic contest.

In order to sustain or improve the intercollegiate athletic programs, the application of the most sophisticated and advanced knowledge of public relations, promotions, and fund-raising is required. Within the past thirty years (since the end of World War II), there has been a steady increase in emphasis on these support programs. This has been due, in part, to rapidly rising costs of operations, expansion of athletic programs, construction of campus facilities for athletics, and severe reductions in financial support from government funds.

Intercollegiate athletics is confronted with vigorous competition for the entertainment dollar. Although national attendance figures for inter-collegiate athletic events continue to increase, neither the greater number of spectators nor higher ticket prices are adequate for maintaining the quality of programs at their maximum levels or for improving them. Major competition for public interest and involvement are television, professional sports, participation sports, travel, and recreational activities. Simultaneously, student financial support of the intercollegiate athletics program has dropped. On some campuses the withdrawal of student government appropriations has been absolute; on other campuses partial but substantial reductions of support have been experienced.

Many administrators of intercollegiate athletic programs have been and remain philosophically opposed to organized and emphasized public relations, promotions, and fund-raising activities. Their point of view can be vigorously defended. However, the harsh reality of choosing between two alternatives must be confronted: the intercollegiate athletic program, as it has been known, will either live or perish with the absence or presence of well-planned and well-conducted public relations, promotions, and fund-raising programs.

The author assumes that the intercollegiate athletic programs characteristic in the vast majority of our institutions of higher education should be—must be—retained. Furthermore, intercollegiate athletics will thrive only if the departments of athletics organize and implement quality programs in public relations, promotions, and fund-raising.

Although the public high schools and community colleges do not, at present, face identical problems with their interscholastic or intercollegiate athletic programs as the four-year institutions, they, too, have a real need and concern for improving their public relations, promotions, and fund-raising activities. Their public relations and promotions pro-

grams needs are more similar, at this time, to the senior institutions than their fund-raising requirements.

Intercollegiate and interscholastic athletics are extensions of physical education; they are accommodations for the advanced physical education student. American success in intercollegiate and international sports competition is due to a great measure to the physical education programs that provide superior instruction and experiences in basic sports skills.

Yet, it is not only the advanced physical education student that is of concern to the knowledgeable professional educator and lay-person. Their major concern is to provide every student with maximum opportunities, facilities, and leadership in physical education activities so that each may derive maximum physiological, psychological, and sociological benefits. Recent inroads on physical education programs are signals that greater stress must be placed on both the quality of the physical education programs and public relations.

Everyone interested in or responsible for intercollegiate or interscholastic athletics and physical education programs will find valuable, detailed ideas and motivation in this book. Specifically, those persons affiliated with a college or university who will find the contents interesting and beneficial include the: Chief Executive Officer or President, University Development Officer, Director of Athletics, Sports Public Relations Director, Athletic Business Manager, Director of Development or Foundation, Board of Trustees, Development or Foundation Board of Directors, Coaches of all sports, Director of Physical Education, Physical Education Instructors, Athletic Trainer, Alumni Director, and Alumni Board of Directors.

Those affiliated with a high school who will benefit greatly from careful reading of this book include the: Superintendent, Board of Education, Associate Superintendents, Principals, Supervisors of Athletics, Supervisors of Physical Education, Director of Athletics, Director of Physical Education, Coaches of all sports, Teachers of Physical Education, Booster Club Officers, and Public Relations Officer.

The American system of competitive athletics and physical education programs conducted by its educational institutions is unique and unparalleled anywhere in the world. Every effort should be made to preserve and enhance this system. This book is dedicated to these aims.

ROBERT T. BRONZAN
January, 1977

ACKNOWLEDGMENTS

Grateful appreciation is expressed to friends and colleagues who have contributed in countless ways that resulted in the content, preparation, and publication of this book.

Special thanks are extended to the following outstanding Directors of Intercollegiate Athletics who willingly shared their ideas, information, experiences, and programs related to public relations, promotions and fund-raising for the purpose of aiding the continuance and improvement of intercollegiate athletics at all collegiate institutions:

University of Alabama   Samuel Bailey
Arizona State University   Fred Miller

University of Arkansas   Frank Broyles
Bellevue Community College   James Harryman
Boise State University   Lyle Smith
Boston College   William Flynn
University of California,
    Irvine   Raymond Thornton
Clemson University   H. C. McLellan
Drake University   Robert Karnes
Duke University   Carl James
East Carolina University   Clarence Stasavich
University of Florida   Raymond Graves
Florissant Valley Community
    College   William Miller
University of Houston   Harry Fouke
Hutchinson Community Junior
    College   Samuel Butterfield
University of Illinois,
    Urbana-Champaign   Cecil Coleman
Indiana University   J. William Orwig
University of Iowa   Chalmers Elliott
Kansas State University   Ernest Barrett
Kent State University   Michael Lude
Lehigh University   W. B. Leckonby
McNeese State University   Jack Doland
University of Miami,
    Coral Gables   Pete Elliott
University of Minnesota   Paul Giel
Mississippi State University   Charles Shira
Montana State University   Thomas Parac
Mt. Hood Community College   Dutch Triebwasser
University of Nebraska,
    Lincoln   Robert Devaney
University of Nevada, Reno   Richard Trachok
University of North Carolina   Homer Rice
Northeast Louisiana University   William Beall
University of Northern Iowa   Stanley Sheriff
Ohio University   William Rohr
University of Oklahoma   Wade Walker
University of Pacific   Cedric Dempsey
Princeton University   Royce Flippen
Purdue University   George King, Jr.

Rice University	A. M. Bale
Rutgers University, New Brunswick	Frederick Gruninger
South Dakota State University	Stanley Marshall
Temple University	Ernest Casale
Texas Christian University	Abe Martin
University of Utah	James Jack
Utah State University	LaDell Andersen
Vanderbilt University	Clay Stapleton
University of Virginia	Eugene Corrigan
Wake Forest University	Eugene Hooks
Washington State University	Raymond Nagel
University of Wisconsin, Madison	Elroy Hirsch
University of Wisconsin, Milwaukee	Thomas Rosandich

Gratitude is also extended to the many high school coaches and directors of athletics who have contributed, directly or indirectly, to my understanding of public relations at the school level. A special acknowledgment of appreciation is made to more than 200 coaches and administrators of high schools and community colleges whom it has been my privilege to have coached during their collegiate careers and to the many other hundreds of physical educators and coaches who, in the process of completing professional courses I conducted, shaped my philosophy and understanding.

R. T. B.

CONTENTS

PART 1 PUBLIC RELATIONS

1. Public Relations—What It Is............................. 3
2. History of Public Relations and Today's Society............. 7
3. Molding Public Opinion 18
4. The Conduct of Public Relations 26
5. The Internal Publics 46
6. The External Publics................................... 51
7. The School Bond and Public Relations—Relationship to
   Athletic and Physical Education Programs................ 56
8. Educational Institutions and Community Communications..... 64
9. Concepts of Athletic Public Relations 73

xiii

10. Concepts of Physical Education Public Relations **80**
11. Job Description of the Public Relations Practitioner **83**
12. How To Find and Tell What Is New **91**
13. Publicity **98**
14. The Tools of Communication **109**
15. Communications and Public Speaking **119**
16. Public Relations and the Coach or Teacher **124**
17. Unique Athletic Public Relations Activities by Colleges and
    Schools **135**
18. Physical Education Public Relations Activities for Colleges
    and Schools **145**

PART 2 PROMOTIONS

19. Unique Promotional Activities for Athletics by Colleges and
    Universities **153**

PART 3 FUND-RAISING

20. Concepts of Fund-Raising **171**
21. Fund-Raising Activities by Colleges and Universities **215**

APPENDIX

A   Checklist for Staging a Sports Clinic **240**
B   Checklist for Staging a Banquet **244**
C   Checklist for Staging a Conference **252**

Bibliography **259**

Index **263**

PUBLIC RELATIONS, PROMOTIONS, AND FUND-RAISING FOR ATHLETIC AND PHYSICAL EDUCATION PROGRAMS

PART ONE
PUBLIC RELATIONS

CHAPTER ONE
PUBLIC RELATIONS—
WHAT IT IS

Few terms are written or spoken with more frequency each day in the United States than "public relations." Yet "public relations" has different meanings for different people. Reasons for this lack of uniform definition stem largely from two sources. One involves the genesis of public relations—because of earlier practices, predominantly confined to press-agentry and propaganda, many people continue to associate or even equate public relations with these activities. The other cause for confusion results when some persons refer to public relations and they think of a management concept, while others use the term to denote a specialized function, formulated and executed only by professional practitioners.

Adding to the general confusion, public relations, viewed either as a management concept or a specialized practice, is still in the process of becoming totally accepted and perfected. Measured by time, public relations practices date back many centuries. Archeologists have discovered public bulletins that were used as early as 1800 B.C. to advise or warn citizens. Yet, public relations as we know it today is less than a century old; moreover, most of the conceptual advances and refinement of applied methods used in its current practice are products of just the last fifty years.

The lack of universal application of the term public relations is further complicated by a regard for its use as a miracle panacea to any vexing situation. For example, when there is any form of misunderstanding or lack of knowledge between two or more persons or groups, the popular remedy prescribed to heal the breach is public relations. Likewise, when there is some friction or disenchantment between a public figure or an institution and the public, many persons depend upon public relations to placate emotions and restore a congenial relationship.

There is ample evidence to indicate that attempts are frequently made to substitute public relations for a quality program or product. This misconception of the use and power of public relations is prevalent —although success is seldom, if ever, achieved by following this course.

PUBLIC RELATIONS DEFINED

In order to constructively discuss the scope of public relations, examine its structure, and evaluate its worth, there should be some consensus concerning the meaning of the term. Many practitioners have presented their definitions of public relations; most have been helpful. A brief, practical definition, expressed in behavioral context, has been developed by the *Public Relations News*, a periodical highly regarded by executives in the public relations field and related areas. This definition seems to satisfy most critics; it can be used as a guide for a comprehensive public relations program.

"Public relations is the management function which evaluates public attitudes, identifies the policies and procedures of an individual or an organization with the public interest, and executes a program of action to earn public understanding and acceptance."

Hereafter, use of the term public relations in this text will correspond to the above definition.

A critical examination of this definition and an interpretation of its content are important for a clear, complete understanding of what public relations really is. To facilitate this analysis, the definition is separated into its key parts.

Public relations is a *management function*. Stated in other words, public relations is not a task or operation to be fully delegated to a lower echelon in an institution or organization. Instead, it is assigned to the top management level where policies and programs are developed and administered.

Public relations cannot flourish or produce desired results unless it systematically and purposively *evaluates public attitudes*. A good public relations program does not depend upon whims, guesses, or wishful thinking. Rather, the foundation upon which a productive, ongoing public relations program operates is in-depth data pertaining to specific publics that is derived from selected instruments used skillfully by an expert.

Public relations should be sensitive to the vital relationships between an individual or an organization, and, in so acting, *identifies* the policies, procedures, programs, and products of an individual or an institution *with the public interest*. This consideration for public interest is what largely differentiates public relations objectives from those of press-agentry, propaganda, or advertising.

The next element of the definition is one that *executes a program of action*. This area is the realm of the professional public relations expert or practitioner. Expertise is required for the selection of the proper tools or techniques of communication best suited for a specific purpose or objective. At this point, the public relations expert may be granted free rein to do what is considered proper and productive, or, in some cases, these plans are submitted to higher authorities for approval and support.

The purposes of the foregoing steps in a public relations program are to *earn public understanding and acceptance*. Emphasis is directed to the methods for gaining understanding and acceptance; these must be "earned" in order to be of lasting value. When public understanding and acceptance are attained, only then can a person or institution be justifiably proud of their public relations program.

THE NEED FOR PUBLIC RELATIONS

No public institution or individual can enjoy major success for a prolonged period without public support or sanction. Once these are achieved, then it becomes somewhat easier to sustain them by the constant application of sound public relations. A word of caution is in order.

Because public support or sanction have been attained at a given time, this is no assurance that they will continue to exist on their own impetus. For this reason, public relations is an ongoing, ever-changing, and adaptive process. To let up or to cease a public relations program is the prelude to failure.

Public relations in a modern, industrial society is a necessity. It is no longer a question of whether or not a public relations program should or should not be conducted but rather what kind of public relations program should be adopted. The very nature of a complex urban environment requires that public relations be vigorously exercised by all persons and institutions that are of public interest, have public responsibilities, or depend upon public support. This includes both profit and nonprofit entities. While it is more obvious that commercial enterprises, governmental agencies, and public utilities must conduct satisfactory public relations programs, it is equally important for colleges and schools to sponsor and operate public relations programs of the highest quality.

During America's formative years, public relations was usually limited to an informal, one-to-one relationship. As an agrarian country with only a few cities of moderate-size population, there was little or no need for organized public relations. The farmer, printer, and general store owner were on a first-name basis. School enrollments were small. Teachers and administrators were known personally by the majority of the citizens residing in the school district. School affairs and issues were regular subjects that were discussed by two persons or small informal groups. School public relations was, in a real sense, practiced daily, as were those of other public concern.

As the nation matured, population swelled, industrialization developed, and urbanization resulted, there became a corresponding need for all segments of the new society to devise new techniques in order to communicate with their counterparts. No longer was it feasible or possible to depend upon interpersonal relationships as a means of communicating needs, interests, information, services, or products. The use of indirect communication through the application of audio or visual aids became necessary in order to contact or reach the large numbers of persons who might have or should have a concern with a specific message. As the competition increased among those entities that sought to have their messages received and favorably acted upon, a new field of varied techniques and strategies developed to maximize this process. The inevitable outcome of this competition led to the need and subsequent development of modern public relations as both an art and a profession.

CHAPTER TWO
HISTORY OF PUBLIC
RELATIONS AND
TODAY'S SOCIETY

In a very real sense, public opinion dates back to the first time two or more members of the human race exchanged ideas, plans, or products. Although it was not until the eighteenth century that the term "public opinion" was coined, the acknowledgement of its existence and importance extends as far back as 1800 B.C. Early civilizations have left evidence of its use. The early Greek orator and philosopher Demosthenes employed publicity in his efforts to stimulate and organize resistance against the conqueror, Philip of Macedonia, by channeling public opinion. Julius Caesar had at his disposal overwhelming resources of men and materials to expand and maintain the Roman Empire. Yet, he relied heavily upon propaganda to lessen resistance from people whose lands he sought. The Roman Catholic Church acknowledged the importance of public opinion in the seventeenth century when it established its College of Propaganda.

AMERICA AND PUBLIC RELATIONS

America has been the unique setting for advanced public relations since the Revolutionary War. American Revolutionists utilized many of the techniques that are still employed to arouse people's emotions and to mold their opinions. The well-known modern flier was produced and widely distributed throughout the Colonies, inciting people to rise up against the British. Public gatherings in the form of town hall meetings were used. Banners, posters, and slogans were popular techniques for creating interest, curiosity, and support. Leaders of this movement, such as Samuel Adams, Thomas Paine, Alexander Hamilton, Thomas Jefferson, and Benjamin Franklin, recognized the power and influence of propaganda to stimulate interest and generate support for their cause. A classic example of a staged event to dramatize a particular situation and shape public opinion was the Boston Tea Party, the product of the fertile mind of Samuel Adams.

PUBLIC RELATIONS AND POLITICS

As the nation was maturing after the Civil War, new problems and issues arose, as did the need to shape or direct public opinion. President Andrew Jackson, who lacked communicative skills, realized this need. Consequently, he obtained the services of Amos Kendall, a former Kentucky newspaper editor. Kendall was a trusted friend and Jackson relied heavily upon him to help mold national policies. To do this, Kendall was assigned to write newspaper articles, speeches, and official news releases. Yet, Kendall was not one to merely depend upon the force of the office he represented in order to have his messages received and followed. He was guided by his own structured public opinion polls—probably the first major application of this instrument. Further, he systematically analyzed newspaper content and editorial comment to determine the mood of the public. His motive for both of these approaches was to learn what people wanted. Then, at his advice, Jackson gave them what they wanted. To dramatize Jackson's actions, Kendall contrived and manipulated press conferences, staged events, organized political rallies, and supervised political party activities. Throughout the entire process, Kendall realized the need for anonymity, and for this reason conducted the scenario from backstage.

Kendall's creative mind and awareness of the potential power of public opinion led to the formation of the Office of Information, which was innocuously attached to the Department of Agriculture. He was among the first to recognize that the power base of politics was shifting from the eastern seaboard to the west, and that the accompanying rise of literacy would soon be felt at the voting booth. Many of his basic ideas and concepts are still followed.

PRESS AGENTRY

Phineas T. Barnum reportedly left a fortune of over $4 million. Barnum, the famous circus owner, was the foremost disciple of press-agentry. At mid-nineteenth century his methods were noted for their successful impact. He was an expert at faking and staging events that fanned the spark of curiosity and intensified the public's interest. Although many of his methods were controversial, bizarre, and at times bordered on the edge of mysticism, they were successful in terms of box-office receipts. Many of his techniques and schemes are still employed today, but with more subtlety.

The earliest recorded use of the term *press agent* is found in the 1868 publications of John Robinson's Circus and Menagerie. By 1880, and for the ensuing twenty years, the term was common in show business and the entertainment world. Later, other commercial enterprises copied the use of the term, notably book and magazine publishers. Because of the questionable methods employed by many press agents, editors formed a lowly opinion of these individuals. To some degree, this mistrust and suspicion exists today toward persons associated with promotional activities.

Soon after the close of the Civil War, there was a great rush to construct railroads, expand industries, and develop utilities. The nation underwent a major upheaval and rearrangement in the twenty-five years between 1875 and 1900. During this time, immigrants arrived by the thousands, adding available manpower and limitless vitality to the burgeoning nation. Transportation facilities and equipment were improved and expanded. Communications experienced tremendous changes due to the development of the telegraph system. Mass production of newspapers and magazines found ready markets. The power base of the nation had changed from the plantation baron to the new prince of industry and finance. The frontiersman was replaced by the factory worker. As wealth accumulated and became concentrated, powerful monopolies came into existence. Many of these paid little attention to the common man and his life, and, in many instances, these gigantic commercial enterprises used, misused, and abused the worker. This was literally the era of the attitude of "the public be damned!" Public relations was nonexistent.

The presidential political campaign of 1880 between Tilden and Hayes marked the first time that election literature was produced and distributed in huge volumes. The public was inundated with all forms of pamphlets, bulletins, fliers, posters, and advertisements. This new approach to political campaigning was made possible or advisable by the vast improvements in printing processes, cheap and available paper, new levels of literacy among the masses, and the importance of winning the support of thousands of newly arrived immigrants.

The Brian–McKinley presidential race of 1896 launched new political campaign methods that were to continue for the next sixty years. In fact, much of the format used at that time can be identified today. Both major political parties established headquarters in Chicago. From them came a steady bombardment of pamphlets, banners, posters, press releases, photographs, and general propaganda. These programs left an imprint upon today's political campaign strategies and tactics.

PUBLIC RELATIONS AND CORPORATIONS

As should be expected in a land of freedom, the working class began to resist the tactics and treatment of the huge financial and industrial empires. Their resistance led to many of the social and economic reforms of the early 1900s. Corporations eventually recognized the folly of their former treatment of the general populace, and at the same time they became aware of the self-serving advantages of removing hostility and replacing it with public favor and support. At the turn of the century, two of the nation's most powerful and well-known financiers, Thomas Fortune Ryan and Harry Payne Whitney, employed George Harvey as their public relations manager. Harvey, a former newspaperman and publisher, initiated public relations strategies and tactics that were soon emulated by others. The Mutual Life Insurance Company, for example, was under public scrutiny and attack when Charles J. Smith was engaged in 1888 to prepare newspaper and magazine articles to counteract these effects.

The United States Marine Corps, observant of the successful techniques employed by private enterprise, used advertisements to attract recruits by the time of the Civil War. And, in the Spanish-American War of 1898, Cuban propagandists were successful in generating America's sympathy for Cuba and opposition to Spain. News releases and mass meetings were successfully used to obtain both moral support and funds on their behalf.

The open recognition of the value of public support was exemplified by the American Medical Association when a resolution was passed in 1885 providing news reporters with on-site accommodations and full cooperation in order to facilitate their coverage of transactions at their annual conventions.

FIRST USE OF TERM "PUBLIC RELATIONS"

One of the new giants of commerce was the railroads. The difficulties of reducing public opposition to the construction and operation of railroads, getting public acceptance of the fees charged for transporting passengers and materials, and seeking political favors induced the Association of American Railroads to launch a massive public relations program. In fact, this organization was the first business entity to use the term public relations when it appeared in the 1897 issue of the *Year Book of Railway Literature*.

At the turn of the century, big business was wallowing in its own greed at the expense of the common worker. This treatment of the working class created an atmosphere conducive to a popular revolt. Inspired by Theodore Roosevelt and Senator Robert M. LaFollette and the revealing writings of Upton Sinclair and others regarding the maltreatment of the working class, there came a period of legislative regulations and trust-busting. During this time, nearly all major corporations had lost touch with their publics. To silence the activities of the revisionists, the corporations wanted to use their power to lash out, speak out, and to defend their actions. But they did not have the know how to do this effectively. Their ineptness is shown by their first action. They withdrew advertising from newspapers and magazines until they could be assured of favorable consideration in the publications. While this effort failed to achieve anything positive concerning its objectives, it did lead to the formation of the first advertising agency.

Faced with a general public uprising, big business was at a loss as to what countermeasures to use until the railroads developed their first press bureau. By 1905, railroads had established press bureau headquarters in Boston with branch offices in New York, Chicago, Washing-

ton, St. Louis, and Topeka. Each office was directed by a former newspaperman and staffed with a full complement of employees. Their primary job was to smother public protests with their own articles depicting
railroads in favorable light.

Observing the successes in directing public opinion by the railroads,
other major industries applied the same formula. Typically, an experienced newspaperman was employed to head a press bureau office and
given an adequate staff. Out of these came workers who were called
publicity men. They reeled out millions of words to offset the charges
levied against their employers. When deemed advisable, many of them
staged various kinds of events to create favorable news.

THE NEW CONCEPT OF PUBLIC RELATIONS

While the format of a publicity bureau was adopted and put into use by
most of the large corporations, there was one person who did not restrict
his field to this method of retaliation. He was Ivey Ledbetter Lee, who
has been called the "father of public relations." Originally a business
world reporter, he became engaged as an organizer for a mayoralty campaign in New York City. With this experience and an interest in expanding the scope of his concepts, Lee assumed a position in the press bureau
of the Democratic National Committee during the 1904 campaign. Real-
izing that much of the efforts put forth in press releases would be offset
by the continuing public cynicism and suspicion, Lee carried this lesson
into business. Following the elections he became established as a specialist in publicity for corporations. This was a new approach for the
business world, although the entertainment industry had earlier employed persons in a similar capacity. Lee recognized that corporations
could only win public favor or at least reduce public hostility by following a straightforward policy. Board meetings were no longer to be kept
secret; the public would be apprised of transactions. Financial records of
corporations would be made a matter of public record. Lee was confident
that press agentry would never be a worthy solution to the problems fac-
ing corporations. As might be expected, corporation executives turned
away from his suggestions and recommendations.

Suffering from this rebuff, Lee dissolved his public relations firm in
1906 and became an executive assistant to the president of the Pennsylvania Railroad. This appointment marked the first time a public relations practitioner was appointed to the policy-making level of any major
organization. From this unusual vantage position, Lee conceived and

experimented with various public relations tools and concepts. Leaving the post in 1914, he became a personal advisor to John D. Rockefeller, Jr. Among his chief duties was to eliminate the persistent public animosity toward his employer.

Lee made it clear that publicity and public relations were *not* one and the same, although the term public relations was not used to any meaningful degree until 1919. He convinced others that both public relations and good works were essential for success, a combination that remains the key concept today.

At about the time that Lee was changing the role of public relations, other practitioners of the same period were becoming active. A publicity bureau was opened in 1900 in Boston for the purpose of publicizing Harvard University, Massachusetts Institute of Technology, the Boston Elevated train, and railroads. In 1903, the American Telegraph and Telephone Company engaged a person to do publicity work. Shortly thereafter, the New York Central Railway, Consolidated Gas, and Standard Oil were employing publicists and public relations consultants.

Industrial and financial corporations were not the only entities that underwent a change in attitude and tactics. Changes or adaptations in political campaign methods were made necessary by the changing technological and demographical conditions. The nation was expanding in land size, and the population was multiplying geometrically. Although the newspapers made various technological adaptations, they were unable to cope with ever-changing conditions. A new form of mass communication arrived on the scene; radio broadcasting by the mid-1920s became a popular and effective way of campaigning. Through this new medium, the candidate could create a more personal relationship. The illiterate or the non-English reading voter could be effectively reached. Aside from a personal meeting, the radio became the most persuasive tool. The net result was that campaign efforts and expenditures were adjusted to accommodate this new and potent medium.

President Theodore Roosevelt recognized this potency. He refined the use of the "trial balloon," and, when the readings indicated approval, he utilized the radio extensively to put across his programs and to obtain general support.

PUBLIC RELATIONS AS A PROFESSION

During World War I, President Woodrow Wilson used the agencies of communication to generate and solidify public approval of his programs.

Following World War I, Edward L. Bernays came to the forefront in the field of public relations. Bernays coined the term "public relations counsel"; he wrote the first book on public relations in 1923 and he taught the first course in public relations while a professor at New York University.

Prior to World War I, several major universities and colleges had operating press bureaus. Following the war, the number increased, primarily as an arm of the campus fund-raising programs. The American College Publicity Association was started in 1915; after 1946 it became known as the American College Public Relations Association. It is now called the Council for the Advancement and Support of Education.

In the 1930s and early 1940s, President Franklin Delano Roosevelt's concept and use of public relations provided a sudden acknowledgement and general acceptance of the field. His utilization of public relations to engender public support and acceptance removed any doubt about the effectiveness and value of a well-conceived program.

During World War II, the federal government started the Office of War Information. This public relations program did much to maximize war efforts on the part of citizens in areas of production, conservation of materials, willingness to sacrifice, and overall morale.

Following World War II, there has never been any doubt about the importance of public relations for any public individual or enterprise. Today, businesses, political parties, public and private educational institutions, governmental agencies at all levels, and other areas of human endeavor have not only accepted public relations but rely heavily upon such programs for their success.

In order to complete the evolution of the communications systems, one must examine the television medium. By 1952, television broadcasting was used in full-scale. One of the first areas to capitalize upon this powerful medium was politics. The elections of 1952 and 1956 established this new device in communication as the most potent single development in shaping public opinion. The extension of the geographic dimensions of the nation, the many more millions of people, and the hectic expectations of a candidate made it physically impossible for candidates to cover the nation and be seen, in person, by even a minority of its citizens. Television was a fully acceptable substitute. With television, the candidate could be heard and seen simultaneously. The intimacy provided by the camera allowed people to evaluate the sincerity and conviction of political aspirants. A new era had begun. Today, judicious use of the press, radio, and television is the key to a political office in most instances.

The evolution of the use of mass communication media in politics is easily demonstrated and generally well understood. Because of its proven effectiveness, business, industry, and other profit and nonprofit organizations, including schools and colleges, have adopted virtually the same approach in promoting their products, shaping public opinion, and eliciting public support.

Most of these commercial enterprises and public institutions are too large for executives to supervise all facets of their operations directly. Public relations practitioners are employed to provide top management with supportive evidence as to what people like or dislike, to help chart proper courses of action to satisfy the publics they consider vital, to share their expertise by offering ways and means of tailoring policies, products, or programs to earn maximum public support, and to appropriately interpret for each of their crucial publics their employer's policies, programs, and products.

PUBLIC RELATIONS AND THE EDUCATIONAL SYSTEM

Education is one of the nation's largest enterprises. It is of paramount importance to the public at-large and to its many separate publics. For these reasons, public relations is of vital concern to educational institutions and to their component departments or divisions.

PUBLIC RELATIONS FOR ATHLETICS AND PHYSICAL EDUCATION

Interscholastic athletics and physical education are two areas within the secondary school that are of unusual interest and concern to the general public. Few, if any, other departments or programs in the high school can elicit public approval or disapproval to the same degree. Because these programs are of keen interest to the general public, and particularly to selected publics, the importance of a public relations program on their behalf is crucial.

What has been said concerning interscholastic athletics and physical education can be multiplied when dealing with the same programs at the intercollegiate level. Of the many departments or divisions within a college or university, perhaps none is as sensitive or dependent upon public approval or support for success, and few are as susceptible to attack from outside the campus as these programs.

Because of these precarious conditions, the remaining portions of this text that deal with public relations will present plans, programs, and methods to successfully cope with them.

PUBLIC RELATIONS AND TODAY'S SOCIETY

In reviewing the history of public relations it is abundantly clear that its emergence into a necessary, important facet of American society parallels the growth in industrial, technological, geographical, population, government, education, and competitive marketplace. As our society became more and more complex and interdependent, the scope and importance of public relations also mushroomed. As a modern, technological nation with a high level of affluency and provisions for freedom of choice in all areas, including self-direction, public relations benefits both the producer and consumer.

In order for any public enterprise, profit or nonprofit, to succeed for any reasonable length of time there are certain fundamental premises that need to be fulfilled. Each enterprise must be ready and willing to accept the obligations of public responsibility that are products of an interdependent society. Each enterprise must seek ways and means of communicating with abstract, removed publics over lines that face physical distance, psychological indifference, and various obstacles. Each enterprise is required to seek ways by which it can become fully integrated in the community that it was created to serve.

To fulfill these obligations requires that any organization or enterprise acknowedge several conditions pertaining to public relations; unless and until such acknowledgement is accorded, the chances of conducting any organization or enterprise with success are quite limited. At least three specific concessions are vital to this phenomenon. First, it is essential that the importance of public relations be accepted; second, it is necessary that one recognize that public relations is a function of a highly specialized staff; and, third, it is imperative for management to realize that public relations is a matter of first importance and that public relations must be assigned to the highest echelon.

The fundamental premises upon which modern public relations rests and the acceptance of public relations as a management function have required several decades to achieve.

The societal revolution in America gave natural birth to public relations. There were many influential changes that hastened the growth of public relations, many of which are still in the process of evolution. Perhaps one of the most significant causes for the growth of public relations was the weight of public opinion. In a nation with guarantees of freedom, citizens individually and collectively formed their opinions and reacted accordingly. The realization that public opinions are subject to direction, control, or modification was a strong stimulant for the emergence of public relations.

It is unlikely that any one element of our life can become big and remain apart from others. Quite the contrary—bigness breeds bigness. Labor, agriculture, pressure groups, government, education, communications, entertainment, and all other areas are big. Each needs the other, and each survives through this interdependency.

We have reached the point in our nation's life when public opinion is undoubtedly the most potent force in our arsenal. Public opinion, directly or indirectly, influences the course of human affairs. Therefore, the need and ability to manipulate and influence this force has become of critical importance. And it is this fact that makes the practice of public relations not only mandatory but of utmost value. Public relations, to a great measure, is the conduit through which humans communicate on a local, national, or international level.

CHAPTER THREE
MOLDING PUBLIC
OPINION

Public opinion is one of the most powerful forces in our society. If this concept is accepted, then it is of great importance to investigate the sources of public opinion, what causes public opinion to be whatever it is, how public opinion can be directed and to what extent, and who can be most likely to succeed in guiding public opinion.

Public opinion can be influenced by either pressure or persuasion. The public relation practitioner depends upon the latter. Through the use of various strategies and tactics, the practitioner seeks to neutralize opinions, change them, arouse latent opinions favorably, or conserve or solidify existing opinions. The practitioner is constantly engaged in striving to start, lead, change, speed, or slow waves of public opinion.

PUBLICS

Practitioners recognize that they will seldom deal with the public-at-large. Instead, public opinion is approached through publics. A general public is comprised of many separate, although often interlocked publics. A public is simply a collective noun for a group of individuals who share some common bond or interest. In any town or city, there are many different publics, although any one person may, in fact, be a member of several at any moment.

ATTITUDES AND OPINIONS

An attitude is an inclination to respond in a given way to a given issue or situation. An opinion is the expression of an attitude. Usually, a person's attitude remains latent until an issue or situation arises that affects the public or group to which he or she belongs. An issue is identified as the cause of conflict, frustration, or anxiety. When an issue is confronted, the individual or public assumes a stance and voices their opinion. Public opinion is the combined individual opinions on public issues.

From where do we derive our attitudes? Each person's attitudes are the product of all conscious experiences. The more common and dominant sources of our attitudes are derived from our various social institutions. The culture in which we are reared plays a major role in shaping our attitudes; for many individuals this force is the most influential. Sources that shape our culture are the family, religion, school, economic class, and social class. At different periods in our nation's maturation, certain of these institutions have played significant roles in shaping attitudes. Changes in family life, relevance of religion, purposes of schools and the composition of students attending them, importance of material possessions, and the stigma of social class have occurred and are in a continual state of flux.

MOTIVATIONS FOR CHANGES IN ATTITUDES

Individuals tend to respond differently to the same social pressures and persuasions. Causes for motivation differ. The appeals of certain incentives will be effective to the degree that the individual has the necessary motivational predisposition to respond. Sources of motivation are important, and the successful public relations practitioner not only recognizes this fact but applies this knowledge.

One of the most powerful sources is that of group motivation.

Groups are comprised of persons who are bound together for some common purpose. Whether or not a person's opinion is changed depends to a great degree on the resistance or support the person encounters with his or her group. A group tends to establish standards for its members' behavior.

Another source of motivation is one's personal drives. These include self-preservation (psychological as well as physiological), hunger, security, social acceptance, and sex. Public relations practitioners are aware of these drives or needs, and in planning and executing a public relations program these are in the foreground.

In order to communicate with individuals in groups, messages must be significant and relevant to a particular group interest in a particular situation. Each public is considered an independent or separate target. And, in public relations planning, one does not employ the "shotgun" method of communication in hopes of striking each of many publics in any particular setting. Rather, one uses the proper "rifle" for each target group. It is well-known that a person's group relationships provide the environment for most of the communication one receives and transmits. And, when a person belongs to more than one group or organization, which is typical, he or she will respond more in harmony with the group to which there is the strongest allegiance.

Unorganized groups are crowds or masses. If the individuals represented are attentive to one thing at a given time, they may be said to belong to an unorganized public. Mass advertising relies upon creating mass behavior; for example, encouraging people to dress alike, to wear certain hair styles, to purchase certain items are goals of compelling mass behavior.

IMPORTANCE OF COMMUNICATIONS

To a great extent our opinions are formed by what we see, hear, and read. It is through communications by which experiences and attitudes are shared, and it is this process that determines our social life. Communications includes all the symbols identified by the mind, the means of conveying them to others, and the processes of preserving them. In order to reach, understand, or influence another, communication is necessary. This obviously simple fact is the hub of public relations.

Our hustling, energetic, and competitive society gives rise to public relations programs from all directions. Everyone is seeking attention and approval. At the same time, each individual has less and less time, attention, and energy to give to more and more demands. One learns to ration time, attention, and energy to those things deserving of support. Appeals based upon known motivational sources and incentives usually have the most success in capturing attention and eventually support.

In addition to satisfying basic motives and incentives, people tend to react to external forces. To varying degrees, persons are influenced by authorities, a respected individual, a popular idol, or others; seldom does one choose a direction based upon research or logical deduction. This circumstance exists largely because life is very complicated—there is little time available to do otherwise.

LAWS OF PUBLIC OPINION
The meaning and content of public opinion has been of great interest to practitioners. Efforts to analyze the phenomena that create or change public opinion have resulted in several accepted "laws." Several of these are:*

1 Opinion is highly sensitive to important events.

2 Events of unusual magnitude are likely to swing public opinion temporarily from one extreme to another. Opinion does not become stabilized until the implications of events are seen with some perspective.

3 Opinion is generally determined more by events than by words—unless those words are themselves interpreted as "events."

4 Verbal statements and outlines of course of action have maximum importance when opinion is unstructured, when people are suggestible and seek some interpretation from a reliable source.

5 By and large, public opinion does not anticipate emergencies—it only reacts to them.

6 Psychologically, opinion is basically determined by self-interest. Events, words, or any other stimuli affect opinion only in so far as their relationship to self-interest is apparent.

7 Opinion does not remain aroused for any long period of time unless people feel their self-interest is acutely involved or unless opinion aroused by words is sustained by events.

8 Once self-interest is involved, opinions are not easily changed.

* Hadley Cantril, *Gauging Public Opinion* (Princeton, N.J.: Princeton University Press, 1944), pp. 226–30. Copyright 1944 © 1972. Reprinted by permission of Princeton University Press.

9 When an opinion is held by a slight majority or when opinion is not solidly structured, an accomplished fact tends to shift opinion in the direction of acceptance.

10 At critical times, people become more sensitive to the adequacy of their leadership—if they have confidence in it, they are willing to assign more than usual responsibility to it; if they lack confidence in it, they are less tolerant than usual.

11 People are less reluctant to have critical decisions made by their leaders if they feel that somehow they, the people, are taking some part in the decision.

12 People have more opinions and are able to form opinions more easily with respect to goals than with respect-to methods necessary to reach those goals.

13 Public opinion, like individual opinion, is colored by desire. And when opinion is based chiefly on desire rather than information, it is likely to show especially sharp shifts with events. The more enlightened people are to the implication of events and proposals for their own self-interest, the more likely they are to agree with the more objective opinions of realistic experts.

PRINCIPLES OF PERSUASION

Persuasion is the approach used to effect public opinion. It is important for anyone dealing with the shaping of public opinion to be familiar with some of the principles of persuasion. Cutlip* has condensed principles from a number of sources and arranged them into a concise, logical manner, as follows.

1 To accomplish attitude change, a suggestion for change must first be received and accepted. "Acceptance of the message" is a critical factor in persuasive communication.

2 The suggestion is more likely to be accepted if it meets existing personality needs and drives, if it is in harmony with group norms and loyalties, and if the source is perceived as trustworthy and expert.

3 A suggestion in the mass media coupled with face-to-face reinforcement is more likely accepted than a suggestion carried by either alone, other things being equal.

4 Change in attitude is more likely to occur if the suggestion is accompanied by other factors underlying belief and attitude. This often refers to a changed environment that makes acceptance easier.

* Scott M. Cutlip and Allen H. Center, *Effective Public Relations*, 2nd Ed. (Engle-wood Cliffs, N.J.: Prentice-Hall, Inc., 1958), p. 72.

5 There probably will be more opinion change in the desired direction if conclusions are explicitly stated than if the audience is left to draw its own conclusions.

6 When the audience is friendly, or when only one position will be presented, or when immediate but temporary opinion change is wanted, it is more effective to give only one side of an argument.

7 When the audience disagrees, or when it is probable that it will hear the other side from another source, it is more effective to present both sides of the argument.

8 When equally attractive opposing views are presented one after another, the one presented last will probably be more effective.

9 Sometimes emotional appeals are more influential; sometimes factual ones are. It depends on the kind of message and the kind of audience.

10 A strong threat is generally less effective than a mild threat in inducing desired opinion change.

11 The desired opinion change may be more measurable some time after exposure to the communication than right after exposure.

12 The people you want most in your audience are least likely to be there. This is the censorship of attention the individual invokes.

13 There is a "sleeper effect" in communications received from sources the listener regards as having low credibility. In some tests, time has tended to wash out the distributed source and leave information behind

BASIC PRINCIPLES OF OPINION CHANGE

Counselor Earl Newsom has effectively taken some observations of public opinion and adapted them into some basic principles that are worthy guides. Cutlip* has extracted these principles from Newsom's published addresses and added his own interpolations. These basic principles are:

1 *Identification Principle:* People will ignore an idea, an opinion, a point of view unless they see clearly that it affects their personal fears or desires, hopes or aspirations.

Application: Your message must be stated in terms of the interest of your audience.

2 *Action Principle:* People do not buy ideas separated from action—either action taken or about to be taken by the sponsor of the idea, or action that people themselves can conveniently take to prove the merit of the idea.

---

* *Ibid*, pp. 72–73.

Application: Unless a means of action is provided people, they tend to shrug off appeals to action.

3   *Principle of Familiarity and Trust:*   We, the people, buy ideas only from those we trust; we are influenced by, or adopt, only those opinions or points of view put forward by individuals, corporations, or institutions in whom we have confidence.

Application: Unless the receiver has confidence in the sender he is not likely to listen or to believe.

4   *Clarity Principle:*   The situation must be clear to us, not confusing. The thing we observe, read, see, hear, and the thing that produces our impressions must be *clear*, not subject to several interpretations.

Application: To communicate you must employ words, symbols, stereotypes that the receiver understands and comprehends.

The foregoing "laws" and "principles" of public opinion apply to nearly all institutions, organizations, or firms. In the commercial competitive world, the extent of success in the application of these approaches is reflected on the profit and loss statement; in the areas of governmental, political, and educational interests, their successful use is noted by the vitality, vigor, and longevity of each.

ROLE OF PUBLIC RELATIONS AND
FORMING OPINIONS

Public opinion is either passive, negative, or positive on most issues. The aim of public relations is to influence the indifferent or neutral persons. One of the most productive ways to influence passive elements is to prove to them that the issue affects their own welfare. Public relations has the responsibility of generating affirmative action on the basis that it is in the interest of the individual. Personalizing the issues usually generates action and support. One of the basic methods to maximize this effect is to first capture the interest, enthusiasm, and support of the leaders of the target publics. These leaders must be brought into the campaign on a partnership basis. While the ratio of leaders to followers varies with the composition of the public, a general guide is one leader for every five followers.

Everyone draws upon past experiences or latent opinions. For those who are concerned with public relations in schools and colleges, it should be emphasized that one's experiences in school, and specifically in physical education and competitive sports programs, will contribute more to opposition or support of a related school or college issue than any other. Pleasant, rewarding experiences in physical education or competitive sports are the greatest assurance for later support at the voting booth, stadiums, fund-raising, or other activities associated with these areas. Exactly the opposite is also true. For this reason, teachers, coaches, and administrators should never lose sight of the fact that public relations begins in the classroom or on the playing area.

Since it is covered in greater detail in later chapters, it is only necessary at this time to state that public opinion is an ever-changing phenomenon and that public relations is a never-ending activity.

More importantly, it is essential for all concerned to recognize that public relations is not an emergency procedure, summoned much as a fire department is to extinguish a conflagration. Public relations should be placed in the hands of experts, or, at least, in those of sensitive, knowledgeable persons who recognize the importance of a continuing public relations program.

CHAPTER FOUR
THE CONDUCT OF
PUBLIC RELATIONS

Examples of attempted public relations programs that have met with disastrous consequences are far too numerous. In many of these cases there was adequate funding for materials, programs, and personnel. However, the most important ingredient for any successful public relations program was either missing or only partially available. This ingredient is expertise that implies a comprehension of the public relations process. Failure of public relations programs can be due to many causes, but the most common ones include attempting to copy some other program without a sufficient background of knowledge, demanding fast action, substituting progress for quality, and getting involved with the mechanics of the public relations process without having grasped the "big" picture.

ANALYSIS OF THE PUBLIC RELATIONS PROCESS

The public relations process is not unlike most other problem-solving activities. Essentially, this process can be defined in four basic steps.

1 *Research* Rely upon opinion, attitude, and reaction of persons concerned. Seek to answer the basic question: What is our problem?

2 *Planning* Bring all the accumulated data from the previous step to bear on the policies and programs of the organization. The purpose of this step is to reach certain decisions on "what can be done" to resolve or eliminate the problem.

3 *Communication* This covers explaining and dramatizing the selected courses of action to all whom may be affected and whose support is essential.

4 *Evaluation* An analysis of the program and the effectiveness of the techniques used are important for long-range purposes.

RESEARCH DIFFERENTIATES PUBLIC RELATIONS AND PUBLICITY

Each of the above four steps are necessary for a successful, complete public relations program. Ordinarily, failure is due to the skipping of one or more steps, or to giving merely passing attention to them. One basic root of trouble occurs because little or no attention is given to research. This step requires expertise, time, and financing. Often the step is omitted because it can be laborious, glamorless, and its importance not fully understood by outsiders, including supervisors or administrators. But, to the successful practitioner, research is the foundation upon which the entire remainder of the steps will depend. The greatest distinction between publicity and public relations is the different degree in the use of research.

It should be readily apparent that succeeding steps in the public relations process are dependent and determined by the research step. In practice, all four steps may be in action to different degrees and at different times; in other words, each step is not necessarily distinct and isolated from the others.

NEED AND IMPORTANCE OF DATA

Human relations problems are just as specific and researchable as those in most other areas, although subjective inquiry can and should be used wherever appropriate. Regardless of the actual methods used in obtaining data, a methodical, systematic program of research is the most effective avenue toward a sound and satisfying public relations program.

The simple process of listening is an important tool in gathering information; this actually provides for an interchange of messages. As simple as listening may be, it is still the taking-off point for communication. To listen thoroughly and with purpose requires humility, patience, and a systematic effort—listening is not an easy task. Empathy is an essential preface to listening, and empathy is achieved by open-minded listening. One must be prepared to listen to both the favorable and unfavorable and to respond to each.

Aside from subjective procedures, such as listening, the research associated with public relations should be as objective as possible. In order to accurately ascertain what people think, what they know or don't know, believe or disbelieve, and actually read or listen to, one must utilize the most sophisticated instruments that have been developed for these purposes. Practitioners employ opinion surveys, attitude studies, and audience reaction probes that pass the most critical scrutiny. To utilize anything less than superior instruments is akin to measuring distance with an inaccurate tape measure. A faulty instrument can lead to faulty or erroneous conclusions. Most practitioners are capable of selecting proper instruments to measure or probe whatever it is they seek; in cases where there is any doubt, the wise practitioner seeks expert advice from others. Regardless of the instruments used or how they are used, the successful practitioner understands that it is important for those who will chart the remainder of the public relations program to be able to look at problems or issues from the public's viewpoint.

Research pays other handsome dividends. Namely, if a public relations program is founded upon good, inclusive evidence that can withstand any or all criticisms, then the chances that the top management will approve the plan is generally assured. On the contrary, a public relations format presented to top management that fails to be based upon irrefutable evidence leads to personal and program difficulties.

Research is also very useful in revealing trouble spots before they explode. Ordinarily, it is an easier, less costly, and more profitable process to remedy the causes of trouble than to attempt to rectify the damage that occurs when they erupt. Continuous fact-finding and purposive listening are means of stemming eruptions. These actions will also uncover ill-founded rumors, allowing for remedial action long before some injury results to the organization.

Only through research can a public relations program reach its maximum potential. For every patient the physican determines the precise instruments and their application for diagnostic purposes. So it is with the public relations practitioner who should select certain publics for study and determine the ways this will be done. Through research, it is possible to identify the leaders of a particular public, and to learn their values, viewpoints, and language. All of these are necessary if the practitioner is to obtain meaningful data. As in the practice of the physician, the extent to which a public relations effort increases in effectiveness is in proportion to the specificity with which it is directed to a special group.

While research offers some answers of immediate value, one should be mindful of the long-range benefits. Knowing a public's attitudes, opinions, and base of information is of inestimable value in charting ongoing public relations programs.

In the real world, a public relations program that is based upon the four steps often meets with resistance. Particularly common is the opposition to a comprehensive research program. This opposition stems from the budget required to provide adequate staff and instruments and from the failure to understand the elements of a public relations program. One must attempt to justify expenditures for the research phase of public relations on grounds that it is an economical action in the long run. This argument must be supported by using examples and graphic presentations.

OPINION RESEARCH
Complete opinion research should entail four separate, but related stages. Each is necessary in order to reap the full benefit of the others. The first stage is that of assessing the current situation, or determining what people think today and why. The second stage is to discover how public opinion operates, or attempt to identify the various forces that help shape public opinion. The third stage is the use of "before and after" testing in order to detect the effects of any given announcement, change in program, advertisement, article, change in personnel, or other variations. The fourth step is that of evaluation of the response to the public relations program, the extent of attitude change, and the action resulting from it.

DEVELOPING A "FACT FILE"
The public relations practitioner understands the importance of fact-finding; when such a public relations specialist is not available, others may be asked to fill this responsibility. Without facts, a satisfactory pub-

lic relations program is a rarity. How does one go about assembling a storehouse of useful facts for public relations purposes? One of the first steps is to start a fact-file. Facts are collected from any and all sources; they are clipped or photocopied; they are analyzed, arranged, and stored according to some meaningful retrieval system. This fact-file becomes a useful resource center for ideas and information to include in speeches, pamphlets, special reports, advertising, exhibits, special events, fund-raising, and background material for special projects. Unless a fact-file is a regular part of a public relations office, certain types of information and facts required to meet some objective will be lacking.

DEFINING PUBLICS AND LEADERS

Another fundamental and essential responsibility assigned to the public relations specialist, or to those assigned public relations responsibilities, is the defining of publics and their composition. Ordinarily it is through research that one locates and defines the publics in a given community. Once they are identified, then one attempts to determine the most effective means of communicating with each. To successfully influence publics, one must determine the exact composition of the public by age, sex, religion, education, political leanings, economic status, attitudes on society, and any other distinguishing characteristic. It is especially important to learn all that is possible about the leaders of each public. Once a public has been identified and its characteristics are known, it is important to realize that publics are constantly undergoing change. Changes occur in attitudes, age groupings, economic interests, political tendencies, and even geographic representation. America has a highly mobile people. Caution should be exercised in pinpointing leaders of a public—often the real leaders are others than those who are perceived as such. A common error is to automatically award leadership roles to lawyers, doctors, clergy, and bankers as the sum total of community leaders. Likewise, the mistake is frequently made of assigning a person a position of leadership in a particular public because that person was a leader in another public or group. One should also be aware that a person may be a leader in a group but not in the total community. Usually each social and economic stratum generates its own opinion leaders. And, since most persons are affiliated with more than one group, the leaders of each group to which a person belongs are looked to for guidance in specific areas. Trying to pinpoint respected group leaders is difficult in many cases, but the effort and time are well re-paid.

The typical community is comprised of many separate groups or publics, yet many, if not all, are interrelated in some fashion. The prudent practitioner needs to know the anatomy of each group, and then must select those appeals that will be most effective for each particular public. There are times when certain appeals to a particular group will offend other groups. At times, it is necessary for the public relations practitioner to choose between groups. Any institution or organization should identify the publics of interest to them, and they should rank them in priority as to their importance; effort, time, and money should be expended according to the relative importance of each public.

THE POWER STRUCTURE

Every community and every separate public has its own power structure that is most important to the public relations expert. This power structure receives the primary attention, and only after this nucleus is persuaded to give its support to the institution or organization does one then attempt to concentrate on the persons outside this power structure but within the group.

The more carefully publics are identified, their character known, and their power structure revealed, the more successful will be the selection and implementation of ways of reaching and influencing them. This is not a simple task. Rather, to accomplish these ends requires the guiding hand of a public relations expert or one who has an unusual interest and knowledge in the field.

Knowing what people think is necessary in order to determine where to start a public relations program. As stated earlier, listening to all is a useful, although nonscientific, way to gain some idea of what people are thinking. In coming to some conclusion about what people are thinking, based upon listening, one must be certain that the persons to whom one listens represents the publics of greatest concern to the public relations objectives.

ADVISORY BOARDS OR PANELS

Other informal methods of ascertaining what people think can be used. Various personal contacts, even if short-lived, can be of aid. The telephone is a vital instrument for increasing the scope of the sources of information. Correspondence received, particularly from acquaintances, can be of value even though many messages are subtle. In this regard, one can and should execute an analysis of mail. This is much more than a mere tabulation of numbers in favor or in opposition; rather, it should be an attempt to seek out the causes for various opinions so that proper constructive steps can be put into action. A favorite way of assessing the opinion of the public is to initiate an advisory committee or panel. The committee should have representation from the various publics with which one is keenly concerned; representatives should be selected from the leaders of the various publics. Advisory committees or panels should be more than a perfunctory aspect to a program. They should meet on schedule, be given meaningful tasks, and their advice, if sought, should be followed except for unusual circumstances.

KEEPING A PULSE ON CURRENT POSITIONS
Another favorite and productive way of determining what people think is to collect press clippings and to monitor radio and television comments. Unless this is approached in a structured form it is a futile effort, but, if done with care and according to a plan, these sources of public information can be of great value to any public relations program.

Speeches and writings of opinion leaders are a source of information. Generally the contents of these are forerunners of what is to follow. They are to some degree harbingers that give indication of what can be expected.

FACE-TO-FACE BENEFITS
There are few, if any, informal methods of obtaining an understanding of what people think that are more successful than face-to-face contacts. Anyone involved with public relations understands this valuable approach. Meeting persons from all facts of the community publics is important; confining oneself to merely associating with a restricted selection of persons can not only be misleading but it can be disastrous. Successful politicians recognize the power of personal contact. Persons associated with institutions or organizations that depend upon public relations, as nearly all of them do, also are aware of the value of personal contact on a broad basis.

USE OF FORMAL METHODS OF INQUIRY
Some of the formal ways of determining what people think are the use of special instruments. Most of these instruments are planned to supply

information on a large public by means of mathematical probability. The structure, content, and application of the instrument must be exact, pretested, and immune to various influences.

One of the favorite methods of assessing public opinion is the use of the cross-section survey. In this instance a carefully prepared set of questions is asked of a cross-section sample of a given public. Three standard ways to draw a sample are by probability, area, or quota. In the case of probability every nth name on a given list is used; for an area, geographic zones are used; and, for a quota, the bases may be any known characteristic such as age, sex, income, race, education, and so on. All of these survey are more quantitative than qualitative.

Another popular method of determining what people think is to select a panel comprised of representatives from crucial publics that is interviewed periodically and in depth.

An excellent method of discovering what people think is the in-depth interview. Time and cost are usually prohibitive and so discourage an excessive use of this technique.

Conducting a content analysis of all stories and articles used by the media is helpful. This is also an excellent way to keep account of the use of news releases.

One of the most familiar techniques is the use of mailed questionnaires. One advantage of this technique is that it is relatively economical. On the other hand, this advantage is offset by the fact that it is never known if respondents are representative of the public you are investigating. When used, allowances should be made to encourage free expression. Often this phase of the questionnaire can be of more value than answers to given questions.

Whether informal, formal, or a combination of both methods of obtaining information are used, the prudent practitioner constantly employs some or all to discover latent problems before they erupt into a crisis. Opinion research is most rewarding as a guide to long-range plans and to improving communications techniques.

PLANNING AS THE SECOND STEP

Planning is the second major step toward completing a complete public relations program. More and more emphasis is placed on planning public relations programs than ever before. Sympotoms of inadequate or lack of planning are "wheel-spinning" or covering the same ground over and over until it becomes sterile, reacting to emergencies that were not pre-

dicted or expected, and using defensive spur-of-the-moment tactics. Lack
of planning or impromptu planning leads to negative results; whereas
good, long-range planning can lead to an integrated program in which
all efforts aid in the achievement of specified goals, increased management support and participation, and a positive rather than a defensive
approach to public relations.

If adequate planning is so important, why is it so often neglected?
Generally the answer is twofold. In some cases, the significance of planning is not fully understood or appreciated; in others, it is omitted due
to the lack of time. Planning takes time, and if pressures of other activities are assigned a higher priority, then inadequate planning of public
relations should be expected.

Planning starts with the determination of realistic aims for the institution or organization. These aims encompass a determination of goals,
strategy, and tactics. Both short and long-range objectives, or targets, are
identified and assigned priorities. Decisions are made as to preventative
and remedial activities for specific situations or problems, although insofar as possible stress is placed upon the former. Planning makes clear the
need for adequate staffing and budget; unless planning is carefully completed, the chances of gaining approval of either staff or operating
budget are reduced.

Any institution or organization should evolve its ideals or aspirations. These should be carefully selected and, once determined, made
cornerstones for all other planning. Generally, ideals are expressions of
the wishes to gain rewards, aid others, be respected in the community,
be supported from within the organization, provide a necessary or desirable service or product, be free from needless outside restraints, and
influence public opinion in a positive way. When an organization has
problems in its public relations, usually they relate to one or more of
these basic ideals, and are traceable in full or in part to a breakdown
of communications.

The institution or organization is rare that is always free of problems, either actual or threatened. How one deals with problems is important in public relations. There is a three-step process that is helpful in
most cases. First determine by analysis the organization's attitudes
toward publics with whom communication needs improvement. Second,
attempt to discover what the attitudes are of the publics involved. Third,
seek to identify those areas of mutual understanding and approval; then

pinpoint areas that must be approached in order to establish a full working relationship and understanding.

The actual act of planning involves two parts. At the start there should be the development of strategy. Strategy is a statement or definition of the overall master plan. Once strategy is firmed, attention is then given to tactics. This involves the skillful use of the precise tools and techniques essential to accomplish each separate portion of the overall campaign. Strategies and tactics must complement long-range and short-term planning. Planning is guided by the ultimate aims of the organization; these aims should be formulated by the top management with the assistance of public relations experts. Aims should be realistic, expressed in simple terms, and fully understood with no likelihood of misinterpretation.

All public relations programs can be categorized as being either preventative or remedial in action. When good long-range planning exists, based upon a set of clear aims, and operating from complete and valid inquires into prevailing conditions, then one can emphasize the preventative type of public relations. Just the opposite situation leads to a public relations program that must react to emergency situations from a defensive posture. Most school and college public relations programs suffer from the lack of planning, even though this approach consumes less time and energy over a long period of time; fulfillment of basic aims is attained less frequently and support of the institution or organization is seldom achieved.

PUT PLANNING IN WRITING

Planning is critical, yet the act of planning is often omitted because an understanding of the process is lacking. Good planning requires putting everything of importance in writing. This includes all that the authorities have approved, and in some cases that which they have specifically disapproved. The institution's policies should be written in clear terms. When these fundamental aspects of the public relations program are placed into writing (and approved of in writing), then several benefits automatically accrue. First, everyone knows the direction of movement; everyone can focus their energies upon movement in the prescribed direction. Second, support and cooperation from within the institution or organization are more readily given. Third, development of tactics to pursue the ultimate aims are more precise and selective. Fourth, there is conservation of resources, time, and effort.

CRITERIA FOR GOOD PLANNING

The art of planning is no easy skill to acquire; it must be developed with experience and knowledge. Often, planning seems to be too abstract; words are used that are either meaningless or subject to virtually any desired interpretation. On the other hand, planning can be overorganized and can hamper logical, intelligent decisions that must be made at various moments. Too informal planning can be disastrous, particularly when some unexpected difficulty arises.

The criteria for a good plan includes the following:

1 Aims of the institution should be stated in adequate terms.
2 All planning should be in harmony with the institution's prime purposes and with its character.
3 Plans should be sincere and contain integrity of purpose and execution.
4 Plans should be stated in affirmative terms.
5 The overall plan and its component parts should be stated in clear and simple messages.
6 The plan should be all-inclusive in scope and execution of it should be continuous.
7 The plan should be mutually beneficial to the institution and the public.

A good public relations program seeks to advance the institution's goals. To do this the program content should be engineered so that it informs the specific publics over a period of time about the history of the institution, its ideals, achievements, policies, services, personnel, and projects it seeks for the future. If this is done with success there can be expected public understanding and support.

WHO DOES THE PLANNING?

Planning done either exclusively by a public relations practitioner or without this expert is fraught with danger. Ideally, planning of the public relations program involves top management, supervisory management, and the public relations expert. The public relations specialist should be able to identify the public's needs, desires, and opinions that are relevant to the institution and in so doing gain a better understanding of the institution's policies and attitudes.

When a plan has evolved out of joint effort and has been launched, it is the responsibility of the public relations practitioner to keep the top executives fully informed of all major steps or events so that they can better understand, support, and transmit them to others.

PLANNING AND TIMING

Good planning implies the use of a timetable. Once the guiding strategy is determined and the specific tactics are identified, then it is essential to develop a chronology of execution. When this is done beforehand it is probable that, whatever the tactic, it will be accomplished on time and in a superior fashion; further, those persons affected will not be shocked. The timing of tactics should adhere to the momentum principle—once movement is started, each tactic should be applied at the proper time to heighten the overall impact. Generally, planning uses tactics in the early rounds of the campaign that call upon the efforts of those persons most intimately associated with the ultimate outcome; as the plan progresses each succeeding tactic relies upon those with decreasing personal involvement. As the plan proceeds it is hoped that those with less than total commitment will be fully caught up in the enthusiasm and aims of the plan.

Timing should seek to produce the right effect at the right time. Every tactic should be examined in light of what has occurred prior to its scheduled time of use and what will occur after it has been introduced. Messages or communications should be transmitted to complement each phase of the program. These messages should be prepared to meet the following criteria:

1 Does the message appeal to individual needs and wants?
2 Does the message provide or point out social support for the desired attitudes?
3 Is the message introduced at such a time that it will reinforce related events?
4 Does the message point out or provide a channel for action along the desired attitude and at the same time point out ways to surmount barriers to such action?

HOW TO PLAN FOR CRISES

Even when the best of plans are made, there will be times when crises or catastrophes will appear. One cannot anticipate when they will occur or what their nature will be. Nonetheless, one can plan for them. During periods of crises or catastrophes, time is of great importance. Something must be done at once; there is little or no time for impromptu planning. Planning for these should be done as part of the total project and during the early stages. A good emergency plan will specifically consider and place into writing who will be in charge of any counteraction, what this counteraction will be, how it will be put into action, when it will be enacted, and any other detail consistent with the institution and the total plan. While it should be taken for granted, it is recommended that all persons involved with the institution or its public relations plan be specifically reminded in writing that they are to refrain from any action except as stated in writing.

In summary, good planning can only be based upon adequate fact-finding. Plans must be consistent with the institution's ultimate aims, basic policies, and objectives; everyone who will have some responsibility in implementing plans should be involved in formulating them. The supervision and responsibility for implementing the plan should be assigned to the public relations expert or to someone who has the necessary conviction, enthusiasm, and technical ability.

COMMUNICATIONS

The third step in a public relations program is as vital as that of fact-finding and planning. This step is communicating. While the public relations practitioner is deeply involved in the first two steps, it is crucial that he or she be the foremost person in the communication step. This step is truly a test of professional abilities. Although others should be called upon to assist in the process of communicating, the final responsibility rests with the public relations expert or to the person assigned this duty.

Before discussing specific techniques of communicating, an understanding of communications is valuable. Communication is the binder that allows a society to function. Words are the first common denominator of this binding capability. Words are symbols. They are either "thing" or "nothing" words. Abstractions like "democracy," "spirit," and others have no simple or universally agreed on references in the real world of physical objects. If people cannot see, hear, smell, taste, or touch something, then it is difficult for them to agree upon anything. To communicate effectively, the sender's words must mean the same thing to the receiver that they do to the sender. The more "thing" words and the fewer "nothing" words the sender uses, the easier it will be for the message to be understood as the sender intended. There are four elements necessary for communications: the sender, the message or symbols, the medium, and the receiver. A breakdown can happen in one or all four. Effective communications requires satisfactory performance by all four components. The sender must have desired information that must be transmitted in symbols that the receiver understands and by a channel that carries the message to the receiver; the message must be within the receiver's capacity to understand and it should motivate the receiver's self-interest.

Communications are affected by many variables. The public relations practitioner consciously or otherwise assesses messages before sending them out. Some of the variables that affect the result of messages are:

1   The exposure, access, and attention given to the communicator's message.
2   The different characteristics of the media of communication.
3   The content of the message, especially its form, presentation, and effectiveness of appeal.
4   The receiver's predisposition that tends to accept, reject or modify the message.
5   The interpersonal relations of individuals as members of various groups.

COMMUNICATING WITH AND THROUGH LEADERS

The significance of the interpersonal relations of individuals as members of groups has been identified as one of the most powerful influences, if not the greatest. This finding has given impetus to the "two-step" flow of mass communication theory. In this instance, emphasis is directed upon reaching the "thought leaders" of a group, rather than relying upon mass communications. Initial targets of communication are the opinion leaders of a group, using the variables listed above. Ideas penetrate the masses through a process similar to osmosis. Opinion leaders might be regarded as the center of a group; spreading of ideas and the forming of opinions emanates from the center and moves in ever-increasing concentric circles. The rate of osmosis is related to the variables cited above.

ANALYSIS OF MENTAL PROCESSES ASSOCIATED WITH COMMUNICATIONS

A primary purpose of a public relations program is to persuade others to accept the same ideas or opinions as promulgated by the institution. Knowledge of the mental processes that are necessary to bring about this acceptance is of key importance to the public relations practitioner or others who seek to accomplish this end. Basically there are five steps involved in the mental process, each of importance and each that must follow the preceding step in sequence.

The first step in bringing people to accept one's ideas or opinions is that of awareness. An individual obviously cannot either endorse or reject an idea until he or she is made aware of it. In order to capture the attention of an individual, the idea must be presented in an interesting, attractive, and possibly unique fashion. Care should be used to make certain that self-interests are aroused.

The second step is one of developing interest. After an awareness is created, then the individual is provided with information that immediately satisfies interests, and stimulates continued interest.

Having been made aware of an idea and having been exposed to sufficient information, the individual then commences to evaluate the merits of the idea, the third step. In many cases the individual makes use of a mental application of the idea as a sort of "dry run" test. Possibly at this stage of mental activity more data are desired. At the conclusion of this step, the individual is now ready to put the idea to trial.

At this fourth step in the total process, the individual actually applies the idea or practice, generally on a restricted scale. During this stage, attention is given to the methods or presentation, techniques of application, and general reactions. If satisfied, then the individual is ready to move to the final step in this mental process.

The final step is one of adoption. If successfully adopted, then the individual often becomes an active participant in spreading the idea or opinion to others.

There is no set timetable for this process to be completed. There are many variables that affect the rate of acceptance. A common influence is the state of readiness of the individual; this state can be altered by one's previous experiences. Other influences may include the extent of self-interest that can be satisfied, the absence of conflicting ideas, the rapport between sender and the receiver, and the endorsement of the idea by opinion leaders respected by the individual.

COMMUNICATIONS AND THE MASS MEDIA

The mass media of communication is a simple method to create awareness. For some projects this is the main instrument used for this purpose; in others, mass media is avoided and emphasis is concentrated upon a personal face-to-face relationship. The second step, developing interest, can also be aided by use of the mass communication media;

however, best results ordinarily are attained by personal relationships. Mental evaluation is influenced greatly by friends and associates, as is the trial step.

Communications is a long, tedious task, particularly when a new idea or practice is involved. Attempts to expedite the process without regard for the "incubation" period can lead to failure or even overt resistance. The public relations practitioner, or others charged with the responsibility of conditioning the public's ideas or opinions, should make certain that this entire process is understood by all concerned with the public relations program.

BARRIERS TO COMMUNICATIONS

There are certain barriers and distortions of the public relations program that should be recognized in order for preventative or remedial measures to be employed in communications. Typical barriers are those of social basis; there are various do's and don'ts for different social strata. Age is often a barrier; interests, particularly self-interests, change with age. Language is an obstacle that often prevents communications from being received in accordance with the sender's intent. Vocabulary difference acts in the same way. A common barrier is a political difference; in this case, the idea or message of itself is rejected because of political overtones. Of course, many communications are rejected because of economic factors rather than because of their own merits.

USE OF SYMBOLS IN COMMUNICATIONS

In our modern, complex society in which everyone is striving to attract attention, derive support, or sell some product or service the competition is fierce. Everyone tends to live within a world of their own symbols. In order to make contact with these people, it is necessary to communicate familiar symbols. Getting the true facts to an individual is often the key to obtaining the desired action. People tend to rely upon stereotypes. An isolated and significant impression is converted into a generalization. These are employed as a form of defense mechanism. The public relations expert develops the ability to recognize the influence and presence of symbols and stereotypes in the seeming contradictions and the antagonisms of public opinion. Additionally, superstitions, prejudices, and vanities are constant barriers to all communications in varying degrees. People tend to believe what they want to believe.

From the preceding discussion it becomes obvious that the act of communicating is complex. There is no single set of sure-fire rules. Productive communications requires specific programming according to the situation, time, place, and audience. Proper selection of media and the use of them are vital. Messages must be repeated over and over again; the message must be simple.

Our society and our way of living demands that we depend more and more on secondhand communication from others for our own needs. As our society becomes larger and more complex, and as we have less time to listen, read, and think for ourselves, the more we are dependent upon others to help us reach decisions. At the same time, the numbers of individuals and organizations who want us to support or adopt some project, idea, or goal also increase. Because of lack of time, we can give less attention to their pleas. It is this real world that a public relations practitioner must face everyday.

COMMUNICATIONS THROUGH MASS MEDIA

Because of the nature of our society and the lives we lead, mass media adjusts accordingly. They give out that which excites and entertains; they tend to headline the sensational, the controversial, and the amusing. Factual and less interesting information tends to be subordinated. Values are attached more to emotion than to reason. Because of this situation, an institution must take the lead in providing positive communications and information that appeals to the mass media agencies. Good deeds may and probably will go unnoticed or misunderstood, unless they are properly told. Misunderstandings about an institution are usually traceable to misinformation or the lack of information; informed persons make for informed support and strong backing.

PUBLICITY AND COMMUNICATIONS

Publicity is needed in our present society. Publicity should not be the only tool, but rather it should play a specific part of the whole process of public relations. The absorption of the message, as measured by the reaction it brings, is the best test of publicity, not the number of column inches. Facts should be told continuously, clearly, and candidly. Negative facts are bound to surface, so in the vast majority of cases it is better for an institution to include the bad with the good news. Negative facts can often be used to an advantage if brought into the open—their concealment eventually leads to distrust and loss of credibility.

SEMANTICS

All forms of communication, of which publicity is just one, should be aware of semantics. Semantics is the science of what words really mean. Word meaning changes, and the communicator should keep aware of current usage, particularly for the publics he or she services. The use of words is steadily becoming more complicated and exacting. As technology develops there is the necessity to develop new words, with their need caused by specialization. With our rapidly changing society, characterized by shifting age groups, mobility, extended education, and the reliance upon sophisticated mass media devices, the public relations specialist must be certain of what he or she releases or talks about. Words can have different meanings for different groups; the ideal use of words is to have the receivers of messages attach the same meaning to them as the sender does. Avoid overworked words in messages; seek a different and interesting way of saying something; avoid complications and strive to make the process of reception exciting and rewarding.

EVALUATION OF COMMUNICATIONS

Communications should measure up to established standards or principles. Cutlip* has suggested that the following meet most high expectations.

1 *Credibility*   Communications start with a climate of belief. This is built by performance on the part of the source, which reflects an earnest desire to serve the receiver. The receiver must have confidence in the sender, he must have a high regard for the source's competence on the subject.

2 *Context*   A communications program must correspond to the realities of its environment. Mechanical media are only supplementary to the word and deed occurring in daily living. The context must provide for participation and playback.

3 *Content*   The message must have meaning for the receiver. It must have relevance to him. In general, people select those items of information that promise them greatest rewards. The content determines the audience.

4 *Clarity*   The message must be put in simple terms. Words must mean the same thing to the receiver as they do to the sender. Complex issues must be compressed into themes, slogans, stereotypes, that have simplicity and clarity. The farther a message has to travel, the simpler it must be. An institution must speak with one voice, not many.

* Scott M. Cutlip and Allen H. Center, *Effective Public Relations*, 2nd ed. (Englewood Cliffs, N.J.: Prentice-Hall, Inc., 1958), pp. 140–41.

5 *Continuity and Consistency* Communication is an unending process. It requires repetition to achieve penetration. Repetition—with variation—contributes to both factual and attitude learning. The story must be consistent.

6 *Channels* Established channels of communication should be used—channels that the receiver employs and respects. Creating new ones is difficult. Different channels have different effects and serve in different stages of the diffusion process.

7 *Capability of Audience* Communication must take into account the capability of the audience. Communications are most effective when they require the least effort on the part of the recipient. This includes factors of availability, habit, reading ability, and receiver's knowledge.

Communications is the life-force of public relations. The importance of communicating effectively, efficiently, and consistently increases geometrically in relation to population growth, urbanization, complexity of life, and the multitude of pressures exerted overtly and covertly.

EVALUATION OF THE PUBLIC RELATIONS PROGRAM

The fourth and final step in the conduct of public relations is that of evaluation. As in the other three steps, often less than adequate time, effort, and money are devoted to evaluation. When evaluation is omitted, the probabilities of improving the public relations program are dim. Most persons learn from both errors and successes. Unless some objective means of evaluating prior or current public relations programs are applied, then it is unlikely that improvement in succeeding ones can be expected.

There is not too much mystery surrounding evaluation. Essentially, one should examine each major function and pose these questions: What specific goals were set for this function? To what extent did this activity contribute to the realization of these goals? What was accomplished by this function? Did we get a fair return for the time, effort, and money invested in this function?

Whenever possible, pre-testing or pre-evaluation should be conducted. Of course, if prior evaluations of programs have been made, these may serve as benchmarks. Post-evaluation should be conducted. Results or the status of any particular concern are then compared. Post-evaluation should provide information concerning audience coverage, audience response, communications impact, and the process of influence.

Audience coverage should reveal how many persons were reached, the characteristics of those persons reached, and what aspects of the public relations program had the greatest and least effect upon them. Audience response should be evaluated concerning the kind of response generated, the amount of interest created, and the extent to which the message was understood. One should seek to learn the extent of the communications impact, the nature of the impact, and the durability of the impact. It is important for the public relations practitioner to know by what process the communication achieved desirable results, the channels of influence, and the mechanisms that achieved a change in the opinions and behavior of its target audience.

Other evaluation devices are generally more quantitative than qualitative. Some of the more common devices or techniques used include the reader-interest survey, readability tests, and radio and television audience levels. Readership does not necessarily equal circulation, nor does it equal comprehension and retention. Readability tests can be of value by shedding light upon the content, format, organization, and writing style.

The critical test of a communications program is the results it produces. In most cases this can be determined only by face-to-face interviews or by impact analysis on a short and long-range basis. Impact can be measured to some extent by noting changes in attitude, tickets sold, funds raised, and general support.

CHAPTER FIVE
THE INTERNAL
PUBLICS

Few, if any, public relations programs have succeeded without the enthusiastic, committed support of the internal publics of the institution or organization. There is probably no other public institution that demonstrates this necessity better than the school or college. Employee relations—those that exist between administrators and staff—is the pulse of school or college public relations. Good internal public relations are founded upon belief and trust, the products of day-by-day actions of those in authority.

A school or college as a social unit has certain special responsibilities. Each person in the social unit has a certain place in its structure; each has specific duties, responsibilities, and expected contributions to the total pattern and each has interrelationships with others. The extent to which an institution can integrate all of these functions determines its success. When each employee understands the internal system and the advantages of maintaining effective cooperation within it, then one can reasonably expect concerted effort and harmony.

RECOGNIZING NEEDS OF INTERNAL PUBLICS

The able administrator realizes that the internal publics have social-psychological as well as economic needs. For some persons and publics, the social-psychological needs are more important than economic needs. Those charged with administration should attempt to carefully and accurately assess the hierarchy of needs for each person and public. The predominant social-psychological needs include the following:

1 *Need to Belong*   Most people want to identify with others; they want to be a part of a group that represents more power and prestige than can be self-generated.

2 *Need for Accomplishment*   Most people want identifiable goals and they want these goals to be attainable; most people want to experience progress toward attaining goals and to have others, usually superiors, to recognize this fact.

3 *Need for Self-Esteem*   Everyone should be expected to have their own sense of worth and standard of pride and dignity; these personal values should be acknowledged.

4 *Need for Acceptance*   Acceptance by the group or groups to which one belongs is vital for most persons.

5 *Need for Security*   Although variations exist among persons as to their dependency upon security, there are few who are immune to this need and there are many for whom this matter is paramount.

6 *Need for Creativity*   Opportunities for creativity should be available to all within defined boundaries; it must be recognized that this need varies among people.

Status and function are critical to a worker. The organization must guarantee, by deed and action, that each person will have equal opportunity to attain status and function. The administrator should seek to develop the understanding that every position is significant in the overall scheme of things. At the same time, there must be the realization that a particular position merits a status that is different from another. Understanding this difference and the symbols attached to it, such as office amenities, titles, and other privileges, is important as reward for those who occupy certain positions and motivation for others who pursue them. Every person should be convinced by actual practice that there is equal opportunity for advancement, based upon certain capabilities that are known and measurable. This understanding is a powerful motivator. When an institution attends to recognizing indiviual status, function, and the opportunity for advancement, the social-psychological needs for security, importance, individuality, and acceptance by others are satisfied. These are the true cornerstones of internal public relations.

FOUNDATIONS OF GOOD
INTERNAL RELATIONS

In order for an institution to realize its highest goals, there must be mutual confidence and respect between employer and employees. Earning the confidence and respect of employees is not a complex matter. First, the employer must be genuinely interested in an employee's personal affairs, to the extent that there is no infringement upon reserved areas. One should be attentive to the employee's expressed desires and fears. Second, the employer should seek to identify areas of concern and take action to remedy known problems. Personnel policies should be developed mutually and then implemented so that equality, fairness, and opportunity apply to all employees. Third, a good internal public relations program assures the free and candid flow of information downward as well as upward. A climate needs to be established that fosters this exchange of information and ideas without fear of reprisal. The "tone of voice" used in policy statements or directives is often more important than the message conveyed. Administrators should have personnel policies in writing so that everyone can be aware of them, that they can be equally administered, and that the rewards for compliance are known.

TWO-WAY COMMUNICATIONS IS ESSENTIAL

Too often the error is made by an administrator in thinking that the role of a public relations program or expert is to "sell" employees. A better method of achieving good internal public relations is to make certain that two-way communication is provided, encouraged, and made a permanent policy. Instead of emphasizing the "selling" of public relations to employees, every attempt should be made to have employees participate in major policy matters and decisions. This can be done on either a one-to-one basis or in open group discussions. Other avenues of communications should be sponsored. Employee bulletins, pamphlets, bulletin boards, handbooks, letters, and questionnaires are examples of methods that have been used successfully when employees are responsible for content.

IMPORTANCE OF INTERNAL PUBLIC RELATIONS

Public relations start at home. Until internal public relations are satisfactory, the chances are next to nil that external public relations programs will be successful. In a school or college setting, internal public relations are vital to any public program. For example, a bond measure faces near-certain defeat unless the staff are avid supporters of the proposal. Nothing will injure a competitive athletics program quicker than if just a few faculty members publicly question its values. A fundraising project is virtually doomed to failure if the internal public is indifferent to or openly opposes it.

The astute administrator of any school or college will make certain that the internal public relations of the institution are satisfactory before allocating time, effort, and money to an external public relations program.

STUDENTS AND PUBLIC RELATIONS

In a school or college, the faculty and staff are vital to any public relations program. However, the students of an institution are of equal importance. The old saying that "public relations starts in the classroom or on the playing field" is valid. Students today are more sophisticated. They are not willing to accept anything presented to them at face value; they want to know why, who, what, when, and how. The best way to develop positive public relations among students is to offer and conduct an educational program that meets the severest tests of quality, content, and timing. On the other hand, the quickest way to create indifference or open opposition to the school and its activities is to present programs that are inferior, unplanned, meaningless, and haphazardly offered.

Students are direct conduits to parents. What students believe about a school or college and any specific program offered is quickly absorbed by parents. Parents, in turn, pass along these opinions to fellow employees, relatives, club membership, or other groups to which they belong.

IMPORTANCE OF PUBLIC RELATIONS
WITH STUDENTS

An athletic program must be conducted so as to contribute to the higher goals and values of an institution. Students must be granted full and equal opportunities to participate. Methods of coaching should be open to any investigation. When an athletic program is conducted ideally, one can expect positive public relations among the participants. Parents will adopt the attitudes of their sons and daughters and will transmit these same attitudes to others among the external publics.

The typical collegiate institution has a number of internal publics; common among these are:

Teaching faculty
Administrators
Support staff
Students
Alumni
Board of trustees
Affiliated supportive agencies
Retired faculty and administrators
Close relatives of each of the above

Each of the above publics can be further subdivided into smaller units. For example, the teaching faculty might be further subdivided according to sex, age, tenured and nontenured, athletics ticket purchasers and nonpurchasers, and academic divisions.

Good public relations practices identify the various publics and then tailor-make certain programs for them.

CHAPTER SIX
THE EXTERNAL
PUBLICS

An institution has internal and external publics. It cannot survive or flourish without the cooperation and esteem of many people, either acting as individuals or in groups. A public relations program is a positive effort to foster favorable community relations. A public relations program, in terms of time and money entailed, is considered a profitable investment—it is a calculated casting of bread upon the water. Effective public relations does not result from gifts, gimmicks, or publicity alone; rather, it involves the products of responsible community service that are made known.

The local community is a microcosm of the entire nation. Community life is organized along the lines of interest groups, whether the

interest is in lower taxes, ecology, higher wages, a new community building, attraction of industry, cultural facilities, or whatever. These groupings come and go, shift, overlap, and change in vigor. Each community
is distinct but ever-changing. This calls for a constant reappraisal of a
public relations program so that particular circumstances can be satisfactorily observed.

Community interests are complex. Individuals join or affiliate with
groups largely on the basis of self-interest. Nothing is more important in
developing community relations than the identification of the decision-
makers of each group. If these leaders can be swayed to your causes, this
usually makes the persuasion of their followers a relatively easy task.
Each stratum of the community develops its own leaders and has only a
few. To identify them may require extensive probing. Do not jump to
conclusions concerning actual leaders. A mayor in one community may
be a leader while the mayor in another may only be a puppet.

PEOPLE DETERMINE PEOPLE'S ATTITUDES

The publicly known policies of an institution are an overt expression of
attitudes. Most often, the opinions held regarding an institution are
attached to the chief administrator. The administrator becomes the sym-
bol. People tend to identify actions and attitudes with people, not with
buildings or products. In addition to the attitudes and personality of the
chief administrator, people tend to judge an institution by the type and
extent of two-way participation used to resolve mutual concerns. In other
words, the chief administrator should become engaged with community
problems, issues, and concerns that may or may not have a direct bearing
upon the institution he or she represents. Similarly, the chief administrator should encourage and provide for public participation in the formulation of goals, policies, and procedures of an institution. There is a
need for continuous two-way communication. When internal matters are
kept behind locked doors, suspicion arises that often is more devastating
than the real facts. The public should be encouraged to ask questions
that should then be answered as forthrightly as possible.

The public is comprised of publics. Each sub-public is distinct to a
greater or lesser degree. Because of their distinctiveness, the persons
identified with a particular public usually read and listen only to that
which is of unique interest to them. As a consequence, it is difficult to
reach or influence the persons representing certain groups merely
through the use of common public relations channels and materials.

SCHOOL OR COLLEGE PUBLICS IDENTIFIED

In analyzing the publics of importance to an educational institution, it is often helpful to group them according to their relationships to the school or college. The National School Public Relations Association has developed a structural analysis of the general public into sub-groups or sub-publics. These are:

1 Groups tentatively classified as "immediate" school publics. The sub-publics within this immediate school public include students, teachers, school employees, parents, alumni, school organizations, and close relatives of persons within these sub-groups.

2 Groups tentatively classified as "associated" publics. The sub-groups within this associated school public includes women clubs, prospective parents, religious groups, clergy, professional and educational associations, civic and service groups, consistent supporters of the school, youth service groups, persons or enterprises engaged in commercial relationships with the institution, and more distant relatives and friends in both the immediate and associated groups.

3 "Disassociated" public that may be in favor or opposed to important school issues. This category is represented by industrial groups, commercial groups, municipal government employees, political groups, taxpayer organizations, banking and financing groups, and special interest groups.

4 "Institutional" publics that are disassociated but with their own immediate groups and all-consuming interests. Examples of the sub-groups in this category are ethnic groups, exclusive social clubs, senior citizens, mobile home residents, industry, military establishments, state and federal bureaus or agencies, and fraternal organizations.

Generally, the farther a group or public is removed from the school or college and their day-by-day problems, the less contact there will be and subsequently the less interest and involvement. Direct contacts with institutionalized publics are practically impossible for school or college representatives; it may not even be possible for them to reach disassociated publics. When there is a satisfactory communication link between representatives of the school or college with either the institutionalized or disassociated publics, it most often occurs indirectly through joint involvement in a service club, social event, church activity, or business action. Thus, the barriers that separate these groups in their relationships with the school or college are bridged by common interests, goals, and friendships that are not the exclusive domain of either the school or college or the primary group to which a person belongs. Public relations programs for schools and colleges should be aware that the pattern for any community is very complex, interwoven, and unpredictable insofar as who or what will be the key to success in obtaining the support of various groups or publics.

EXTERNAL PUBLICS OF A COLLEGE
The typical collegiate institution has the following external publics:

Women clubs

Parent clubs

Religious organizations

Clergy

Professional associations

Educational associations

Civic clubs

Service clubs

Booster clubs

Commercial firms (engaged in business with the institution)

Distant relatives and friends of internal publics

Industrial firms and associates

Commercial firms and associations

Labor organizations

Municipal government employees

City council

Political groups

State legislators

Taxpayer associations

Banking and financing groups

Ethnic groups

Social groups

Senior citizen groups

Military

State employee groups

Federal employee groups

Fraternal groups

Each of the above named publics can be subdivided into units. For example, women's clubs might be separated into units based upon age, affiliations with other organizations, graduates of colleges or universities, ethnic differences, and other classifications. Identifying a separate public and possible sub-groups is a necessary function. Care should be taken to avoid distinguishing too many "splinter" units. The public relations program should be developed to appeal to any significant group in the community; certain aspects of the public relations program must be specifically designed for a particular public.

CHAPTER SEVEN
THE SCHOOL BOND AND PUBLIC RELATIONS— RELATIONSHIP TO ATHLETIC AND PHYSICAL EDUCATION PROGRAMS

Although the primary concern of this book is not school bonds or tax levies, there is much that is revealed in these activities that focuses upon public relations. *Often the outcome of school bond issues affect athletic and physical education programs.* Physical education and athletic facilities typically represent 50 per cent or more of the total capital investment of a public high school. Because of this percentage of costs and the tendency for both educators and administrators to curtail or eliminate facilities, program, and personnel necessary to conduct physical education and athletic programs during financial crises, the wise, alert, and imaginative physical educator or athletic director seeks to understand the processes involved in school bond elections. The better these processes are understood, the better public relations programs can be designed to bring about desired results. The public relations involved in a school bond election is very little different from public relations for an athletic program, physical education program, or any other phase of the school or college offerings. School bond elections are to a great degree an objective measurement of the effectiveness of school or college public relations. Few other actions are so definitive as to whether or not the public accepts and supports the school or college.

CAUSES OF BOND FAILURES

The causes of bond failures vary from school to school, yet the most common cause is that the parents and patrons of the school have not been involved in decision making. People who have a keen interest in the outcome of a tax levy campaign should be part of the structure for its planning from the very inception of the proposal. The most effective way for schools to conduct a tax vote campaign is to rely upon intermediary persons or groups who are at least once removed from the school or college itself—this comprises the associated groups (see Chapter Six). They should carry the message to the public, and should activate the general campaign. The school or college public relations department must provide them with all the factual information possible, as well as campaign literature, campaign materials, and overall guidance pertaining to strategies and tactics. These intermediaries establish contacts with the disassociated and institutionalized groups in order to obtain their interest and support. Of special importance is for the intermediaries to solicit and gain the support and active participation of the community opinion leaders. Whenever school personnel themselves become openly engaged in the direct advocacy of a high tax levy, their motivations become suspect immediately.

OVERREACTION TO DEFEAT

After a tax bond has been defeated two or three times, school administrators often utilize a threat approach. Dropping or curtailment of extra-curricular activities, including athletics, special services, transportation, and supplies are typically noted in the threat. Such a strategy generates fear and the end-results are either resentment, disbelief, indifference, or retaliation. In some instances, there are citizens who would agree that such cutbacks are good. It should be clear that threat is a poor strategy;

in many cases its use denotes frustration. And this frustration can be traceable to a lack of a good educational program or a failure to employ a good public relations program, or both.

The internal publics of a school or college should be involved in determining any major decision, or, at the very least, they should be among the first to hear whatever has been decided. People need to be given the opportunity to identify with problems and suggested solutions.

REASONS FOR DEFEAT

Bond elections during the late 1960s and the 1970s have been defeated two-thirds of the time. Each bond defeat has some special feature, but there is a consistent series of reasons for most; these are:

1 A high percentage of voters over 45 years of age vote against bond issues.*
This is attributed to their concern about their own future economic status.

2 Some voters believe that the financial responsibility for school costs belongs to the state or federal government.

3 Some voters cast their ballots to express their resentment with the lack of information or involvement with school or college problems, issues, and solutions.

4 Some voters cast their ballot exclusively on the basis of their own potential gain or loss.

WHO SUPPORTS BOND ISSUES?

The broad base of support for school bond issues comes mainly from new residents, parents of school-age children, persons employed in skilled, clerical, or sales occupations, and from those who read school bulletins and publications. An examination of the publics who generally support school bond issues and levies reveals that they have a self-interest in the outcome. This underscores again the importance of having people involved in school activities on a continuous basis.

It has been demonstrated that from 20 to 30 per cent of voters who cast their ballot will support any issue concerning the school. About the same percentage of voters will vote against any issue pertaining to the school. This means there is from 40 to 60 per cent of the voter popula-

---

* Adolph Unruh and Robert A. Willier, *Public Relations for Schools* (Belmont, Calif.: Fearon Publications, 1974), p. 72.

tion that can be influenced by a public relations program.* Many people change their mind during a campaign. Many vote according to their opinion leaders, or membership in some particular public. The most important influence upon the 40 to 60 per cent of the voters who are neither for or against any school issue is the opinion leader.

A growing public that is becoming more and more vital to the passage of school levies is senior citizens. Presently over 10 per cent of our total population is 65 years or older; this relative proportion increases dramatically when nonvoting youth under 18 years of age are omitted. Senior citizens tend to remain behind and live where the population is at a standstill or declining; exceptions occur when senior citizens move into a separate community for elderly persons. In either case, the senior citizens comprise a forceful voting bloc. About two out of three senior citizens own their own home; these homes are of low valuation, and about one-half of the senior citizens, as a family unit, have incomes of less than $3000 annually. Any increase in property tax poses a real threat to their economic condition. Almost 60 per cent of those citizens over 65 years of age live in the major rapidly growing states—New York, California, Illinois, Ohio, Texas, Michigan, Massachusetts, New Jersey, and Florida.

Senior citizens have been the victims of a changing society. They have become disengaged and out of touch. Few productive efforts have been made to motivate the re-entry of senior citizens into the mainstream of America, particularly in its school systems. The astute school administrator will initiate programs that will encourage the utilization of the wisdom, skills, and the time to pass these along by using senior citizens as resource persons. Other avenues of establishing favorable attitudes include the provision of adult education, selected according to interests and conducted at the most favorable time, formation of "golden-age" clubs that can use the school facilities for many of their activities, and the inauguration of specialized recreational activities conducted on the campus. Granting free or reduced tickets to senior citizens so they can attend athletic events, drama productions, musical events, exhibits, and similar attractions can be valuable in gaining support.

BOND CAMPAIGN STRATEGY

Campaign strategy to assure the passage of tax levies deserves the attention of all those who care about schools and colleges and what they can

* Ibid.

or should offer students. A summary of successful campaign strategy
includes the following.

1 Opinion leaders must be identified early, convinced that the program or
cause is worthy of their support, and motivated to become personally and
actively involved in communicating their feelings to others.

2 Endorsement of proposals from key publics and groups, such as the civic
and service clubs, elected officials, professional, business, and labor organizations, and others that are important to the specific community must be obtained.

3 Opposition or indifference to a school measure is found to be greater among
the less educated, for they often perceive the school to be opposed to the
values for which they stand. These persons can best be influenced by opinion
leaders.

4 People who feel they have been alienated, have no power or authority, or
who are not involved in meaningful school-related activities will either not vote
or will vote negatively. These people should be identified and steps taken to
remedy the cause of their attitude.

Ironically, parents and voters tend to evaluate the school on the most
recent information or previous interaction. When information reaches
them in adequate amounts and on a consistent basis, a positive mind-set
is cultivated. On the other hand, when information is skimpy and inter-
spersed with negative reports, they tend to believe the worst about the
schools. Today, citizens and parents are better educated and more sophisticated. They want to know more about the internal operations of the
school and are interested in the curriculum, the content of subject matter, and methods of teaching. At the same time, our modern society has
made it difficult for personal involvement in the school. The development
of suburban communities and refinement of transportation has created
the so-called bedroom communities where one or both parents only sleep,
yet they have the right to voice their opinions and the right to vote. In
suburban communities, the voter turnout is less than 50 per cent of those
registered and eligible to cast a ballot. Because of bedroom communities, it is hard to develop enthusiastic support. Therefore, a good ongoing
public relations program is all the more important in seeking support of
these voters for schools.

SOURCES OF INFORMATION FOR
BOND PROPOSALS

Of the various publics that are important to schools, few can be of more
value than those persons affiliated with banks and financial institutions.

These persons and agencies have a great impact upon community projects, particularly school tax campaigns. Financial institutions know much of what is going on economically within the community or that which is scheduled to take place. They should be consulted for this purpose and also for determining the calendar date of the school bond election. They can be a prime source of information and advice as to major pockets of opposition.

SCHOOL BONDS FACE COMPETITION
School bond elections face stiff competition. In a recent Gallup Poll of the American Institute of Public Opinion, the ten top priority problems in the United States are crime, inflation, air–water pollution, race tension, drug addiction, overpopulation, low educational standards, labor–management disputes, inadequate housing, and low productivity standards. Education is in direct confrontation and competition for the tax dollar and public support.

CAUSES FOR OPPOSITION TO BONDS
Much of the taxpayer's opposition to additional school tax levies is due to the expenditure of the school monies. About 70 to 80 per cent of the school budget is assigned to salaries. Construction costs have increased dramatically, but so has insurance, utilities, equipment, supplies, and transportation. Seats of opposition are found among the retired or pensioners, parents whose children have completed school, parents who are not interested in sending their children to college, private school parents, citizens without children, the economically poor who do not understand the value of an education, and the struggling small business owner. Some interests groups organize in order to more effectively oppose school expenditures. Other interest groups organize and lead efforts designed to curtail school improvements; these groups may be opposed to sex education, vocational education, frills, or other school activities. Some persons are alienated by their understanding of school discipline or lack thereof, juvenile delinquency, top-heavy administrative staff, costly frills, or other real or imaginary conditions. Militant teachers offend many voters, regardless of the final justification of the cause for their actions; the militant teacher should be brought into the decision-making processes so that he or she will have the feeling of belonging and also become aware that solutions are often subject to long-term planning and action.

One of the major causes of alienation or indifference is traceable to the high level of mobility in our citizens. Families are seldom located in one home, instead they move so frequently that they do not develop any sense of belonging or being accepted. The typical American changes the location of his residence at least once every four to five years. Families seldom become interested or concerned with the educational problems or issues within a community.

Suburbia has also created some new problems for the school system. In bedroom communities the tax base is relatively small due to the lack of industrial and commercial enterprises. As a result, the home-owner taxes must assume the major portion of the tax burden.

Other changes in our schools are underway. From a peak of over 100,000 school districts there are now just a few more than 20,000. A dilemma confronts many school districts; they wish to decentralize or remain autonomous, but they cannot support schools of acceptable quality. Another change is being felt by public schools. In 1971, nearly 800 elementary and secondary parochial schools were closed, leaving some 10,500 operating. The enrollment in these schools has dropped from over six million to approximately four million. Obviously, this shift has added to the costs of public education.

SCHOOL BONDS AND PUBLIC RELATIONS

Successful school tax levies are the end-result of a good educational program combined with an effective public relations program. Many schools neglect the latter until the eve of an election, then launch bulldozer tactics. With rare exception, failure to obtain public support is certain. Public relations must be practiced every day, every month, and every year. Schools can learn from public utility companies. When these companies seek a rate increase, they plan for it nearly two years in advance. They prepare the public for the increase by providing volumes of information and every conceivable and reasonable justification for the rate change.

RELATIONSHIP OF SCHOOL BONDS
TO PROGRAMS

The capital investment devoted to athletic and physical education facilities in a typical high school campus represents approximately 50 percent of the total cost. When the land requirements, buildings, playing fields and courts, swimming pool, stadium, gymnasium, locker–shower rooms, equipment rooms, and other amenities needed for these programs are subtracted, the investment is drastically reduced.

Since school bonds are either directly or indirectly related to facilities, their passage or defeat is of vital concern to athletic and physical education departments. Also, since these programs are of such high public interest, it is clear that school administrators, coaches, physical educators, and program directors need to recognize the importance of public relations to school bond acceptance.

CHAPTER EIGHT
EDUCATIONAL
INSTITUTIONS AND
COMMUNITY
COMMUNICATIONS

In any form of communication there are four essential ingredients; all are necessary. They are the sender, the message, the medium, and the receiver. If the message is unclear, it may convey unintended meanings. The use of certain words trigger tensions and emotions in the receiver, and these reactions may block out the intended meaning. The receiver accepts, decodes, critically searches for additional cues, and then adds a personal interpretation of the words, perception of the sender, and association with the unintended meanings of the message. One's own status, function, and cultural dispositions are influential in the interpretation of the message. The astute sender knows that this process of communication will take place, consequently the message is prepared as accurately, meaningfully, and specifically as possible. This same process takes place whether the situation is formal, informal, face-to-face, or indirect.

EFFECT OF OPINION LEADERS

In nearly every distinct group or public there is at least one opinion leader who frequently influences the attitudes of followers by passing on to them his or her evaluation of a communication, which is then usually accepted by the entire group. This opinion leader is the focus of communications research. Since this person is the key, the prudent public relations specialist will locate and utilize this influence.

COMMUNICATIONS INSIDE AND OUTSIDE

There are two environments in which channels of communication take place. One is inside the institutional environment, and the other is outside. Both environments have formal means for disseminating information as well as informal, person-to-person networks of communication. In schools and colleges, the formal communications system starts with the board of education or trustees, the superintendent or chief executive officer, and then flows downward. The same flow of information takes place among the support staff—except that it may move upward or downward. The informal method of communication tends to carry messages within its own members or level. Communications between different levels of groups are more difficult to observe. Information is shared among the same level or social class, but it is seldom transmitted above or below. The same principle applies to ethnic groups.

CITIZEN GROUPS AND COMMUNICATIONS

A school or college should have established citizen groups with whom a close and reliable association is formed. These groups are usually started by the board of education, board of trustees, chief executive officers, or others; some are self-starting. The size of the citizen group or committee varies in number from 15 to 100. A larger committee can be divided into subcommittees and assigned specific tasks; an executive committee can be formed, and a steering committee can be structured. Subcommittees can be assigned to enrollment projections, financial support, curriculum trends, public relations, objectives and philosophy of the school, policies, legislation, or any other area of importance. Membership on committees should be limited in size so that each member will feel the importance and distinction of the appointment; periods of service should be staggered and membership should be changed systematically so that new ideas and enthusiasm can be combined with experience.

It is most essential that the leadership of all committees understand their role. Among the main guidelines should be emphasis upon the specificity of the committee responsibilities, avoidance of becoming a pressure group, the danger of circumventing the board of trustees or main body and going directly to the public. All committee memberships should represent a cross section of the community as much as it is feasible to do so; care should be exercised to avoid stacking the committee. Committees and their work should not interfere with regular school or college processes. Assignments to committees should not overlap. Communication channels should be carefully explained; allowances for feedback should be built into any plan. Early arrangements should be considered for constant monitoring by the steering committee and the professional staff.

In secondary schools care should be taken not to select a citizen's committee from only the Parent–Teachers Association or the Home and School Club. While the members of these organizations often represent the utmost interest in the school operations, it is possible that the broad scope of the community will not be represented. If such organizations exist, then it is advisable to comprise the committee from its membership along with nonmembers within the community.

A citizen's advisory group or committee can be of great value to the school or college, particularly in conveying the attitudes of various publics toward the institution and its policies and procedures. Furthermore, members of the committee become instrumental as communicators of the institution's public relations program. A sure way to immobilize or cause dissatisfaction by committee members is to encourage them to participate in meaningless assignments and either avoid or ignore their recommendations on serious, significant matters. If a committee is established, one should be ready to heed its advice or recommendations. While it is not absolutely necessary to follow this advice in every instance, the committee is entitled to an explanation of the reasons for not doing so.

The purpose of school–community communications is to inform citizens, parents, and patrons of all the activities, innovations, achievements, and possibilities of the educational effort of the schools. A second category or purpose of equal importance is to provide ample opportunities for feedback from the community. This can be accomplished by encouraging two-way communications through citizen participation in the decision-making processes of the school, community sponsored studies, surveys, and interviews with the opinion leaders in the community.

Other objectives or purposes of school-community communications are to help the citizens appreciate the value of a good educational program and the importance of a good education for the individual.

MEANS OF RECEIVING COMMUNICATIONS

The majority of citizens find out about their schools from the local newspaper. Personal contact with school personnel is the second most widely used form of communications; and radio and television are next in importance. This ranking can vary from community to community. An astute public relations practitioner discovers the situation for the community served. Television is fast becoming the most powerful medium in many communities. Kovalick[*] found that the greatest dispenser of news was television, in fact more important than either direct information from school personnel or the radio, even though both latter sources are vital. Neighborhood newspapers usually report on local schools in a favorable way. The least effective means for the school to communicate with the community is through public meetings. In the case of public meetings, two factors tend to depress their effectiveness; first, many persons who need to know about events are not present, and second, the format used for conveying messages and stimulating action often leaves much to be desired. Take-home materials, particularly for students in secondary schools, is not effective since many students either do not carry these to their intended destination or they screen them.

SCHOOL PUBLICATIONS AND COMMUNICATIONS

School publications can be effective if they are prepared correctly, distributed efficiently, and are timely. All school publications should meet the highest standards, particularly in the use of language, spelling, and grammar. Of course, the message or information conveyed should be

[*] Jerome G. Kovalick, "Somebody Better Do Something," (Washington, D.C.: National School Public Relations Association), 1970.

subject to as little misinterpretation as possible. Some of the key criteria for school publications are the following.

1 *Form* The material should be readable, have sensory appeal, utilize a newspaper layout, and have a broad range of reader interest.

2 *Content* The material should have cognitive appeal, inquiry satisfaction, source credibility, contrasting points of view, factual information, comprehensiveness, and personal interest.

3 *Response* The object of the publication is to stimulate action in many cases; this action may be either overt or covert, but in either case one seeks to instill certain attitudes and opinions. The use of slogans, phrases, or axioms that are easily remembered, repeated, and have meaning is a forceful method. Tact, diplomacy, and friendship are used.

ASSESSING RESULTS OF THE
COMMUNICATIONS PROCESS

Finding out what the community thinks about the school or college or any of its programs, personnel, or procedures is critical to any public relations program. Without this knowledge, the likelihood of counterproductive efforts is increased. Some of the most successful methods of inquiry into what the community thinks include the following.

1 Analyze the articles, editorials, and letters to the editor.

2 Analyze local television programming, especially that pertaining to education and the educational institutions.

3 Maintain a record of telephone calls and letters from citizens that pertain to the school or college.

4 Maintain complete and accurate files and statistics of the number of dropouts, flunk-outs, scholarships awarded, distinctions earned by individuals or programs, won–lost records, percentage of graduates attending advanced schools, and other significant data.

5 After a school bond fails or succeeds, attempt to determine the basis for the outcome so that this knowledge can be applied at a later time.

6 Keep a record of the platforms announced by both successful and unsuccessful candidates for the school board or board of trustees. An analysis of these platforms can offer meaningful cues.

7 Use valid and reliable questionnaires and opinionnaires—an established method of gaining insight to what people think.

8 Conduct purposive interviews with parents and patrons. These can reveal information and attitudes of persons that may not otherwise be learned.

9 Use the so-called "exit" interviews with teachers who are leaving the school or college for whatever reason and with parents who are departing the community.

10 Use Parent–Teacher Associations. Home-and-School Clubs, or informal meetings of parents and patrons for open discussions. These should be planned beforehand in order to isolate various topics and to prepare factual information adequately.

11 Recognize that the school or college advisory committee can be of utmost value to any institution in ascertaining the feelings that citizens have toward their educational systems and personnel.

12 Rely upon opinion leaders from the various segments of the school or college's publics. Discussions should be on a face-to-face basis. Mutual confidence and trust must be fostered over a period of time and experiences.

13 Seek information from a core-sample of community leaders on an informal face-to-face basis, preferably at a breakfast or luncheon.

14 Foster the use of informal face-to-face discussions, limited questionnaires, discussion groups, reliance groups, reliance upon opinion leaders, and other appropriate methods of gathering information and gaining insight to be employed among teachers, staff, and students.

SCHOOL BOARD AND COMMUNICATIONS

Public relations programs start with the school or college's policies and performance. These are largely determined by the governing board and the chief executive officer, although the prudent leader will incorporate the contributions of the faculty, staff, and lay-persons. Basically, the school board or board of trustees form the bridge between the institution and the public. For this reason, among others, the board of governors and the chief executive officer should come to an agreement about the role of public relations. This agreement generally includes the understanding that the governing board will interpret the community to the school or college staff, and, in turn, will also interpret the ideas and policies of the school and staff to the community.

STUDENTS AS COMMUNICATORS

Students are the most influential of the school or college's publics. Much of the current information and the attitudes held by the general public are transmitted by the student to parent to the public-at-large via the community grapevine. The old adage that public relations starts in the classroom or on the playing field has proved undeniably accurate. Students should be involved in the development of policies, implementing courses or activities that meet their needs and interests, and in all areas of concern. Students who have pride in their institution and its accomplishments are potent public relations aids. The obvious is often overlooked. Students of today who have reached eighteen years of age are eligible to cast ballots, they will become the parents of future school children, and they will provide the money to operate the educational institutions. In the instance of physical education and competitive athletics, the attitudes toward these activities formed during student days tend to remain indefinitely. When it is necessary to reduce operating costs or find time for curricular additions, a negative attitude toward either physical education or competitive athletics is a forerunner to their curtailment or elimination. Of course, a positive attitude towards these activities formed during student years leads to support at all times.

IMPORTANCE OF INFORMATION
DISSEMINATION

School and college administrators should recognize the fact that the main cause of public pressures on their institutions, in most instances, is due to the public being uninformed or misinformed. When effective agencies exist to assist the institution's public relations program, key public leaders and groups should be involved in changes of policy, organization, curricula, or other major shifts. Leaders should be encouraged to carry the full message to their publics and to the public-at-large. In some cases, it is advisable to hold public hearings on important aspects; key opinion leaders should have all the necessary information and data necessary to make a good case for the desired changes. Providing the general public with as much information as feasible is desirable, along with the stated support of key leaders and publics. When an issue requires considerable space or more than the community newspapers can assign to it, the use of a printed supplement to go along with the paper can be helpful.

COMMUNICATIONS AND
HIGHER EDUCATION

Higher education has some public relations interests and needs that are not shared fully by the elementary or secondary schools. Public relations at major universities started after World War I, when institutions found the need to solicit funds to accommodate the growing number of students. After World War II, collegiate public relations accelerated and expanded; the Council for the Advancement and Support of Education is today an extremely vital organization.

Most people fail to understand the purposes, programs, and methods of colleges. Blame for this condition can be placed upon many; however, the primary responsibility for this state belongs to the institution's public relations program.

It is of paramount importance for the college administrative personnel to recognize that the institution belongs to the public, and belonging to the public obligates the administration to communicate fully with the public. No institution of higher education is self-supporting. Support comes more completely when the public is totally aware of issues, program, and plans. During the 1950s and 1960s, institutions of higher education were recipients of the greatest financial outpouring of all time. With the onset of the mid-1970s, the situation changed dramatically. Enrollments started to level off and, in some cases, actually drop. Competition for public dollars by mid-1970's reached new heights. Federal taxes reached a new peak. National programs of defense, environment control, transportation, welfare, employment, and others absorbed much of the taxpayer's dollars. On the local level, increased programs or new programs in crime control, ecology, special programs for the disadvantaged, health, welfare, government, operations, and others have added to the burden of the taxpayer. The end-result of the high costs of these programs has made it much more difficult for the institutions of higher education to receive the necessary support to conduct curricular offerings and related activities. If higher education is to obtain its rightful share of public financial support, then it must convince the public that what it has to offer deserves a high priority. This can be accomplished best by conducting quality education programs and by carrying on an aggressive, imaginative public relations program.

STUDENT COMMUNICATIONS

The chief executive officer is the key to the college's public relations program. This individual must understand its significance. And, maximum support and enthusiasm should be attached to it. College students deserve to be treated as adults. As such they should have a voice in policy matters, curricular affairs, and sponsored activities. Students generally represent a wide geographical area and when they return to their home localities during college holidays, they become the broadcaster of the college, positively or negatively.

ALUMNI COMMUNICATIONS

The alumni of a collegiate institution has a lasting relationship that may be for better or worse. Students who have been included in the core content of the institution are more likely to be constructive, helpful alumni. Serious efforts should be made to introduce senior students to the alumni program so that their eventual transition will be more likely and desirable. Alumni should be motivated to maintain a keen interest in the institution. This is done best by keeping the alumni fully informed of all phases of the institution's programs. An active alumni organization can be of great assistance to the institution, but care must be exercised to make certain that its leaders do not have a vested self-interest or a selfish motive. While the sentimental ties between alumni and the institution should be propagated, the alumni should be granted opportunities to perform challenging tasks for their alma mater. The administration should seek to have alumni carry out programs that lead to the fulfillment of principles, not things. When this is done, loyalty, interest, counsel, and money will usually follow.

COMMUNICATIONS AND POLITICIANS

The college administrator should recognize the importance of good communications with the state legislators, state officials, and governmental agencies. All of these persons will, at some time, have an influence upon the institution through curriculum content, financial support, and primary charges or purposes.

CHAPTER NINE
CONCEPTS OF
ATHLETIC RELATIONS

Among typical secondary schools and colleges there are vast differences in the public relations programs conducted by their respective athletic and physical education departments. At most collegiate institutions the emphasis on athletic teams requires an aggressive public relations and promotions program because the financial basis for the department depends so heavily on gate receipts and contributions and both are directly related to win–loss records. Inevitably, public relations, win–loss records, and revenues are inseparable. Few, if any, other institution-sponsored activities are as self-dependent upon deriving their own funds as the intercollegiate athletics program. Thus, necessity compels action. Caution should be used to universally condemn an athletics program because of this necessity; rather, in many instances, commendations are in order for the energies, commitments, and results achieved by the dedicated, talented, and successful individuals attached to the athletics department.

AUTHORIZATION OF PUBLIC RELATIONS

The director of athletics or chief administrative officer for the athletics program should have a complete understanding with the president or chief executive officer of the institution concerning the role and responsibility of the department. Included in this understanding should be an agreement pertaining to the type of public relations program to be conducted. A written document should be prepared enumerating the major goals of the institution and the specific ways that the athletics department can and should contribute to their realization. Included in this document should be the primary objectives assigned to the athletics department. There should also be a clear statement concerning the role of the athletic department's public relations, any limitations under which the public relations program should operate, and a delineation of the specific areas of responsibility. This agreement serves many useful purposes, but primarily it grants certain rights and states specific responsibilities and restrictions. The athletic department's "staff manual," "operating code," or similar in-house guide should contain this information for the benefit of all members of the staff.

ATHLETIC DEPARTMENTS ARE UNIQUE
IN PUBLIC RELATIONS

Collegiate athletic departments have long realized the need for a vigorous, well-conceived public relations program. There are only a few four-year institutions that are presently without at least one public relations specialist assigned full or part-time to this responsibility; community colleges are moving in the same direction. Larger universities employ from one to three full-time experts in addition to employing part-time help. Annual budgets for public relations activities ranges from a few hundred dollars to over $100,000. These expenditures are looked upon as an investment with expectations of profitable returns.

The title of the public relations specialist used most often is "Sports Information Director." This title became somewhat standardized by actions of the National Collegiate Athletic Association. Yet this title seems too restrictive; the connotation implied by persons both on or off-campus is that the office is solely responsible for publicity. Perhaps the titles "Director of Athletic Public Relations" or "Sports Public Relations Director" more fully describe the actual functions of this office.

SELECTION OF THE PUBLIC RELATIONS PRACTITIONER

The selection of the public relations practitioner should be done with as much care, planning, and judgment as used to employ a head football or basketball coach. A serious error in selection can cause great and long-lasting harm to the institution and its athletic program. By making the proper selection, the athletic program will be bolstered by improved public relations, local and national recognition, desirable scheduling, and increased revenues. The office of public relations is one of the last places that one should attempt to squeeze budgets. To some degree, the public relations office can be compared to the marketing and sales operations of a commercial enterprise, and, in the same way, eventual success is related to the public acceptance of the final product presented.

An ideal combination background for a public relations director for the athletic program belongs to a person who has completed specialized training and education in the field and who has a close affinity or identification with sports teams and programs. Simply employing a "mechanic" or someone who is familiar with public relations techniques should be avoided. The ideal person should have a grasp of the technical phases of public relations plus an understanding of the role of the institution in society and the part that athletics can and must fill to aid the institution. While public relations experts should be congenial and adaptable to a given situation, they should also have strong convictions and deep feelings and be unafraid to present their opinions at the proper time and place. One should always be cognizant that the specialist is employed to give advice and guidance, among other things; preventing the expert from expressing opinions is self-defeating.

ACCEPTANCE OF THE PUBLIC RELATIONS PRACTITIONER

The public relations practitioner should be granted the same working amenities as those provided the highest echelon within the department. This is recommended for at least two important reasons. First, certain amenities will aid in attracting the highest caliber specialist. Second, the fulfillment of responsibilities is facilitated when other staff members in the department and persons outside the department recognize that the public relations practitioner is considered part of the top management level.

ROLE OF THE DIRECTOR OF ATHLETICS
IN PUBLIC RELATIONS
Regardless of who is employed as director of athletic public relations, the shape and direction of the public relations program will be determined largely by the director of athletics. Fortunately, most directors of athletics have a positive understanding of public relations. Yet, there are several who have a limited knowledge or understanding of just what public relations is, how it can be developed, and what its importance is to the athletic program and to the institution. When the latter conditions prevail, the tasks of the public relations expert are more difficult. If possible, attempts should be made to slowly and progressively educate the director of athletics in public relations.

PUBLIC RELATIONS AS A TOTAL
STAFF RESPONSIBILITY
At the time of employment of a newly appointed director of athletic public relations (or equivalent title) and at least once a year at all other times, the director of athletics should conduct a review of the objectives of the athletic program in general and those of public relations specifically. Depending upon the number of the athletic department staff, the director of athletics may have all members of the staff engaged in this process; if this is not preferable, the assignment to complete all preliminary work may be given to a committee. All members of the department should have direct involvement in the process. Such an experience educates or enlightens some, and it applies the principle that when persons are involved they are more supportive and receptive to final plans. A word of advice may be in order. It is usually a gross mistake to conduct this review in a perfunctory manner, allow the course of review to become chaotic or haphazard, or attempt the project without allotting sufficient time.

PUBLIC RELATIONS HANDBOOK FOR STAFF
All prior decisions or conclusions regarding department public relations objectives, policies, procedures, priorities, and responsibilities concerning

the intercollegiate athletic department should be in writing and distributed to each staff member. Each staff member should be requested to review this document by a certain date before the department undertakes any project. Further, each staff member might prepare a written summation pertaining to their opinion of each section in the document. Staff members should be reassured that all comments or objectives will be treated objectively and without reprisal; freedom of thought and expression within a department are crucial to good internal public relations. The purposes for this review and written reaction are to expedite matters and to encourage full attention to the task. Also, no one can claim that they were not allowed to participate in the formulation of the operational guidelines.

OBJECTIVES OF PUBLIC RELATIONS

Objectives of athletic public relations programs may vary somewhat from situation to situation, although most of the basic objectives remain constant for all institutions. Some of these objectives are listed below with the foreknowledge that they may be altered to meet certain circumstances, some may be eliminated, and others added.

1 Inform all relevant publics about the athletic program.

2 Develop confidence in the values of the program for the participants and others.

3 Create moral and material support for the athletic programs.

4 Stimulate an awareness of athletics as an expression and vital contribution to our way of life.

5 Contribute to psychological, social, and recreational needs of the masses.

6 Foster understanding of the operations of athletic programs in order to prevent misunderstandings.

7 Encourage the conduct and content of athletics program to meet the interests and needs of the participant and relevant publics.

8 Develop a proper perspective of athletic competition by everyone participating in or associated with the athletic program.

DIRECTOR OF ATHLETICS' RESPONSIBILITY
FOR PUBLIC RELATIONS

The director of athletics cannot assign the responsibility for the public relations program to anyone else; he may delegate certain functions and duties to the public relations practitioner. However, even after such delegation, the athletic director is held accountable for planning and coordinating the public relations program. The talents of staff members should be utilized in the public relations program to the same extent that they are for the sports program itself. Recognition of the importance of personal and department public relations expressed by the director of athletics is assimilated by the department's staff members. For this reason the athletic director should be a leader in this area.

COMMUNITY COLLEGE AND SCHOOL
PUBLIC RELATIONS PROGRAMS

While this discussion has focused upon the college or university program, many of the same precepts and principles apply fully to the secondary school and community college. Essentially the main difference is that the secondary school or community college can not or does not appoint a full-time public relations specialist for the athletic program. Under these conditions the athletic director, staff, and the institution administration must confront the issue of whether or not a structured public relations program for athletics will be attempted. The common error—and one to be avoided at all times—is to make public relations activities, other than personal actions, the responsibility of a coach in each sport. The axiom to the effect that "everyone's job is really no one's job" applies perfectly. An athletic department that relies upon each coach to conduct the public relations program for his or her own sport eventually leads to confusion, conflict, and collapse.

When it is absolutely certain that no person can be employed either full-time or part-time as a director of athletic public relations, alternate plans should be considered. One such plan that has been a worthy substitute involves an agreement by all staff members and the administration of the instituton. This plan provides for some member of the athletic staff to have a basic knowledge of public relations or be willing to develop an acceptable level of competency. Furthermore, this individual should display some zest for working in public relations. Although employed as a regular teaching and coaching staff member, anywhere from one-third to two-thirds of this member's working time will be devoted to the public relations program of the department. All members of the staff must be willing to allow for such an arrangement. Staff members must also be willing to absorb this individual's normal teaching and coaching duties that are relieved due to attention to public relations. For example, if the regular teaching load of all staff members is five teaching periods plus afterschool coaching, the individual may be relieved of anywhere from two to five teaching periods and coaching. The remainder of the staff would proportionately share in absorbing the individual's regular duties on an equitable basis spread over the school year. Depending upon the number of staff members, this "overload" might vary from an average of one additional working hour per day for the entire school year to as little as one additional working hour for every week.

Under this arrangement, the individual assigned to public relations is responsible for the typical duties of that office. Other staff members are relieved of attempting to conduct their own public relations program and instead all actions and activities are channeled through this individual. Efforts become cooperative.

Under this operation, the athletic public relations director seeks assistance from other school or community college departments. Properly conceived and supervised, valuable practical experiences can be gained by students involved in the program. Arrangements should be completed with certain departments on campus. These would include departments of journalism, typing, photography, and art. A plan could be devised so that the experiences received by students in these departments are meaningful, particularly for those who plan careers in the respective areas. Specific work assignments should be planned for students to be attended at specifically scheduled times. Work quality of students must be evaluated and reported.

It is advisable to house the athletic public relations director and the students assigned to that office in separate accommodations. Do not install this office in the staff's general office. The entire operation of this public relations office must be conducted in a businesslike manner.

While this substitute plan is not as desirable as one in which a public relations specialist is employed, it is a most feasible and productive substitute. Public relations activities are assigned to one person, although all members of the staff must cooperate in such ways so as to maximize the efficiency and results of the office. As indicated earlier, when public relations is everyone's job, it then becomes no one's job.

CHAPTER TEN
CONCEPTS OF
PHYSICAL EDUCATION
PUBLIC RELATIONS

Perhaps one of the most misunderstood programs at high school and college levels is that of physical education. Contradictions abound throughout school systems and collegiate institutions. Nearly every reputable and recognized itemization of the primary aims of education includes the physical and emotional well-being of students and the need for preparation of leisure time activities. Yet, whenever there is a cutback on funds, or periodic changes in emphasis upon academic subjects, or the launching of new programs, physical education is subject to sacrifices in time, staff, and budget.

There are several basic causes for physical education becoming the victim in order to accommodate various academic changes and emphases. It is not the purpose of this discussion to enumerate these causes. However, one of the fundamental reasons for physical education's precarious standing is the lack of public relations or the presence of a weak public relations program.

PHYSICAL EDUCATION PUBLIC RELATIONS PROGRAMS

Unlike competitive athletics at either the high school or college level, physical education programs do not enjoy a public relations expert or office. The absence of a public relations expert assigned to the physical education department is understandable. Nonetheless, the absence of an acceptable substitute is not only unfortunate but tragic. Physical education must sponsor at least a minimal public relations program if it is to withstand the inroads and opposition it is sure to face. How does a physical education department, without special funding, approach a public relations program?

Actually, there is very little difference in the approach used for a nonfunded athletic public relations program from that used for a nonfunded physical education public relations program. The basic strategy is the same. At the outset, the chief administrative officer must give personal approval to the need for the public relations program and the proposed plan to implement it. Secondly, the physical education staff should be enthusiastic and unified concerning the need for the public relations program, how it is to be implemented, and their willingness to contribute their time and effort to allow it to succeed. Once approval is granted by the proper authorities and the physical education staff endorses the plan, the following format, or one adapted to meet a local situation, is made effective.

An inventory is made of the scope and content of the proposed public relations program. Both short-range and long-range objectives, strategies, and tactics should be identified, recorded, and assigned priorities. This master plan requires a relatively long time to develop. Haste at the expense of quality and detailed consideration should be avoided. Simply enumerating the various public relations activities is insufficient. A cooperative effort must be made to consider all possible activities. The question is not merely to identify these activities, but also to evaluate each concerning its appropriateness for the specific institution, expense, time commitment, risks of failure or misinterpretation, objectives realization, and immediate and long-range benefits. It is obvious that the public relations program cannot undertake an unlimited number of activities. Decisions on these matters are crucial.

After a master plan has been approved, then an evaluation is made of the estimated time investment necessary for the director or person assigned to implement the program. The conclusion may be that a staff member would require from two to six hours of released teaching time daily in order to carry out the program. The physical education staff members are then requested to absorb a fair share of this released time. For example, the school day may consist of six class periods and there are six physical education teachers, in addition to the proposed public relations director and the chairperson of the physical education department. Thus, if a staff member was to be granted six hours per day of released time, then each of the remaining six teachers would add one additional teaching hour per day to their load. If there are twelve physical education teachers, then each might add one additional teaching hour for one semester or half the academic year. If there are more or fewer teachers, then some equitable formula is applied.

The person appointed as the physical education public relations director (or coordinator) should have a separate office or an area that can be isolated. While regular teachers spend most of their working hours in a classroom or at a teaching area and only use the general staff office short periods of time between classes, the public relations director is located at a desk most of the working day. There will be too many distractions for the public relations director to complete tasks if forced to share an office with the remaining staff members. Also, the public relations director should seek to involve student assistants.

Student assistants can be valuable. A carefully planned program should be evolved with the chairpersons of the journalism or publications department, typing or business department, art department, and others who may be involved. A high set of standards must be incorporated for the selection of students and for the evaluation of their work. This arrangement should seek to benefit the student as an internship program for those who intend to pursue the related career. In addition to the previously cited reasons for a separate office or workroom, the presence of students on a regular basis makes it desirable to have a location removed from the regular staff.

The job description and explanation of the various public relations activities that apply to the public relations director are noted in detail in ensuing chapters.

CHAPTER ELEVEN
JOB DESCRIPTION OF
THE PUBLIC
RELATIONS
PRACTITIONER

Specific duties of the public relations practitioner for the athletics or physical education departments at schools and colleges are covered in subsequent sections of this book. Before considering specific duties, an overview of the public relations activities or job description of the practitioner is advantageous.

INTERNAL RELATIONS HAVE TOP PRIORITY
The initial objective of the public relations practitioner is to earn widespread, enthusiastic support for the public relations concept within his or her department. This is of critical importance, yet it is a task often

very difficult to accomplish. Surprisingly, there is often a great amount of built-in skepticism, indifference, or antagonism. Some of the roots for these attitudes may involve personality clashes, old wounds, jealousy, or pride. Quite often the cause is lack of understanding or misunderstanding of the functions and benefits of a good public relations program. Whatever the reasons, the public relations practitioner should attempt to identify them; various staff members may have quite different reasons for their position. Fortunately, not all staff members will be negative in their attitude toward public relations. Time, patience, and due caution should be taken to identify the attitudes of each member. This is done best, in most cases, by establishing a cordial, candid relationship with each staff member. Usually a department staff has a "power bloc" or opinion leaders. These need to be pinpointed, and the highest priority given to soliciting their support and enthusiasm.

ADMINISTRATOR'S SUPPORT IS ESSENTIAL

The chief administrator plus immediate staff should be won over concerning the importance and needed support of public relations. This task is facilitated by having data, evidence, facts, and information about the various publics and what they think of the institution and specifically of the athletics or physical education program, depending upon which program is involved. To simply attempt to "brainwash" administrators concerning the importance of public relations is an error. If backup materials are adequate and of high quality, they will be of much more value in gaining support.

Once the top administrators approve of the public relations concept, it is advisable to obtain a signed statement regarding purposes, responsibilities, and authority. This statement serves in several ways: the public relations practitioner is recognized on campus and off-campus, the athletics (or physical education) staff accepts the role with more cooperation, and the practitioner operates with more confidence.

RELATIONSHIPS BETWEEN PRACTITIONER
AND STAFF MEMBERS

Public relations practitioners should convince staff members that their purpose is to aid programs, that they are willing to expend time and energy on their behalf, but that mutual cooperation is a necessity for full success. Trust and candor are required of all persons for a public relations program to function properly. A clarification of the rights, responsibilities, and duties of staff members to the public relations practitioner needs to be discussed in open meeting, with agreements reached, and written statements prepared; similarly, the rights, responsibilities, and duties of the public relations practitioner in reference to staff members and their programs must be detailed and approved in writing. These final documents are used as guides, not weapons.

It should be emphasized that the most frequent cause of conflict between the public relations practitioner and the staff members is the lack of fixed boundaries or the disregard of established guidelines. The best preventative to avoid conflict is respect, trust, candor, and a sense of teamwork. Any indiscretions should be discussed and settled as early as possible on merits, not on personalities or power plays. Conformance to established guidelines should be commended by the director of athletics (or physical education).

Public relations is mainly a staff function. Essentially, the staff position is to support or assist the line officer. This can be done best by helping the staff members with their problems and their solutions.

In addition to performing the unique duties of the position, the public relations practitioner can be of special benefit to the director of athletics (or physical education) by maintaining a high level of loyalty under all conditions inside the law, help in preparing messages, speeches, or other public statements, offering inspiration and motivation to reach the stated goals, and aiding in restraining line and staff persons from doing anything detrimental to the department or institution.

OBLIGATIONS OF THE PUBLIC RELATIONS PRACTITIONER

Broadly stated, the public relations practitioner has many major responsibilities and functions. One is to serve as the central source of information and as the official channel of communication between the institution and its publics. This entails communicating both the good and the bad. Frequently staff members are eager to be spokesmen for the good, positive, and innovative news or information, but these same individuals have the tendency to remain silent, unheard, and unseen during episodes that are difficult and distasteful. The public relations practitioner should have the full authority to be the official representative for all purposes, subject only to direction by the director of athletics (or physical education).

The public relations practitioner also has the responsibility to determine how a story will be released, to whom, when, and where. When more than one person has the leeway to issue a story, it may be done in such a way as to cause negative results, particularly on the part of the media who may rightly or wrongly believe that the release was inappropriate in one or several ways. This is another strong reason for clearly establishing a policy within the department of athletics (or physical education) concerning the authority and responsibility for issuing news releases; this policy should be clearly stated in writing and made a feature section in the department handbook or guidebook for staff.

The public relations practitioner is responsible for coordinating all college activities related in any way to the athletic program that have a public relations impact. All department publications should either be prepared under the direction of the public relations specialist or, at the very least, should be subject to his or her approval before being printed and issued. Further, the institution and department policies should clearly spell out these conditions in writing and make them a part of the guidebook or handbook. At the secondary school and community college level these same lines of responsibility and authority are assigned to the person serving as the public relations director.

GOOD PUBLIC RELATIONS
REQUIRE RESEARCH

Any good public relations program operates from a base of facts, evidence, and data. To collect this material in ways that it is valid and reliable requires a high level of sophistication, otherwise the collected materials can be misleading and cause disastrous results. The responsibility and the authority to collect these materials rests with the public relations specialist. In the event that the public relations specialist does not have the resources, time, or understanding to do this satisfactorily, the task may be assigned to another person. However, the public relations specialist remains in charge and retains full responsibility for the final results. In addition to collecting information pertaining to attitudes, facts, evidence, and other information, the public relations specialist is charged with analysis of all materials. Again, outside assistance may be obtained; however, the final findings are the responsibility of the public relations specialist. The reason why responsibility for the collection and analysis of materials cannot be transferred is that they provide the foundation for a good public relations program. Dependence upon another person to complete this highly important and sensitive task is too risky. Furthermore, it is too easy to assign blame for any subsequent failure upon insufficient or inadequate background materials prepared by another person.

WHO IS RESPONSIBLE FOR PUBLIC RELATIONS?

The public relations specialist is also given complete authority and responsibility to plan and execute the public relations program, subject only to supervision by the director of athletics (or physical education). As a matter of operating policy and for the protection of both persons, the public relations specialist should present a plan for public relations and the intended method to implement it to the director of athletics (or physical education). This procedure has much merit. The public relations specialist can operate more confidently, seek help when needed, and be able to withstand criticism or opposition. Likewise, the director of athletics (or physical education), knowing the entire picture, can defend or support the public relations specialist with more confidence, can anticipate various activities and methods, and can better plan to offer emergency assistance in the form of funds, personnel, or time.

BUDGET FOR PUBLIC RELATIONS

To expect a public relations program to function without an adequate budget is foolhardy and self-deceiving. There will be certain expenses, in addition to salaries, that are necessary. Stationery, postage, printing, photography, duplicating processes, telephone, and travel costs are ordinarily involved. The public relations practitioner should prepare a budget for each major activity as well as a total budget. This procedure once again emphasizes the value of preparing a master plan for the year. Often, merely on the basis of cost, certain preferred activities may have to be changed or postponed. Unless the public relations practitioner prepares a comprehensive budget and obtains approval of it by the director of athletics (or physical education), it will be impossible to operate the program with any degree of security, confidence, or continuity.

One of the most difficult areas to obtain finances is for research or the collection of data. Persons who lack sophistication in public relations affairs often fail to recognize the need and significance of this phase of the program. The public relations practitioner should be well-prepared when presenting this budget request to the director of athletics (or physical education) and perhaps to the staff.

OFFICE LOCATION

The physical location of the office of the public relations practitioner should be adjacent to that of the director of athletics (or physical education) and accessible to the staff. This proximity and accessibility, yet separateness, encourages free interchange and a sense of "oneness." In many institutions this arrangement allows the secretarial office to assist the public relations practitioner by serving as a reception center for visitors, telephone message center, and information outlet.

IMPORTANCE OF PERSONAL ATTITUDE

A good public relations practitioner portrays confidence in his or her own ability and in the persons and programs represented. Conveying an attitude of defeat or skepticism can harm the public relations efforts. These attitudes must be genuine and consistent; any attempt to fake these feelings usually fails. On the other hand, genuine enthusiasm and confidence can be somewhat contagious. Staff members, administrators, other department faculty, students, and publics off-campus soon are affected by a positive, confident attitude. Unless the staff of the athletic (or physical education) department has confidence in the public relations practitioner and his or her efforts, minimal success can be predicted.

KNOW YOUR PEOPLE AND THEIR PROBLEMS

Communications between the staff and public relations specialist are essential. The public relations specialist should learn the language used by the staff, so that their messages are interpreted properly. Specific efforts should be made to learn about the problems confronting each staff member as they relate to their program. Knowing the problem helps the public relations specialist in shaping the program for that particular sport or activity. Each staff member is unique; individual personality and philosophy of the administration of the sport or activity under his or her direction should be studied by the public relations practitioner. This examination aids the public relations specialist in interpreting the actions, events, and needs of the staff member and it also assists in intercommunication.

A public relations practitioner must resist certain normal human tendencies. Unless restraint is exercised, the public relations specialist may tend to favor certain staff members over others merely on the basis of personality. Or, there may be a bias toward certain sports. The safest method is to treat each staff member and the sport or activity represented as equally as possible.

SUPPORT OF DIRECTOR OF ATHLETICS

The director of athletics (or physical education) should reflect respect and confidence in the public relations practitioner. When these are present, other staff members are more likely to react in the same manner. Of course, reciprocal respect and confidence of staff members by the public relations specialist are essential. Should the public relations specialist be universally popular this would be most unusual. While one should strive for this status, the chances of attaining it are quite remote. In any case, personality clashes or petty differences should be avoided as much as possible.

KNOW THE PAST

Upon accepting the position of public relations director, there are certain actions and recommendations worth heeding. A careful study should be made of the entire environment, including the people, program, and working conditions. If prior research or accumulation of data are available, these are reviewed. Previous public relations procedures, events, and programs should be examined. Visits are made with each staff member who has any seniority in the department. These are informal but structured so as to obtain information and answers about past practices and current needs. Such visits should occur in the offices of the staff members or at a neutral site, such as a faculty lounge, coffee shop, or other location conducive to the realization of objectives. Attempts should be directed to learning about personal experiences involving public relations and those pertaining to the department as a whole. An attempt is made to capture the general changes in attitude and policy over the years and the reasons for them. Efforts must also be made to learn about interdepartmental relationships. Try to determine if there is any animosity between the athletics (or physical education) department and any other department on campus. If animosity exists, seek to determine the causes and what can be done to rectify the situation. This is important. As so often stated, public relations starts at home. By contacting most or all of the campus departments and either formally or informally expressing the objectives of the athletics (or physical education) department to their chairperson or entire staff, much resentment, suspicion, and antagonism can be reduced.

A thorough review should be made of all matters on file. Special attention is devoted to examining the files of complaints, letters of commendation or criticism, reading of minutes of meetings, statements of policy, faculty handbooks, copies of letters mailed, various notices, financial reports, and printed materials. If there is a "morgue," one should look for historical materials, basis for legends, and keepsakes. These actions help the public relations practitioner to understand the present in the light of yesteryear.

THE PRACTITIONER ON STAGE

Although it should not be necessary, the public relations director must be reminded that he or she, probably more than any other single staff member, will represent the department and institution publicly, and if not personally at least indirectly. There will be attendance at press meetings, regular visits to members of the media, attendance at meetings of a wide span of publics, speeches at various public functions, appearances on television or radio, and many other activities. Social graces, manner of speaking, dress, appearance, and content of conversation are all consciously or unconsciously evaluated by those with whom one comes into contact. In one sense, the public relations director represents the athletic (or physical education) department at all times, at all places.

CHAPTER TWELVE
HOW TO FIND AND
TELL WHAT IS NEW

In our modern society with its sophisticated communications media, our citizens are virtually bombarded incessantly by millions of words, pictures, and publications. Among this myriad of messages, public relations programs for athletics (or physical education) must seek to be read, viewed, and heard. Ideally the merits of the athletic (or physical education) program should be sufficient in determining people's attitudes and actions. Yet this is not the case. One must fight for survival and advancement. Some consolation exists in that all other public enterprises or institutions, such as the church, government, and political entities, must face the same challenge. Education, in general, needs to realize that the support enjoyed for decades is fragile and the need for improving its public relations programs is obvious. Within the scope of education, athletics (and physical education) becomes the most threatened since their foundation is not as firm. It is for this reason, in addition to the fact that athletics is financially self-dependent to a large extent, that the director of athletics (or physical education) should launch an offensive strategy.

IMPORTANCE AND USE OF MASS MEDIA

Due to our large urban population centers, the use of mass media for communication of our messages is necessary. This has several advantages: greater numbers can be contacted, it is cheaper, and the messages conveyed by this means are generally accepted by those who read or listen. Disadvantages also exist in their use. These include the important lack of feedback; it is a one-way process. Other weaknesses are that the receivers may not perceive the message in the same way as the sender. Information, especially of technical nature, is subject to misinterpretation, slanting, or distortion.

NEWSPAPERS

The community or suburban newspaper ranks high in importance in carrying communications from the school, including those of the athletic (and physical education) department. Community newspapers are the most influential and powerful force for developing public opinion about schools and their programs.* Additionally, the community newspaper usually takes a positive stand regarding school issues and news. Large metropolitan newspapers play a powerful role in shaping opinions concerning education in general and athletics (or physical education) in particular. Both the metropolitan and community newspapers are important to schools and to athletics (or physical education).

RADIO AND TELEVISION

Radio and television are also very important. Radio is still a giant in shaping people's attitudes and conveying messages. There are over 336

---

* Merle R. Sumption and Yvonne Engstrom, *School–Community Relations—A New Approach* (New York: McGraw-Hill Book Co., 1966), p. 120.

million radio sets in use. Over 200 million American homes have at least one radio; some have several. Contrary to some opinions, radio is still a growing medium. Since 1950, more than 500 new radio stations have commenced operations. Today there are more than 4300 AM stations and 2700 FM compared to 650 TV stations. A large extent of our population depends upon radio for most of their news. Over 85 million automobiles have radios. The nature of the medium allows one to be engaged in travel, performing routine tasks, or engaged in many other activities while still receiving the messages carried by radio. This is particularly true in the case of automobile traveling. Strangely, most school administrators and athletic public relations directors have stressed television use more than radio use. This is partially explained by the attraction of television and its obvious impact. However, obtaining television time is more difficult because of the pressure of all educational, charitable, and nonprofit organizations seeking exposure. Alert and imaginative public relations practitioners have used radio communications to a great advantage. In addition to normal news releases, radio has been employed to carry talk-shows, taped interviews, panel discussions, quiz shows, and public service announcements pertaining to athletic programs with much success. An added advantage of radio over printed media is the personal touch that is added. Though not as effective as television, listening to a spokesman on radio can be persuasive. Various programs can be attuned to meet the needs and interests of various publics in the community. In a typical community, one can transmit a message by radio to more people in just one hour than if one spoke simultaneously to every public meeting place in the area. Surveys have shown that the average person listens to radio every day from two to five hours. Radio programs need materials written especially for them; these are written for the ear, not the eyes. The most effective radio programs are those that are informal, conversational, to the point, and accurate.

The latest mass communication medium is also the most potent. Television is the next best substitute for personal face-to-face contact. In many ways, television can be more influential than a face-to-face meeting because it can employ motion, color, music, animation, and sound effects. Research studies have demonstrated that television is the most potent medium in terms of audience interpretation of a commercial sponsor, remembrance of and understanding of the sales point in the commercial, and greater sales. The average American watches television three hours each day.

USE OF RADIO AND TELEVISION

Radio and television operate according to federal regulations. These regulations specify that a certain portion of their time on the air can be filled with programs of their own choice. Under Federal Communications Commission licenses, television and radio stations must provide public service to the communities in their viewing or listening range. Most operators of radio and television stations are interested in community development, and schools are accorded a high priority in this process. Sadly, the majority of schools fail to capitalize upon this favorable situation. Athletics has been the most active in this area, yet, athletics does not utilize the possibility to any significant extent. A knowledgeable and energetic public relations director will explore these possibilities to the fullest. Special programs will be planned; use of free spot announcements and "hitch-hiking," the addition of complimentary brief messages to regular commercials or programs, will be stressed.

MEETING THE NEEDS OF MEDIA

The editor, manager of the radio or television station, and other persons concerned with mass communications must seek programming that is fresh, appealing, and of interest to their audiences. Stale news, especially when the subject matter is the same, day after day, month after month, and year after year, does not excite the editor or program manager. These people are engaged in a competitive business; their job is to sell subscriptions, advertising, or time. To do this, they must meet the interest and needs of their audience. Readers, viewers, and listeners demand fresh, vital, and interesting materials. Schools and colleges are tradition bound to send out messages that are limited to enrollment, budget, and current issues. While these are of value and considered as such by all, they only tell a part of the story. For news to be effective, it must contain human relationships, personal items of success and failure, new programs, and reports on the rare or unusual events.

Athletic public relations is frequently a victim of repetitiveness and reliance upon cliches. Typical news releases or articles appearing in various institutionally prepared publications stress the win–loss record, individual statistics, weaknesses and strengths of one's own and opponent's teams, and the hackneyed comments by coaches before and after games. Only the most enthusiastic booster is vitally interested in these areas; others have heard or read them ad nauseam.

WHO CARES?

Studies have shown that in a typical community only one per cent of the citizens can identify the superintendent of schools and at least two school board members. About one-half of the citizens have no interest in school affairs, do not participate in school functions, and have no desire to do so. Only about three per cent of the citizens in a typical community believe that they learned about school affairs from school representatives, although over fifty per cent indicated they would like to have this occur. The lesson is very clear: if one is tuned out, one cannot be reached. People must be attentive to receive messages, and attention comes with immediate personal or self-interest.

SOURCES OF NEWS

Where does one search for school news? The list is endless, but the following serves as a review of typical sources:

New teaching or coaching methods

Counseling or guidance services available, planned, or expected

New equipment or facilities and the uses to be made of them

Humorous incidents involving students, teachers, or staff

Services rendered to the community, such as fund drives, charity activities and so on

Participation by students, teachers, and staff in community affairs

Citizens' awards and recognition ceremonies for participation, contributions, or support of school-related activities

Student awards, prizes, and recognition

Staff member trips, conference participation, and extended education and the values thereof to students and community

Unusual field or study trips, stressing their educational values

Special evening, summer, and extended education programs and their value to local citizens

Testing programs and their purposes and uses

Exhibits or demonstrations in drama, music, dance, athletics, physical education, creative writing, wood and metal shop, and others

Participation in campaigns of civic importance, such as ecology, pollution, special programs for the economically, educationally, physically, or mentally disadvantaged, and others

Success stories of current and past students, particularly in the areas of military, politics, religion, professions, athletics, entertainment, writing communications, and other fields

Books, articles, creative activities, and other related participation by teachers, students, and staff

Visits to the campus by celebrities and experts

Personnel changes and importance to the educational program

Financial statements, cost of operating, and projections

Speeches made to layperson's groups and professional groups

Community relations activities, such as recreation programs for children, adults, and senior citizens

Use of local experts as guest speakers or teachers

Proposals of community-related projects, such as use of library, use of facilities, joint traffic plans, reduction of delinquency, and other mutually concerned projects

Reports of anything unusual

Celebrations of various anniversaries, such as 50th year of operation, league champions, and so on

Announcements or coverage of something that is planned or was done for the first time

Any records of significance, such as the number of students graduated, number graduating with honors, number graduating with scholarships, least number of days absent for entire enrollment, first-time winners in various sports, etc.

Special events to be held or that were held, such as speeches by a renowned public figure, reunion of various classes, and so on

Contests of all kinds, such as athletic achievement, singing, drama, debate, art, science, mathematics, home making

Results of surveys, such as community or student interests in occupations, extracurricular events, facilities, school calendar, discipline, athletic competition, required subject matter, and so on

Historical items, such as date of construction of facilities, academic achievements, athletic achievements

Campus visitations, tours, parents' meetings, and other similar events

Summer vocations of students

Summer travel or educational experiences of students

Part-time employment survey of students, revealing the numbers or percentages of students involved and the nature of jobs

Athletically related stories, such as personal motivation, overcoming certain handicaps, personal values attached to athletic participation, background of training or preparation, correlation with academic pursuits, and other human or personal interest areas

Personnel changes, emphasizing the anticipated benefits to the students and to the institution

Community use of facilities, for example the jogging track, swimming pool, rehabilitative rooms, tennis courts, and other activities

Summer recreation and athletic programs, stressing the contributions to fitness, curtailment of delinquency, improvement of skills, and other positive factors

Employment internships, emphasizing the importance of this program in preparing students for vocations and the contributions to the employers in the community

Clinics, workshops, and other special teaching and learning activities

Economics affected by the institution

The above list of potential news gives some indication of the broad base of newsworthy sources on a typical campus. The athletic (or physical education) public relations specialist must have a "nose" for news. Waiting for news to come to you is a practice to be avoided. Search for news is a definite responsibility of the public relations specialist. The athletic (or physical education) public relations director can adapt most of the items listed above so that they have relevance and interest to athletics (or physical education). News is where you find it.

CHAPTER THIRTEEN
PUBLICITY

Publicity is one of the most important tools used by public relations. Publicity is very important, but it is not all-important. In and of itself, publicity cannot be substituted for good works or desirable action. However, it can be used to bring attention to them and to develop an institution's personality.

OBJECTIVE OF PUBLICITY
The primary objective of publicity is to make someone or something known. Basically, it is to draw attention to a person, institution, or function. With all the pressures brought upon the typical person, an effective

publicity program is required to obtain one's fair share of attention. Publicity will not sell tickets (at least no more than once), raise funds, or win supporters; these require a good product, an approved cause, and a good public relations program. Yet publicity can be helpful in conveying ideas to people so that these ends can be more easily attained. However, just being read or heard is no guarantee that the message is either understood or accepted. Nor can simply turning out reams of publicity assure success.

EFFECT OF PUBLICITY

Publicity should be planned with these guidelines in mind: (1) too much publicity can be poor public relations in that at a given point people tend to react negatively to excessive publicity given to one subject; (2) what really counts is the amount of the content of publicity absorbed, not the amount released; (3) the amount of publicity disseminated does not necessarily equal the amount received or used; (4) the nature of the publicity eventually tends to reveal the character of the institution or department it seeks to promote, for better or for worse; (5) some publicity an institution or department receives originates from some outside source; and (6) all public relations activities do not result in publicity, nor should everything be so designed.

NEWSPAPERS

One of the reasons that newspaper publicity is a potentially effective tool is the American custom of reading newspapers. Newspapers reach more people than any other medium. Newspapers are not imposed upon readers; the reader purchases the paper, or reads one that someone else has purchased. At the outset there is some assurance of readiness to accept or expose oneself to the paper's content. Generally, readers are interested in this content and most influential citizens make it a practice of reading the paper daily, in some cases several papers each day. Newspapers are read at leisure, usually. There is more time to digest the content of the items read and to formulate at least tentative opinions. Of course, newspapers are valuable in calling to their readers' attention other forms of communication, such as forthcoming speeches, radio, or television programs. As in most things, there are limitations in depending solely upon newspapers. The typical reader spends only about twenty minutes reading from one-fifth to one-fourth of the editorial content. About eighty per cent of American adults read newspapers; men and women read newspapers in about the same proportions. About twenty per cent read only the main news, sports pages, and the funnies; stated negatively, some eighty per cent usually do not read other sections of the newspaper.

REFERENCES

The collegiate public relations specialist requires several basic aids. These include the *Editor & Publisher International Yearbook Number* and the *N. W. Ayer & Sons Directory of Newspapers and Periodicals.* These references contain detailed information concerning the names of newspapers, addresses, circulation, staff members, and other data.

The collegiate public relations specialist also should have at hand the *National Directory of Newspapers,* published annually by Weekly Newspaper Representatives. State press associations also provide directories that can be efficiently used.

ETHNIC PUBLICATIONS

One greatly overlooked major outlet for publicity is the black newspapers throughout the nation. There are approximately 200 of these, and, although they cover items of general interest, they feature news that involves black members especially. With the high level of participation by black students on college and school athletic teams, the collegiate public relations director should be certain that this segment of newspapers is properly serviced.

HOW MUCH PUBLICITY IS WASTED?

Newspapers live on news. That is their business. The more news they print that is interesting, timely, and unique, the more receptive their readers are. It would be hard to imagine how many tons of publicity releases are never read or used each year. Most of today's publicity output never appears in print anywhere. The University of Wisconsin studies[*] showed that out of 300 press releases received in a five-day period by a typical morning paper, 242 were rejected; out of 339 releases in a five-day period by a typical evening paper, 218 were discarded, 32 used as received, 42 were rewritten and used; out of 113 publicity re-

---

[*] Scott M. Cutlip and Allen H. Center, *Effective Public Relations,* 2nd ed. (Englewood Cliffs, N.J.: Prentice-Hall, Inc., 1958), pp. 252–53.

leases received in one week by a typical weekly newspaper only 3 were used! These findings make it clear that simply grinding out words is a costly waste of time and money.

IMPORTANCE OF PERSONAL
INTERRELATIONSHIPS

What must be done to increase the probabilities that your publicity release will be used? Obviously, there is no single, simple answer or else the rate of rejections would not be so high. Yet, there are some basic principles, guidelines, and practices that will improve chances of them being used. Fundamental to any publicity program are the public relations practitioners. They must develop confidence not only in the organization represented, but also within the press corps. This may take time in the latter case.

MAJOR COMPLAINTS BY MEDIA

What are some of the major reasons why the press may be displeased with a publicity program? Common complaints are that the purpose of some publicity actions is to seek free advertising. Experienced newspaper personnel are quick to recognize this guise. A familiar complaint is that publicity directors often attempt to color or censor the free flow of news. When things are bad, they attempt to control the news; newspaper personnel rightly believe that it is their duty to their readers to report the news as it is. A sure way to strain relationships with a newspaper is to attempt to use influence or pressure tactics to get something in or out of the paper; this is considered a slap in the face by professionals. Then, there is the complaint of gross ignorance concerning the media's requirements; there is no conception of what is news, or how it should be written.

PRINCIPLES OF GOOD PUBLICITY AND
MEDIA RELATIONS

The public relations practitioner can develop confidence and respect by newspaper personnel by adhering to some basic principles or guidelines; these include the following.

1   Be honest.
2   Don't try to block the use of news by use of evasion, censorship, pressure, or trickery; don't win the battle and lose the war.

3   Be cooperative at all times; be accessible by telephone or in person at all times.

4   Be candid; don't seek trouble, but don't try and hide it.

5   Don't pad a weak story; this tends to weaken your credibility.

6   Rumors are usually worse than facts; nip a rumor as soon as it is known; use facts, although initially they may be more detrimental than the rumor. Remember, facts limit the story; rumors tend to remove all boundaries.

7   Don't stress or depend upon off-the-record accounts. Remember, the job of the reporter is to get facts and report the story. Asking the reporter to abide with off-the-record requests is unfair and, in time, will be costly.

8   When news occurs, get the story out as fast as feasible. "Hot" news is desired by newspapers.

9   If a reporter uncovers a story, supply him or her with answers to questions or other materials; do not give the same story to another reporter. Treat this as an exclusive.

10   Give as much service to newspapers as possible.

11   Be willing and ready to supply newspapers with the stories, pictures, statistics they wish, as they want them prepared, and on time.

12   News is a highly perishable commodity. Be available or have all bases covered at all times. Remember that newspapers want news, not publicity.

13   Don't beg or demand to have your story used. This is the prerogative of the newspaper.

14   Don't complain about why a story is not used or how it is used.

15   Don't ask editors for tearsheets or clipping files.

16   Don't try to frame the story in the style that you prefer it; that is the editor's choice.

17   Don't try to obtain publicity by threatening to withdraw advertising or to seek support of advertisers; newspapers consider this coercion.

18   Don't ask a newspaper to kill or suppress a story except for the most dire circumstances; when this is necessary, if ever, meet with the highest echelon of the newspaper and state your request and all the facts pertaining to it. One should always be reminded that if at least two people are aware of the story, it will probably leak out if not in one paper, over one radio or television station, it will in another. The only basis for asking for a "kill" is some potential great harm to the community, institution, or public.

19   Don't ask the newspaper to act contrary to their own policies.

20   Don't ask the newspaper to engage in some private argument or conflict.

21   Do become acquainted with the publisher, the highest ranking officer who is the executive editor, the editor, the editorial page editor, and the managing editor. The latter is the working head of the staff engaged in handling news under him; these are usually divided under the city desk and the copy desk.

In addition to these individuals, a much closer working arrangement is necessary with the sports editor, Sunday desk editor, and the society editor. Of course, it is advantageous to also know the editors for the amusements, arts, and business sections.

22 Do act promptly to commend all persons involved in carrying a special story, promotional activity, or unusual action; copies of the commendation should be mailed to all members of the newspaper who should be aware of the recognition.

23 Do publicly commend at luncheons, banquets, and other group meetings the newspaper and the personnel who have been supportive of your efforts.

24 Do arrange to honor newspaper personnel at public functions, such as graduation, dedication ceremonies, and special events.

25 Do not employ publicity stunts that border on press-agentry.

26 Do not offer presents, gifts, or other material things to editors or reporters.

27 Do expect to grant complimentary tickets to reporters to all events they are expected to cover; grant complimentary tickets to editors and reporters to any activity you hold if they reply in the affirmative to your invitation.

28 Never ask for a "retraction" as such; if necessary, and only if significant, ask for a "correction."

29 Do not "double-plant" or give the same story to two different departments; if the coverage angle is different this may be permissible but it is your responsibility to personally notify each department of your action.

30 Do not expect the newspaper to carry a story for your personal gain, such as a rumored position, threat of resignation, or other uses.

CRITERIA FOR NEWS RELEASES
AND PROCEDURES

As explained earlier, the public is bombarded with publicity stories. The news media must sort through daily stacks of news releases in order to select those stories they believe to be of most interest or benefit to their clients; the quality of presentation has a bearing upon whether or not a release or story is used. One must face the fact that competition is intense. One method of improving the chances that your release will be used is to meet the standards expected in preparing and delivering the story. Some of the most critical areas in meeting these standards are the following:

1 In the first sentence or soon thereafter the story should state who, why, where, when, and how. Good writers will vary the sequences or emphasis, but the essential facts will be included.

2 Use full names, correct initials, and addresses.

3 Be accurate in purported facts—correct spelling, correct grammar, and good sentence structure are minimal expectations.

4 Generally use short sentences that are more readable and understandable. Depending upon the classification of words used, the length of the sentence may vary but it should seldom exceed seventeen words. Sentences that incorporate technical terms, figures, or unusual nameplaces should be shorter for clarity and understanding. Paragraphs should be short; use of a new paragraph for each separate point is preferred.

5 Arrange paragraphs in descending order of importance; include all material that you consider important. The newspaper will cut the story to meet their needs.

6 Select a main point or angle for your story; this should stand out in the first paragraph and never beyond the second paragraph.

7 Express or state the facts pertaining to the story; if opinions are included, cite the sources and use quotations.

8 All news releases should be double- or triple-spaced on white paper; use 8½ by 11 inch paper; use only one side of each sheet of paper; allow a minimum of one inch on sides and bottom and four inches at the top of first page; sender's name, address, and telephone number should appear on the upper left-hand corner; the release date or "For Immediate Release" should appear on the upper right-hand corner of the first page; use a black typewriter ribbon; use unwatermarked white typewriter paper; don't use onion-skin paper for sheets after the first page; if a letterhead is used on the first page, make certain that it is clearly indicated as such by some form of separation or by using a divider-line. At the bottom of every page except the last one use the word "More"; number pages; mark the end of the story by the word "End" or a series of $\#\#\#\#\#$.

9 Do not write a headline for the story; identification of the story can be stated in a brief phrase or sentence appearing on the margins that must be increased in width to accommodate this method.

10 Do not use carbon copies; use of mimeograph or duplicator copies is generally acceptable.

11 Do not mislead the editor or anyone else that the story is exclusive if, in fact, it is not.

12 Fasten pages together with paper clips unless you are advised that the use of a staple is acceptable.

13 Do not use all capital letters; do not use some rare form of type.

14 Address mailing pieces to the "Sports Editor" so that it will be opened by anyone occupying that desk at any given time; of course, it is necessary to address special pieces to individuals.

15 Know your mail distribution time systems; generally allow for the story to arrive two days before its release date for daily papers and at least six days for a Sunday edition. Delivery by mail, messenger, or self must be selected to meet specific needs. If you deliver the story, hand it to the proper person; use civility and depart without attempting to influence the use of the story.
16 If an oral story is required at times of emergency or because of distance or time factor, write out the story and read it as written; retain a copy for your own reference later.
17 Usually Mondays are the best day for stories; analyze your own papers to determine which day or days are best. These days may change according to other activities, particularly nationwide interest in some sporting event, local professional results, or some other influences. Chart the calendar for the best and poorest days and plan accordingly.
18 Sunday papers are able to devote more space as a rule, however, there is much more material for the reader so the impact may be dulled. Saturday papers are not usually read in full.
19 In preparing advance stories, hold less essential details for follow-up purposes; do not expend everything in an early advance story.
20 Provide photographs whenever possible or feasible; avoid the use of more than two or three persons in one picture; attempt to employ some form of action in the picture. Be certain that all subjects in the picture are properly identified, names fully used and spelled correctly. A gloss-finish still-picture is preferred. Usually the less descriptive material required to understand the significance of the picture, the better the picture. When people are posing for a picture they become conscious of their hands and feet; to assist them to relax and contribute to a better picture, have them hold some item, point to something, shake hands, or be involved in some manner. Place something in front of their feet, if compatible.
21 For television, a matte-finish still-picture or a one to two minute film clip is preferred.
22 Identify photographs by typing the information on the lower half of a standard sheet of paper, then paste the upper half to the photograph so that the caption material will drop down below the picture when it is withdrawn from the envelope. Do not write on the back of the picture.

Press conferences should be avoided as much as possible. Only when circumstances warrant it, should a press conference be called. If a press conference is to be used, the following guidelines are in order.

1 Written invitations should be received from five to seven days in advance of the conference; these should be a formal invitation or a letter on official stationary of the institution, signed by the host. The invitation should contain all the basic information such as the purpose, time, place, speakers, refreshments, and any other item of interest.

2 The day before the conference, each invitee should receive a telephone call as a reminder to underline the importance of the conference.

3 A press-kit should be prepared in advance for all who attend the conference. This should contain a news release about the main subject of the conference, a full text of any important explanation or statement that is to be delivered at the conference, several photographs of the primary subjects, and some historical reference material.

4 Establish a check-in desk; send a press-kit immediately to all those who were invited but did not appear.

5 Arrange to have a photographer on-hand; announce to all that the photographer's services are available and when; arrange to have the photographer's products delivered immediately in person or by messenger.

6 Newspaper and television photographers should be accorded full courtesy; if possible, assign a representative of your institution to each photographer to help contact subjects and to fully and properly identify them for the photograph.

7 If the press conference is to be combined with a social function, consider the advantage of having the social function before or after the main purpose of the conference. If before, then the function can be adjourned at one time for all; if the social function follows the main purpose of the conference, some persons will leave immediately in order to prepare materials for the newspaper, radio, or television and the value of the social function is depreciated.

8 Know the deadline of the newspapers that are most important to you; complete the conference no later than four hours before the deadline; adding any travel time to the four-hour leeway.

REQUIREMENTS FOR RADIO

Radio publicity requires a tailored release. An entire 15-minute broadcast uses only about the same number of words equal to two columns of a newspaper. A 48-page newspaper contains 348 columns of material of which 25 to 50 per cent may consist of news and features other than advertising. A radio release must focus upon the crucial facts. Short announcements or spot announcements consist of from 25 to 100 words. Words used should be easily understood and presented in a conversational style. These announcements are timed to run from 15 to 45 seconds, as a rule. Only one announcement should appear on a sheet with the average reading time shown in the upper right-hand corner.

MAJOR CAUSES OF REJECTION
OF NEWS RELEASES
The high rate of rejection of news releases can be traced to some common errors or omissions; these are:

1 Stories with limited reader interest
2 Stories poorly written
3 Conflicts with newspaper policies
4 Distinguished advertising
5 Materials obviously faked or exaggerated
6 Apparent inaccuracies in the story
7 Duplication of stories previously used
8 Materials stretched too thin

WHAT TO DO IF REJECTIONS OF
RELEASES PERSIST
The public relations practitioner should be ever alert that news releases meet expected professional standards. When stories are rejected, complete a self-inventory before looking for other causes. If a full attempt is conducted and the reasons are still in doubt, then arrange to have a conference with the sports editor, reporter, or others involved. Set the tone for this conference by suggesting that you wish to improve your service to them. Perhaps this can be accomplished by a frank, open discussion and exchange of viewpoints. If such a conference is held, regardless of the outcome or gain from it, send a personal expression of gratitude immediately; if considered proper for the local circumstances, send a copy to the person's supervisors.

NATIONAL AND INTERNATIONAL COVERAGE
In addition to local and regional newspapers and radio and television outlets, the collegiate athletic public relations director is concerned with national coverage. The two major press services are the Associated Press (AP) and the United Press International (UPI). Stories with heavy local angles are seldom used by press services. However, a good story can be

spread across the nation and the world at little cost and immediately. Story material given to the press services is usually rewritten into a more concise form. Each press service has national trunk lines, regional wires, and state wires in the United States. Headquarters of each press service is in New York City. In most instances the best approach to the press services is through their nearest bureau or "stringer"; the latter is a paid local correspondent for a press service.

SPECIAL COVERAGE POSSIBILITIES

Other areas of concern to the collegiate athletic public relations director are the feature, photograph, and specialized news syndicates. The Newspaper Enterprise Association (NEA) serves about 800 daily papers in the United States and Canada, plus about 500 weekly newspapers. Other major syndicates are the King's Feature Service, United Features, Central Press Association, and McNaughts. A complete list of feature and specialized syndicate outlets for publicity is published annually in the *Editor and Publisher International Yearbook.*

MAGAZINES

Another important outlet for the collegiate athletics public relations director are the sports magazines and other publications that carry featured sports stories. A file of these should be formed in the public relations office so that essential information is available at any time.

PUBLICITY CAN BE A VALUABLE TOOL
WITHIN LIMITS

Publicity is a valuable tool in communications. It can be used correctly or misused. When the latter situation prevails it is often due to the fact that the person relying upon publicity completely fails to have a broad concept of public relations. It might be analagous to a plumber being compared to an architect. Having a good product is the first requisite to a good publicity program or overall public relations program. Good works and good products deserve to be told to others, and they deserve to be told in ways that are beneficial to both the sender and the receiver. Publicity cannot make up for a poor product or a weak public relations program. When publicity is used correctly to tell others about a good product, everyone benefits.

CHAPTER FOURTEEN
THE TOOLS OF
COMMUNICATION

The heart of public relations, both internal and external, is human relations. Interaction between the school and community is essential; interaction between the college and its publics is also essential. Interaction must be continually cultivated, otherwise it will atrophy and eventually cease to exist. Communication is a social process. It is a necessity for the improvement of human relations. People have different values, needs, interests, and attitudes toward nearly everything. These attitudes become the basis of social and political action, control, or persuasion. The task of public relations is to bring people together on some issue or objective. In our democracy, everyone should be treated equally. Schools and colleges are provided to educate the public and the mass media is expected to disseminate knowledge and information; these are cornerstones of a free people. Through the use of information and reason, people can be influenced to change their attitudes and behavior. When there is the proper use of reason, communication, involvement, individual differences, mutual respect, and freedom, then change is possible that results in progress.

PUBLIC RELATIONS OFFICE AS COMMUNICATIONS CENTER

The public relations department of an educational institution is its public communication outlet center; the public relations department of the athletic (or physical education) program is its communication center. The public relation specialist is responsible for each respective operation. Public relations uses the printed and spoken word and the image. They are transmitted by three main channels, namely, personal contact, the controlled media, and the public media. Personal contact is the most forceful method, but it is impractical in today's society in dealing with large numbers of people. The mass media—namely, newspapers, magazines, radio, and television—are used as communication tools, but their use is subject to approval and acceptance of their administrators. The public relations specialist has full control over only one of the channels of communication, which is commonly referred to as controlled media. Controlled media takes in all the publications, advertising, audiovisual projects, displays and exhibits, campus tours, staged events, and other activities that are conceived, completed, and implemented by the public relations specialist or others on-campus or subject to campus direction. It is the latter area, the controlled media, on which we now focus our attention.

CONTROLLED TOOLS

It is highly unlikely that any single institution or athletic public relations office can sponsor all the various controlled media tools of communication. As in many other instances, a full review should be made of available tools, a master plan for public relations should be completed, and the proper tools of communications should thereafter be selected on the basis of cost, time, and appropriateness. The following survey of communication tools is presented for general understanding and stimulation of ideas.

1 *Campus publications* This is one of the oldest and most productive tools. There are generally three types of campus publications, namely, internal, external, and a combination of both. Campus publications are made available for campus publics or affiliated publics. Special publications are prepared for faculty, students, staff, alumni, or other distinct campus public. The broader the coverage, the more generalized the content should be. There is no prescribed format for these publications. Some are prepared as newspaper format, news magazines, or slick magazines. They can be printed by letterpress, offset, or multilith processes. Some may or may not have special covers, a self-cover, or no cover. Usually this publication is a monthly production. Some carry paid advertisements or exchange advertisements for printing costs. Surveys show that the most popular items are employee progress, promotions, service anniversaries, distinguished awards, announcements of new developments, and policy changes or services. Athletic publications feature personal accounts of players, coaches, administrators, and opponents; other areas include present and future scheduling, reports on finances, facilities, records in competition; names of persons and organizations from off-campus who have contributed time, energy, and money to the athletics program; testimonials by present and past athletes. Questions should be invited and answers provided. Generally speaking, the publication attempts to disseminate information that the organization wants known and information that the publics want to know. There should be some clearly stated objectives for the publication that then will serve as guideposts.

2 *Handbooks and Manuals* These are usually in-house publications and they fall into three main categories. First, an indoctrination booklet for new employees that contains a formal welcome, general orientation, rules, and an effort to convey the theme of teamwork as the key to a "winner." Second, a reference guide is available that contains all policies, procedures, personal benefits, and items pertaining to the position. Third, the institutional booklet is used to motivate an idea or philosophy, rather than a product or a service. This contains information about celebrations, traditions, awards, history, successes, growth, position papers, facilities, and future expectations.

3 *Letters and Bulletins* These publications are used to expedite communications with specific publics. They may be produced on a set-time schedule, or they may be used on a spot-news basis. Letters are inexpensive, direct, important-looking, intimate, quick, and informal. Letters may be reproduced in quantity by typewriter, multigraph, mimeograph, printing, or automatic electric typewriters. Letters are usually mailed to home addresses for better readership and a good climate for persuasion. Letters may focus

upon any subject of importance, for example, changes in policy statements, financial status, personnel information, new ventures, and any other area of interest.

4 *Bulletin Boards*   Bulletin boards are only as effective as they are maintained. Maintained properly, bulletin boards can be of great assistance in disseminating information, corroborating information, killing rumors, and calling attention to some other course of information. Bulletin boards are most effective if they are strategically placed; reading light is acceptable; they are organized into sections for quick reference; messages are kept brief; and, all information is kept current.

5 *Posters*   Internal posters can be used to help draw attention to some particular event, program, or policy. Messages must be kept brief. Changes must be made at proper time intervals.

6 *Outdoor Billboards*   This can be an effective way to convey information or advertise some event. By preparing one's own materials that can be applied quickly and efficiently, the public relations specialist should contact the outdoor billboard companies with the proposal that as a matter of public service they might agree to use the prepared materials on boards that are not in present use.

7 *Information Racks*   The use of information racks both on and off-campus is an inexpensive way of distributing materials. These can be used at various places on campus where students, faculty, and visitors concentrate. Off-campus, they are placed in banks, supermarkets, barber and beauty shops, golf and tennis clubs, and other places people frequent.

8 *Institutional Advertising*   This is a very expensive method of communications and generally it should not be considered. A good way to obtain similar results is to "hitch-hike" your message without charge onto the major commercial advertisements; a brief message, slogan, or statement should be used. For example, "State University versus Western University, Saturday, November 7 at 1 P.M." or "For State University Season Football Tickets or Information, Telephone 777-6161."

9 *Public Meetings*   Studies have found that *typical* meetings are generally nonproductive. However, a public meeting that fulfills certain criteria can be a useful means of communication. Opportunities exist for two-way communication, which in itself is important. Prior preparation in full detail is absolutely essential. A meeting should be programmed from start to finish as precisely as possible; however, the atmosphere and conduct of the meeting should be such that this is not a distraction. A comfortable environment, adequate parking, interesting visual materials, getting everyone involved in

some way, painstaking care concerning content, length, and style of presentations, refreshments, and other details must be planned carefully.

10 *Speaker's Bureau* This is a planned method for providing speakers.
Everyone in the athletics department should be encouraged to be a speaker.
The inexperienced or less capable speakers should be involved in assignments pertaining to youth or children groups, special publics, or other groups
that may not be as sophisticated as professional groups. The public relations specialist should prepare a "fact-sheet" for all speakers that contains
information regarding the institution, the athletics program, and specialized
areas. The public relations specialist should also arrange to have audiovisual
materials available. These would include film clips, slides, flip charts, flannel
boards, and other aids. News releases should be issued before and after the
presentation. (For details on preparing a speech, see Chapter Sixteen).

11 *Public Address System* For internal public use, make certain that the
messages are brief, adjusted for the audience, and delivered properly. Use of
humor, admonitions, anecdotes, and mystery have their place. For external
publics, primarily at athletics events, the public address messages are most
important. Try to obtain and retain a competent announcer; do not rely upon
student announcers, since they are constantly changing. Set forth governing
policies regarding use of language, types of messages, lengths of messages,
use of humor, and other areas. Remember, the public address system is your
tool of communication; it can be harmful or helpful.

12 *The Grapevine* Both good and bad news travels fast over the nebulous
grapevine that attends every school or college. As soon as any false rumor is
made known, take steps to stop it by presenting facts by other means.

13 *Motion Pictures and Slide Films* This is one of the most effective
means of communication. Based on longevity, numbers of persons who may be
exposed to the films, and overall impact, these tools are relatively inexpensive.
Caution should be taken to prevent the production of too long a film. Any
film over seven or eight minutes should withstand close scrutiny. Films should
be edited so that a clear, simple message is presented with maximum impact.
If necessary, produce more than one film. The value of a film is that it brings
to the public what otherwise they may never see. Films can be financed
through the cooperation of commercial enterprises; if this method is used,
the commercial firm should settle for only a brief statement of appreciation.
Advertisements, as such, should be avoided. If possible, film sponsors should
be organizations or public associations.

14 *Television Clips* Based on the same premise as motion pictures, television clips will reach more people at less cost. Local television stations may be

encouraged to film their own products. The public relations specialist should provide the television management with a list of potentially interesting topics or subjects. When a selection of these is made, then the public relations specialist coordinates the action of the television production personnel with the campus activity.

15 *Displays and Exhibits* Exhibits and displays should be planned for both on and off-campus. When conducted on campus, attempt to have exhibits and displays set up at the student union or other centers of activity. Ordinarily, do not set up displays or exhibits in the gymnasium or fieldhouse. Remember, you are trying to expand your base of support. Exhibits and displays entail a great deal of planning and work. Do not limit their use to only a brief campus exposure. Instead, arrange with commercial firms, industrial plants, civic centers, fraternal and social organizations, and other centers of public gatherings to have the exhibits and displays shown for a period of time. An exhibit and display should be in progress every week of the year somewhere in the community. The purposes of exhibits and displays is to communicate what your athletics (or physical education) program is doing. Emphasize the objectives sought. Include humor, action, and novelty in order to attract attention.

16 *Campus Tours and Visits* Campus tours and visits can be a forceful means of communications because what is seen leaves little room for misinterpretation. As in most other cases, poor or inadequate planning of these events can be counterproductive. Every possible detail should be planned in advance. The groups invited to the campus may be a particular public, or it may be a representative mixture of several publics. Do not overlook certain job classifications. For example, two of the most important job holders are the barbers and beauticians of the community. Often the most successful tours or planned visits combine a breakfast or luncheon. Some groups that meet either for breakfast or luncheon on a regular basis may wish to arrange to have the campus cafeteria provide the meal.

17 *Staged Events* These are special events designed to attract the attention of specific groups. Typical staged events include homecoming day, oldtimer's day, reunions, dedications, festivals, and others. Each of these require considerable time and effort to be properly planned and conducted. Although the public relations specialist is very important to these events, others are usually assigned the primary roles. Nonetheless, the public relations specialist should make certain that the event is properly planned.

18 *Inserts* The public relations specialist should plan the use of inserts or "stuffers" several months in advance. The utility companies should be contacted as a possible avenue of distribution. Newspapers should also be considered. Company payroll departments are another good source. The insert should be brief, attractive, and designed to cause further action such as filling out a reply card for tickets, information, placement on a mailing list, schedules, and so on.

19 *Photographer's Day* Each sport should set aside a time period for the taking of photographs of players. The public relations specialist supervises the arrangements for this event, although the assistance of others is required. A contest for the most unusual or best pictures can be held as a followup.

20 *Essay Contests* The public relations specialist can arrange with the campus English department, creative writing department, or school journalism department to co-sponsor an essay contest. The subject matter may pertain to sports, players, or related areas. Criteria for the judging must be established; some form of awards may be planned. The top essays may then appear in the community newspapers and other publications produced by the athletic department.

21 *Banquets* There are two kinds of banquets—good and bad. Good banquets are the result of minute planning of every possible detail. The environmental factors must be considered. The program must be pre-planned as to who will speak, what the topic will be, how much time the talk will be allowed, and when it will be given. Other details such as menus, tickets, serving, lighting, public address systems, entertainment, and dozens of others must be carefully anticipated. (See Appendix B for a checklist.)

22 *Student Liaison* One of the most productive programs for communications between the athletics (or physical education) department and students is for the public relations specialist to take the initiative in arranging for a breakfast or luncheon meeting for representatives of the athletics (or physical education) department and students. For example, a breakfast involving the officers of the student government and the representatives of the athletics department can do much toward establishing a two-way communication. Another student group that can be hosted separately involves the editorial staff of the student publications. A special group might include all the presidents and vice presidents of recognized campus social and professional organizations.

23 *Alumni Groups* Arrangements should be made at least annually for the governing board of the alumni association to convene at a breakfast, luncheon, or dinner meeting. If alumni representatives are dispersed over considerable distances, perhaps this can be arranged in conjunction with homecoming, a regular alumni board meeting, or any other event that would attract members to the campus area.

24 *Invitations to Board of Athletics Meetings* On campuses where intercollegiate athletics functions with an advisory board, public invitations to attend the meeting can be issued via the usual channels of communication. In most cases, few, if any, persons will attend the meetings, but an atmosphere is created that the athletics program is subject to the public's approval and that it is not a closed corporation. Of course, matters to be covered at meetings may, at times, be subject to executive hearings when only the designated persons may attend.

25 *Participation in Community Affairs* The public relations specialist should attempt to persuade the Director of Athletics (or physical education), if necessary, that staff participation in community affairs is most valuable. A list of all civic and service clubs in the area should be compiled. Staff members should be encouraged to select the club of their choice. Staff membership dues and costs of participating should be considered as a legitimate item in the public relations budget. Many of the community opinion leaders are members of these clubs, and developing a friendly liaison with them is important for long-range goals.

26 *Senior Citizen's Guest Day* At present, over ten per cent of the nation's population is over 65 years of age; the numbers in this age group are steadily increasing. Special days should be considered when senior citizens are invited guests to a sports activity. Pre-arrangements are necessary, particularly those pertaining to transportation and parking. Special attention and tribute should be given to those present; the game program might be dedicated to them along with featured artwork and editorial content.

27 *Pioneer's Day* Using the same approach as above, this day is designed to honor all former members of the board of trustees, teachers, administrators, and others who were instrumental in the growth and progress of the institution.

28 *Open House* Parents who attend an open house leave the institution highly satisfied and amazed, or they leave as antagonists. Much of their reaction depends upon the content of the program during their visit and how it is conducted. Much time and effort are required for a successful event. (See Appendix C for a check list.)

29 *Faculty–Student Sports Contests* Arrange for one or more faculty-student sports contests, such as bowling, volleyball, swimming, basketball, or other.

30 *Tributes to Support Staff* Arrange some special acknowledgement to support staff. This can be held at a game, banquet, assembly, or awards ceremony. Prepare personal stories, pictures, and awards in advance.

31 *Letters to Parents* At the start of each year, prepare a letter to the parents of players. Briefly explain the policies and philosophy of the athletics (or physical education) program. Invite questions. If the enrollment of the institution is not excessive, a similar letter can be sent to the parents of all students.

32 *Invitation to Parents* Parents of participants in sports should be sent invitations to witness practice. Additionally, it is most desirable to set aside one day for a "parent's clinic." The coach or coaches utilize this event to explain their basic coaching philosophy, team regulations, and basis for selecting players. Also, the rudiments of their offensive and defensive strategy and tactics are explained. Questions are solicited.

33 *Participation in Faculty Affairs* Staff members are urged to be engaged in faculty affairs by serving on committees, attending faculty meetings, and faculty social functions. Each of these contacts can be productive public relations.

34 *Club Awards* Seek to have civic and service clubs honor an athlete- and coach-of-the-month. This event would not be designated to be the sole program for the day; rather, alloting a few minutes to the introduction of the recipients and their response is all that is necessary. Such an event would give listeners a better perspective of the activities and the people involved. Of course, it would be worthy of an appropriate news release or television film clip.

35 *Publications Distribution at Selected Sites* A copy of all publications prepared by the athletic (or physical education) public relations specialist should be made available to all community barber shops, beauty salons, physician's and dentist's offices, and other ·locations where people have time to read. These should be physically prepared to maintain good appearance.

36 *Professional Publications* Encourage staff members to prepare materials for professional publications. The public relations specialist can provide some technical assistance. This enhances the stature of the staff member when this action becomes known to the institution's publics.

37 *Letter Writing* Next to face-to-face meetings and personalized tele- phone calls, letter writing is an individual's most potent public relations tool. Public relations practitioner not only should produce many letters in the con- duct of their duties, but staff members should be given tips on letter writing. These would include such advice as do not try to sell a thing, but rather what the thing can do for the person or community; present your message in the fewest words possible; keep the beginning short, with impact, and attention-getting; tie the opening sentence as closely as possible to the personal interests of the recipient; use the right amount of "showmanship" with your letter; use good taste in artwork, color, and layout; remember that a P.S. is usually the most powerful mover in the letter; if the letter seeks something, never ask "if", but instead ask "which" by offering a choice; never use high-pressure selling tactics. Letters can be chiefly informative, persuasive, reminders, or covers for other enclosed items.

CHAPTER FIFTEEN
COMMUNICATIONS
AND PUBLIC SPEAKING

Although speaking to publics is one of the main communication tools used in a public relations program, it is treated separately. Everyone on an athletics (or physical education) staff along with the athletics (or physical education) public relations director will have many occasions to speak to various publics. The impressions left at these times are long-lasting and more significant than most printed communications. Furthermore, there is a direct personal gain that can be made by speaking successfully. The difference in the personal advancement of one staff member over another of equal technical ability and experience often lies in their public speaking. Few, if any, recognized public speakers were "born"; so far as we know, there are no genes that carry this ability. As with artists, musicians, actors, and aviators, a great deal of study, experimentation, introspection, and practice are essential for success.

AVOID CLICHES

All of us tend to be tradition-bound to some extent, some more than others. One of the poor traditions in the realm of athletics is the expectation that all coaches will confine their talks to the usual cliches. How many times have you heard a coach refer to win–loss records, opponent's strengths, own team's weaknesses, injuries, assessment of individual abilities, and statistics? All of these topics are interesting or pertinent at some time, but they are overused and overworked.

CONTENT AND PRESENTATION

There are two main sections to any talk: content and presentation. Content of a talk should cover areas that are new, interesting, unusual, factual, philosophical, and related to values. The public relations specialist can and should assist in providing a "fact-sheet" that pertains to the institution, the athletics program, and the specific sport.

The coach should capitalize upon the opportunity to discuss the real merits of competition. Unfortunately, either due to tradition or lack of understanding, coaches tend to emphasize the specific skills of an athlete. This is not objectionable so long as there is equal emphasis upon the importance of playing the sport. A coach who comes across to an audience as one who believes that the sport is the only important thing is suspected of exploitation, rightly or wrongly. By contrast, there is the coach who makes it clear that the main objective of school or college sponsored activities, such as sports, is to develop the whole person; that sport is merely the vehicle, in this instance, employed to reach this end. Emphasis should be given to helping each student in self-realization. This does not detract from the desire or objective of winning. It merely adds some balance. Parents and others who hear a coach speak of developing the entire person are more receptive, particularly when it comes to asking for program support. The coach who makes it clear that there is much more concern about the future of the student than merely their current athletic ability finds an attentive and responsive audience. Of course, the coach must practice these beliefs, otherwise the hypocrisy can be harmful to all.

INFORMATION AND CONTENT FILE

Each staff member should initiate a "content file." Into this file should be placed everything relevant that is read, heard, or observed. In a short time, this file provides much background material for the content of a talk. As the file expands, it may be advisable to subdivide the contents according to specific areas.

IMPORTANCE OF THE MANNER OF PRESENTATION

The second section of a talk is the presentation. Before discussing the actual presentation, a few words should be stated about personal grooming and appearance. The coach or athletic (or physical education) department representative should be aware that the audience will consciously or otherwise be aware of grooming and appearance. Slovenly appearance or radical clothing may be acceptable by some, but for most listeners it creates a prejudice, thus making the reception of the message impossible or difficult. It is a gross waste of time and effort to prepare a fine talk, deliver it expertly, but have it fall short of the goals due to dress and grooming.

In preparing your own speech, do so in words that are "comfortable" to you. Phrase your speech in familiar words. If you are going to use a complete script and read from it, then use double or triple spaced lines and large executive type. Talk about an area in which you have knowledge and confidence.

Check beforehand to make certain the various aids you wish will be on hand, such as a lighted rostrum, electrical outlets, tables for projectors, and all other needs. It is advisable to bring all the essential needs with you, so that if there is some oversight you can use your own equipment.

Arrive at the site ahead of time so that you can become familiar with the environment and the actual location where the talk will be presented. This leeway allows you to meet many of the committee, leaders, and parents. Since this talk is a communications mission on behalf of the public relations program of your institution, the opportunity to meet and visit with these persons may be as important as the talk itself. Before arriving, attempt to learn the full name, occupation, and relationship to the club of all key persons; commit them to memory, if possible. Upon being introduced to these persons, repeat their names.

If appropriate in your opening remarks, in the heart of your talk, or at the conclusion of the talk, use the names of these key people.

People can be more attentive to your message if they are at ease. One of the first actions upon assuming the rostrum is to create an atmosphere of friendliness and ease. Some of the basic ingredients for a good presentation include looking at your audience. Establish eye contact with all sections of it. Avoid random movement that is not related to the talk; it tends to distract. Create the notion that you are conversing with the audience; use names, "we," "you," "all of us," and other personal references. Orally underline the main points of your talk by shifting volume of voice and rate of speaking. Speak with your entire body; avoid the impression that someone wound you up. Refer to your notes in a casual manner; notes on cards are usually most effective; at least 80 per cent of your time your eyes should be on the audience. If questions are to follow your talk, be prepared for silence. A successful way to bridge this gap is to ask yourself questions. For example, use of the form "People always want to know. . . ," or "Have you any idea what the . . . ," is helpful. Somewhere near the close of your talk ask your audience to do something, mentally or physically. Motivate them to make a decision, if only in making a mental choice. Challenge them to tell others about what they heard and believed.

If speeches are to be written, there are several techniques that can be helpful. Use large executive type, double or triple space lines, do not use all capital letters, and use only the upper two-thirds of the page to reduce head bobbing. Start out any specific or new section on a separate page; key the beginning of the new section on the preceding page so that you are prepared. Leave the pages loose or use a ring binder, allowing holes large enough for easy turning. Fold bottom of lower right-hand corner of each page to facilitate turning. Use marks, colors, or other cues as needed. Rehearse sufficiently so that the emphasis is on the delivery and not on the content. Make certain that enough light is available.

SEEK OPPORTUNITIES TO SPEAK

The importance of public speaking as an effective communications tool cannot be overstated. Every staff member should be involved. The public relations specialist should strive to notify civic and service clubs, fraternal organizations, private clubs, labor unions, professional organizations, company employee groups, Parent–Teacher Associations, Home-

and-School Clubs, Boy Scouts, Girl Scouts, religious groups, alumni, senior citizens, taxpayer associations, Little League, "Pop" Warner Football, age-group sports clubs, and all other identifiable groups of the availability of speakers.

Perhaps this example can illustrate the potential impact of an organized public speaking program. Assume there are ten athletic (or physical education) staff members in the department. Further, assume that each staff member gives only an average of one talk per month or twelve talks per year. Figure that the average audience for each talk numbers 50 persons. Each staff member will address 600 persons per year, and the ten staff members will have talked to a total of 6000 persons in one year. Assume that this program is carried on continually from year to year. At the end of ten years, there will have been 60,000 listeners. Of course, out of this total number the same person may be counted more than once. Even so, this exposure in a typical community will have a tremendous impact. Obviously, a staff of 20 would reach 120,000 listeners!

To minimize the importance of a public speaking program is foolish and an extravagant waste of communication potential.

CHAPTER SIXTEEN
PUBLIC RELATIONS
AND THE COACH OR
TEACHER

Public relations is a major concern of leading manufacturers, political parties, religious organizations, entertainers, and nearly every other aspect of our life. It would be simplistic to believe that public relations is unimportant to the coach (or physical education teacher). In fact, public relations of the coach (or teacher) is often directly related to his or her own professional success.

Public relations for the high school or community college coach is as important as it is for the university coach. The main differences in the public relations programs at these levels is that the university usually has a public relations expert to plan and execute a large segment of the program, whereas the high school or community college coach must often carry the full load of the public relations.

Whether or not coaches agree, everything they do has some relationship to their public relations program. The public relations program carried on by a coach is often the only direct contact between the community and the schools. The public relations program of the school, generally resting in full upon the coach, is to tell the story to the community. This is done in many ways. A subtle public relations activity, ordinarily not considered as such, is the way that the public is treated at games they attend. How they are guided to parking lots, the courtesy of ticket sellers and ushers, and the general conduct of the sport are all important in shaping the attitudes of the public. In many cases, this contact with the school is the only time the public has an opportunity to evaluate the school and its programs.

The coach deals directly with sportswriters and sportcasters. There are some simple guidelines that should be followed to develop public relations. First of all, the coach must be honest in dealings with representatives of the media. Statements should not be made that mislead, lie, or exaggerate. Giving the actual weights and heights of players is best. When asked to give an appraisal of a player or team, be honest. Do not ridicule a player. All medical diagnosis and prognosis should be referred to the team physician; restrain from making any announcements about illness or injury until two days before the contest instead of doing so five days in advance and then finding it necessary to explain the recovery.

Coaches will often need to prepare and distribute their own news releases. Set up some systematic way of reporting in regard to time, delivery, and content. Only up-to-date statistics are of any value. Attempt to maintain some form of publicity program all year, including the summer periods. Write about player hobbies, aspirations, summer jobs, and other human interest angles.

Develop a broad range of interests; participate in community affairs. When giving talks, do not limit remarks to traditional subject matter; use the occasion to talk about basic values and philosophy and how participation can help a student attain success in all phases of life.

Develop consistency in your public relations. Don't believe that you can be successful by attending to public relations on a part-time basis.

Under all circumstances remember that you are a teacher of the whole person and not merely a coach of some particular skills. Unethical practices are to be avoided at all costs.

Qualities that news reporters appreciate are honesty, reliability, and accuracy. An intelligent coach attempts to meet these standards at all times. The coach should respect the reporter's professional obligations, as should the reporter respect the coach's. The coach should be available to the reporter at any time, so long as it does not interfere with responsibilities to students. Reporters support coaches who provide them with newsworthy items, such as election of captains, statistical leaders, recipients of scholarships, and other events. When traveling, the coach should attempt to make prior arrangements for telephone coverage. To do this, the reporter should give the coach a clear-line telephone number, clearance to have calls placed collect, and the deadline. In telephoning from out of town, be prepared by locating a public telephone accessible at all times. Have handy the score of the game, scorers, key plays, statistics, attendance, and an appraisal of certain individuals and the team. Make certain that all data are accurate; especially that names are spelled correctly, and the correct score is given.

For home contests, the coach should make certain that parking, seats, refreshments, statistical summary, and other conveniences are provided for members of the media. Members of the media are invited to visit the dressing room immediately after the game has ended; answer all questions. Do not place defeat nor victory on the team except rarely; be more specific in explaining defeat or victory. Avoid "no comment" answers; if there is some special reason for not providing a specific reply, it is better to level with the reporter and let him or her use their own judgment, making certain the reporter understands all of the ramifications. When asked a question in regard to some strategy, such as passing, stalling, or other decisions, do not give a weak answer; explain the basis for the strategy.

The coach should refrain from using the reporter as a means to arouse player emotions, change game outcome expectations, or mislead the opponent. This tactic may be used once successfully, but the penalty of loss of respect and credibility is too great a cost.

If your game is to be broadcast over radio, then the same accommodations provided for newspaper reporters must be available to the announcer. Send or deliver a game kit early; include tickets, parking passes, complimentary tickets, roster of players, brochure, and a map showing where the broadcast will be held. Also, include the name of the person who is responsible for physical properties. Allow at least four seats. Assign a person to serve as a runner for half-time interview guests; suggest various persons to be interviewed, such as school administrators, city officials, booster officers, and representatives of other departments.

Use every opportunity to be interviewed on radio. This can be the next best contact to personal meetings. Anticipate questions, give full and complete answers regardless how trivial the question, speak positively about your team, the opponents, and their coach. Mention your players by name as much as possible; use objective evidence in discussing players, if appropriate. Regardless of outcome of any game, find specific areas to compliment your team. If your game was lost, speak about good points to be maintained and weak points to be improved in an optimistic vein.

Game officials can become ambassadors of good will for you and your team, or they can deprecate your coaching and character. Most officials are engaged in the activity because of personal enjoyment they receive. They are interested in young people and their actions. Officials should be considered as allies, not opponents. They should be accorded courtesy, with arrangements made to provide them well in advance with game tickets, complimentary tickets, parking passes, map, location of dressing quarters, security of dressing quarters, half-time refreshments, and medical attention. Prior plans should be made for providing police escorts off the field or court and from dressing quarters to their transportation. In selecting officials, two guidelines are suggested. Never have a close friend officiate your game, and avoid the use of the same officials over and over.

Explain your precautions and procedures of conditioning. Show parents the protective equipment to be worn by players. Clarify the steps followed in case of injury or illness. Make it clear by careful explanation and practice that the welfare of each player has a higher priority than any victory.

No public is more concerned with your team and players than their parents. Because of this special affiliation, it is likely that this group will be your most vociferous critic or your most devoted supporter. Special attention should be given to establishing a common base of understanding with parents before the playing season begins. Arrange to have a social gathering of parents at which time you can transmit your philosophy of coaching. Your concern for the total welfare of each player should be stressed then as well as your interest in the academic success of each player; give facts or statistics about previous teams. Clarify your point of view on conditioning and its importance to the welfare of the student. Assure parents that their sons or daughters will often appear physically drained after an intensive practice, but that this condition is only temporary. Recovery is near complete within a very brief number of minutes. Advise parents that this temporary fatigue should not be an excuse to reduce or avoid academic responsibilities. Suggest to parents that they might cooperate with their sons or daughters in establishing study periods. For some, completing academic assignments on weekends may alleviate some pressures. Explain to parents the methods you use to select team members; explain the objective measurements that you employ but also explain the subjective, intangible assessments that must be made. Assure parents that the squad selection occurs only after the most careful evaluation of all possible factors, and that, except in the most unusual case, the decisions are final for that season.

At another parent's meeting, feature the technical aspects of the sport. Present your overall offensive and defensive strategies; explain the basis for your selection of them. Have the team demonstrate major maneuvers of each. Also have them demonstrate various offensive and defensive tactics or skills and the practice drills used to perfect them. Provide a question and answer session.

The third step in developing parent–coach relationships is the personal conference with the parents. At this conference, discuss the student's academic status, study habits, vocational ambitions, recreational interests, close friends, social adjustment, personality traits, and any other area that can be helpful in assisting you to have a better understanding of the student, to help parents focus upon important areas, and with the ultimate objective of assisting the student to maximize self-realization.

A pre-season personal conference with each team candidate can be successful in preventing serious problems or aid in understanding them. An informal meeting with each player should cover such topics as hobbies, friends, studies, ambitions, social acceptance, personality inventory, and any other areas that are relevant.

Parents should be treated with respect and courtesy. Care should be taken not to become too friendly with parents while the student has playing eligibility remaining. Caution should be exercised in making any kind of promises, such as if the student does so-and-so he or she is assured of a first-string berth, all-conference selection, a grant-in-aid or scholarship, or other. Do not expect or accept gifts from parents.

Regulations that pertain to team activities, such as training, travel, academics, or other areas must be developed with player input. These regulations should be limited in number, simply stated, and the penalties for their violation left to the discretion of the coach. Whatever the regulations, they should be strictly enforced. Penalties should be fair, consistent, and without punitive intent. The same action should be taken for the star of the team as it would for the last substitute. As in so many other areas, actions speak louder than words. You will be judged by your fairness and consistency. Do not try to enforce regulations by the use of fear or threat, rather seek to establish a mutual concern for each player and for the team.

Each coach is generally interested in increasing the popularity of the sport in which he or she is involved. At a typical high school or community college, and in some four-year institutions where public relations budgets are limited severely, the coach must also be a "promoter." The coach takes the initiative in having pocket-size schedules printed through the compliments of some local firm. Season passes are prepared for distribution to the members of the media, school administration, player's parents, school faculty, school staff, and other publics that are vital to the operation of the sport. For special events, issue written personal invitations to the key persons in your community, including city officials, opinion leaders of various publics, and persons who have supported your endeavors. A special seating section could be provided for these guests.

In Chapter Fifteen, recommendations were offered for the content and presentation of a talk. These basic principles apply to almost any speaker. However, the coach, by nature of position, should capitalize upon the opportunity to communicate personal ideas and thoughts.

Your own team banquet should be viewed as a public relations tool. Although the affair is intended to be a social event and to pay tribute to various persons, the real purpose of the banquet is to communicate your concepts, ideas, and reasons for competitive sports. Most banquets are poorly planned and conducted. Every possible detail should be planned in advance. (See Appendix B for a checklist.) Invitations should be extended to the community leaders, media representatives, and institution representatives. The entire program should be assigned specific time allotments, and these should be followed. Acknowledgements of appreciation must be limited in time; the printed banquet program can be used to detail contributions of various persons. Player introductions and comments should be very brief; the printed banquet program or supplemental material can provide specifics. Make arrangements beforehand to personally thank all persons who attended as guests or participants; these should be mailed as soon as possible.

Another positive public relations activity that can be of personal and institutional benefit is to send a personal note to any person who is mentioned in the newspaper or on radio or television for some achievement, moment of sorrow, or other personal matters of interest. This is especially important regarding former players. These persons can be either your staunchest boosters or greatest enemies. Knowing that you are still concerned with their personal welfare goes a long way in cementing a lasting friendship.

In a typical community, the high school or community college coach must generate most of the public support; this is also a role filled by many four-year college coaches who lack a full-fledged public relations department. Developing a good relationship with various clubs can be helpful since these clubs can be sponsors of luncheons, banquets, special awards, ticket sales, campaigns for improving facilities, and many other activities. An alumni club can be used to help scout opponents or to provide pre-season competition. A parent's club can be instrumental in selling game tickets, banquet tickets, arranging transportation, as well as other ways. The cheerleader's club can arrange to be present at home and away games, help organize post-game activities, obtain posters, attend rallies, attend luncheons, participate in parades, and other activities. A school booster club can be active in ticket sales, raising funds for some special purpose, and in general promotion. Civic and service clubs may sponsor luncheons, solicit game program advertisers, and provide special awards. The faculty club may be employed to sell tickets, supervise game and post-game activities, travel as supervisors to away games, supervise auxiliary organizations such as the band, cheerleaders, and others.

Ironically, many coaches devote many hours and units of energy to off-campus public relations but tend to ignore on-campus interests. Perhaps the most important public for most coaches is their own faculty. In some cases, coaches have ignored the faculty or antagonized them. Some faculty members believe that coaches receive special consideration, undue publicity, and preferred status. Coaches must take the initiative in correcting these and other false assumptions. This can be done by several actions. First, coaches must regard themselves as regular faculty members with all the rights, responsibilities, and privileges accorded to others. Coaches must, by actions and words, convince the faculty that their main concern is the general welfare of the student. The coach should seek to meet with other faculty during lunch hours, coffee breaks, or other free moments. At these times the focus of conversation should not be on the coach, the team, or the game; attempt to discuss the concerns of the teacher or some significant neutral topic. Coaches are often stereotyped; one of the stereotypes is that the coach has a "one-track" mind. Attempts should be made to obliterate that impression by being willing and able to discuss politics, economics, social trends, community projects, educational trends, hobbies, literature, arts, music, and other subjects. At social gatherings of the faculty or at the faculty luncheon room, seek out faculty members whom you may not know or know only casually. Get to know them and have them get to know you. Whenever possible, either in a formal or informal meeting, at the right moment express your philosophy of education and the role of sports in it. Don't ask faculty for preferential treatment for your players; inform players you will not seek such treatment. Provide teachers with a roster of your team, and request that you be notified when any student encounters difficulty or fails to attain normal standards. Nor should you request teachers to excuse students for your benefit; expect teachers to assign homework to your students, and notify students that you expect them to fulfill academic responsibilities. When a faculty member is singled out for some achievement, send them a personal note of congratulations. Write a letter of appreciation to each faculty member and each school staff member who contributed to your program in any way. The importance of developing good relationships with your faculty cannot be overstated.

Some of the other school staff are vital to your program. The school nurse, team physician, supervisor of publications, director of music, art teacher, cafeteria manager, custodial staff, industrial arts instructor, and others are responsible for helping your program. Each of these persons should be acknowledged by a letter, special award, or public presentation.

The telephone is your direct link with the outside world. Impressions are often formed by the manner in which telephones are answered or employed. Unless it is absolutely a necessity, then develop some system of controlling the students who will do this and then provide a period of indoctrination for them. In this indoctrination, stress the public relations value of the telephone. Point out that the voice should be friendly, cheerful, interested, and helpful. Know the location of the coach at all times, when he or she can be reached, and be ready to take all messages. If a question is asked to which the answer is unknown, assure the caller that someone will return the call who can provide the answer just as soon as possible. If a caller protests some action or other thing, do not argue or attempt to explain; listen fully, take notes, and assure caller that someone will call them soon, if they prefer. If the school has only a main switchboard operator or a single office where all incoming calls are received, develop an efficient system to be notified of all calls.

In many high schools and in some colleges, the coach must take the initiative to have a sport brochure prepared. Such a brochure is an important tool in communication. In one sense, this is a publication that attempts to describe the "product" you have. There are many physical variations of brochures; examination of different samples is suggested. Brochures may range from mimeographed 8½ by 11 inch sheets to a slick, multi-colored pocket-size one with printed type. Brochures should contain all the essential information pertaining to the school and sport. Included are comments and/or pictures of the board of trustees, school administrators, history of the school, coaches, conference, past records, current outlook, player profiles, complete roster, schedule, press facilities, and any special item. Brochures should be distributed to members of the media, parent's club, community leaders, faculty, administration, board of trustees, and others who are involved in the direct operation of the sport.

PARENTS AS A PUBLIC
Next to students, parents are the most important public for the typical school. Although conventional parent-teacher or parent-coach relationships do not exist at the college level, many of the basic ideas and practices are employed. Of all the communication methods, probably none is more meaningful or as impressive to parents as a private conference with the coach (or physical education teacher).

PARENT–COACH AND PARENT–TEACHER CONFERENCES
Since parent-coach (or physical education teacher) conferences are so vital, one should attempt to maximize their values. These conferences can be of utmost value to the student, parent, and to the coach (or physical education teacher). An examination of the basic reasons why these conferences fail or are less than satisfactory include coaches (or teachers) talking too much, talking down to parents, failure by coaches (or teachers) to listen, and coaches (or teachers) being ill-prepared. When planned and conducted properly, parent-coach (or teacher) conferences can be very productive. The following recommendations are conducive to successful conferences.

1 Clarify the purposes of the conference
   a Define the problem, if one exists; if no problem exists, define the assets
   b Assemble all information
   c Attempt to define the causes for the problem or nature of assets

   d Develop some tentative causes and solutions or recommendations for use of assets

   e Note the areas of agreement that can be reached by parent, student, and self

2 Prepare for the conference

   a Review purpose of the school and the program

   b Review student records and performances

   c Review any notes of a prior conference

   d Have all test data at hand

   e Outline what should be covered with parents

   f Have a preliminary conference with student and discuss content of conference with parents

3 Conducting the conference

   a Create a spirit of friendliness

   b Be informal; do not sit behind a desk

   c Use simple language

   d Define the problems and objective of the conference

   e Be objective and tactful; enumerate strengths of student and make suggestions for improvement areas

   f Do not counterattack parents; stay on objective

   g Limit suggestions for improvement to no more than two or three

   h Do not become emotional; listen intently; what you don't hear said may be the most important

   i Encourage parents to talk; ask leading questions, if necessary

   j Give assurance of confidentiality of conference content

   k Do not engage in discussion of other instructors or students

   l Do not make promises that may not or can not be kept

   m Do not blame parents or condemn them for student's status; compliment parents when appropriate

   n Allow enough time for parents to be heard; if necessary, meet another time

   o Do not ask personal questions

When the conference is completed, extend your appreciation to parents for their interest and cooperation. Part company on a warm, friendly basis and sense of common interest. After parents have departed, make a brief summary of the conference and place in student's file.

Coaches who make time for parent conferences can contribute to the welfare of the student. A student who is free of tension or problems ordinarily is better prepared to learn and to direct energy toward constructive academic and athletic endeavors.

WHAT CONFERENCES CAN ACHIEVE

At the outset, the conduct of parent conferences seems to indicate an excessive investment of time. The experienced coach (or teacher) can conduct a typical conference in ten to fifteen minutes. For a coach who has fifty players on a team, this means an investment of from ten to fifteen hours. If spaced over a period of ten months, the average investment of time per month is only sixty to seventy-five minutes. The rewards are ample repayment for this investment. In addition to aiding the student attain greater personal, academic, and athletic heights, the public relations link established with parents is strong and lasting. Long after the students graduate, these parents will be boosters of the institution, the sport, and the coach (or teacher); further, these same students will soon be voters and potential boosters of schools and athletic programs.

Few programs in public relations cost so little yet yield so much.

CHAPTER SEVENTEEN
UNIQUE ATHLETIC
PUBLIC RELATIONS
ACTIVITIES BY
COLLEGES AND
SCHOOLS

A survey was conducted by the author in 1975 among 150 institutions of higher education that have had a history of successful athletic accomplishments. Each director of athletics at these institutions was requested to share the unique public relations activities of his or her department. An analysis of activities presented tends to confirm the thesis that imagination, experimentation, and adaption are essential to a public relations program.

At the University of California at Irvine, over 500 posters were mailed to youngsters who attended the summer sports program on that campus. These youngsters were asked to distribute the posters to their neighborhood merchants, community bulletin boards, and so on. A suggested guide for selecting locations was included. Posters were also mailed to the area's junior high schools. Youngsters who attended the summer sports school were formed into a club and in the first year of operation there were 125 members.

At Drake University in Des Moines, Iowa, a special program was conducted for the purpose of emphasizing the "town-and-gown" relationship. Game program covers depicted pictures of players and coaches photographed at various locations in the city. The football programs saluted banking, insurance, the city, agriculture, and government. The basketball covers featured publishing companies, an amusement park, insurance companies, savings and loan associations, the municipal airport, municipal sports arena, and major industries. Photographs were taken during the summer. The objectives of this program were to mold good will and an interest in football and basketball programs.

At Kent State University, Kent, Ohio, a series of meetings were arranged with all phases of mass media. Coaches and athletic administrators met with the staff of each separate newspaper, radio, and television outlet in the area. The objectives of these conferences were to express appreciation for past support, become better acquainted on a personal basis, seek suggestions for improving services to the media, and discuss major policies, goals, and methods.

At East Carolina University, the head basketball coach invited junior basketball players to try out for the "Pirateers" basketball team. The number of youngsters retained was 30. The head basketball coach then devoted time and facilities to conduct basic basketball drills. This team now performs regularly at home basketball games during half-time and the project has caught the imagination and enthusiasm of local fans. Presently the youngsters have purchased various pieces of wearing apparel in the university's colors.

At Wake Forest University, the varsity football team played two games in Japan—one in Tokyo and the other in Osaka. The university calendar is on the 4-1-4 plan, which made it possible for players to complete their fall semester. A chartered airplane was used to transport 70 university personnel and 95 Deacon Club members. Players paid $400 each for the privilege of the trip and Deacon Club members paid $1100. A university professor of Far East History accompanied the team. One unit of credit was earned by players on the basis of reading materials provided beforehand, guided tours in Japan, and living in Japanese homes for four days. Coaches and players conducted football clinics. The net result was tremendous good will between the university delegation and their Japanese counterparts. Deacon Club members developed even a closer relationship with the athletics program.

At Montana State University, a positive step was taken to cultivate understanding between the athletics department and student leaders and organizations. Student leaders are kept current on developments in the athletics program by personal letters. Coaches are made available to speak to any campus club, dormitory, or group; films are shown. The objective of cementing relationships between students and the athletics department has been achieved to a great extent.

At the University of Utah, a decisive effort has been made to sponsor a speaker's bureau featuring coaches and athletics. A coordinator has been designated. His duties are to actively solicit opportunities for the department's representatives to speak at social and business groups, churches and schools, professional and labor organizations, and others. Improved donor contributions, ticket purchases, and good will are the objectives of this program.

At Boise State University, Boise, Idaho, the varsity basketball team spearheaded the March of Dimes Walkathon. The entire basketball squad participated, each dribbling a basketball the entire distance. The presence of the basketball team stimulated community interest and participation for this worthy cause. The greatest number of participants ever was recorded, and considerable good will was generated on behalf of the university.

Also at Boise State University, a football clinic was sponsored for junior football teams in conjunction with the local Optimist Club. Over 1000 youngsters spent an entire day on campus. In the morning, the young students sat in the stadium seats and observed the varsity football team during practice; Optimist Club members served as supervisors. At lunch, the Optimist Club provided hot dogs and cold refreshments. In the afternoon, youngsters met on the stadium turf by positions. There members of the coaching staff organized and conducted learning drills. Obviously a great amount of enthusiasm resulted on the part of the youngsters and their parents, Optimist Club members found considerable enjoyment in the day, and the media gave extensive coverage to the event.

Boise State University also allows various community organizations and agencies to make presentations of their awards and recognitions to recipients during half-time at football and basketball games.

At Purdue University, the 14,123 seat basketball arena is sold out for each game. However, when games are conducted during university recess, some 7000 seats are available to the public. Rather than sell these seats on a random basis, the university undertook a program to invite large corporations to purchase blocks of tickets for their employees. The program was successful in terms of selling all tickets. The objectives of this program were not only to sell tickets but to attempt to generate new Purdue University fans and boosters with the expectation that this would benefit other sports.

At McNeese State University, their "Cowboy Club" members meet at the university cafeteria in a separate dining area. Each member goes through the cafeteria line and pays for his or her own meal. Members of the media are given complimentary luncheon tickets. This plan has the advantages of bringing the public on campus, accommodating any number without pre-planning, and making it convenient to hold a press conference and general discussion meeting, plus films.

At Kansas State University, a concerted effort was made to arrange for members of the coaching staff and administrative staff to visit each chapter of the "Wildcat Club" throughout the state. Simultaneously, free baseball and football clinics were held during this tour. Another project was the inauguration of the "Gibson Girls" and "Diamon Darlin's" who were active in ushering members of the "Wildcat Club" at games and to assist as hostesses at special events, including recruiting activities.

The University of Florida produces a special four-page, slick publication called "Gator Tales for Students." The purposes of this publication are to disseminate information regarding the athletics program and its operations, squelch rumors concerning the athletics program, and to explain the program's policies and philosophy. The extent of student support generated by this means, and others, is depicted by the sale of over 17,000 student ticket books for home football games at $5 each.

The University of Wisconsin at Milwaukee carries out a publication program somewhat similar to that at the University of Florida. At the University of Wisconsin at Milwaukee an 8- to 24-page monthly tabloid newspaper is published; editions are printed for every month from September through May. It is distributed by a van to over sixty area high schools, all university departments, and mailed to members of the athletic booster group, state high schools in Wisconsin and Minnesota, universities appearing on all the various sports schedules, and civic opinion leaders. Additionally, the newspaper is given free in conjunction with home football and basketball game programs. This publication was funded primarily through advertising copy. The objectives were to distribute information regarding the university's sports program, give recognition to athletes, teams, and coaches, pay tribute to university sponsors, feature various faculty members and academic accomplishments, and strengthen the image of the institution and its athletics program.

At South Dakota State University, a weekly sports column, called "Time-out for Sports," is mailed each week to all weekly newspapers in the state. Emphasis in this column is upon some particular high-school event, athletic skills, physical fitness, and recreation. No attempt is made to promote the university's athletics program directly, but indirectly much appreciation and support of the institution are developed.

Utah State University solicits events at which their marching band may appear, particularly parades. Throughout the state there are various types of community celebrations and recognition events; efforts are made to include the university in these, especially the band. Nearly every athletics staff member belongs to at least one or more service clubs in the community. Athletic clinics are held for young people in season, conducted in full by university athletes; complimentary refreshments are served to attendees.

At the University of North Carolina at Chapel Hill, a buffet breakfast is held in the fall, winter, and spring. The major portion of the cost is charged to those in attendance. Coaching staff members, administrators of the athletics department, and student-athletes attend. Invitations are extended to all faculty and staff of the university. The feature of the program includes an invocation, introduction of special guests, coaches, and students. Coaches speak very briefly about current events. Student-athletes are allowed to speak for longer periods about what athletics has meant to them and their attitudes toward athletics. Normally another phase of the meeting is a brief message from the Director of Athletics. Finally, a question and answer period ends the meeting. This project is designed to strengthen internal public relations.

In order to obtain better media coverage of their sports activities and to develop a broader base of support, the University of Illinois assigns one assistant football coach and a team co-captain to one-half of the state. These individuals visit the larger cities within their geographical area. Breakfast, luncheon, or dinner meetings are scheduled beforehand with the media. At that time, a press-kit is distributed with special features about student-athletics from the particular area. Questions and answers are a part of the program. The working members of the media are appreciative of these meetings and react accordingly.

Vanderbilt University launched a special program in 1973 to change negative attitudes to positive ones. All news releases, letters to friends, supporters, and prospective clients emphasized the positive; nothing was said or written with a negative tone or reference. All speaking engagements stressed the positive. A full-fledged effort was made to speak to every possible public, and every opportunity was used to invite their support and attendance. The result has been an upward surge in ticket sales, notably by nonalumni who caught the positive "fever."

Clemson University in South Carolina took advantage of a radio network with some 50 radio stations that blanketed the state plus areas in adjoining states. During the summer and early fall, radio tapes were made by varsity football players discussing the Clemson football program and upcoming season. A sample tape would be "Hello football fans, this is _____ _____, tight end for the Clemson Tigers. We've got our most attractive home schedule ever slated for 1974, and I'd certainly like to have your support in the stands when we take the field. But when you can't make the game in person, be sure to tune in to Radio Station _____, right here in _____, for all the excitement of Tiger football." Each player cut three separate tapes, with different messages, and these were mailed to the radio stations. In this way, a local gridder was heard over his local radio station. All costs were borne by the university. The outcome was pleasing to parents, townfolk, and local high school and its coaching staff, and the radio stations.

Recognizing that women make up at least half of the potential ticket market, Rice University at Houston, Texas sponsored a "Football Clinic for Women." The event was hosted in the university stadium club. The head football coach explained his philosophy, basic rules, playing equipment, and a summary of his offensive and defensive game. Questions and answers completed the event. Early indications are that new or added interest and support are forthcoming.

On press and photographer days for football and basketball, the University of Houston invites grant-in-aid donors and potential donors to the practice area. They and their children are introduced to players and coaches; colored photographs are taken of coaches with parents and children. Photographs are then autographed and framed and either a player or coach will deliver them in person to the donor or prospective donor. These photographs are noticeable in many offices throughout the city. Some of the players have gone on to professional stardom, and these, in particular, are treasured by many people. This project has improved the close relationship between donor and university, and it has helped to attract new donors.

The University of Nebraska at Lincoln, Nebraska, schedules a golf-stop tour of the state each year. Coaches travel to the club for luncheon, golf, and dinner with invitees. Coaches speak briefly, show a limited number of highlights of the past season, and answer questions. The entire atmosphere is one of fun. These meetings are scheduled one a week, at eleven different cities from the last week in May to one week before fall football practice starts. The end result is to personalize relations between members of the boosters club, alumni, and prospective donors.

A spring brunch is held at the University of Iowa just prior to the spring football game. All donors of $100 or more are guests in the press box. Each donor is invited to bring at least one prospective donor as guest. Coaches mingle with the crowd, and the head coach gives a brief summary of what to expect during the spring game, players to note, and changes made. This has been so successful that the site will be moved to the fieldhouse for the brunch.

The University of Minnesota has installed a Code-A-Phone. Taped interviews are made with coaches, players, and others. The telephone number is distributed along with weekly news releases. Media members can call the number to obtain more information or statements from the speakers. A novel method of taping on cassettes allows interviews to take place on the field, in the dressing room, classroom, dormitory, or other places; this feature adds "life" to the interview. This service has been warmly received by all, particularly by members of the media.

The University of Miami in Miami, Florida, installed a "recognize Miami" campaign in 1975 with fine success. The university colors of orange and green were used throughout, with a significant size "U" in the background of every item. Brochure and other publications carried this theme, as did booster lapel buttons, bumper stickers, windshield stickers, and all other items under the supervision of the athletics department. The same format was adopted by the various academic departments for use with their publications and so on. The city and surrounding area became awakened to their university.

Ohio University at Athens, Ohio, has sponsored a Scouts day at one home football game. Some 2000 to 2500 boy scouts, girl scouts, and cub scouts attend. Written invitations, in letter form, are mailed to each organization. The letter contains specific instructions relative to logistics. The objectives of this event are to build good will from the general public in addition to scouts and their families, to have seats occupied that would otherwise be empty for that particular game, and to build future fans.

Developing a radio network to carry its football games has been a target for the University of Virginia. Arrangements have been made with a major oil company to sponsor the games. In order to maximize the coverage of games, a coordinator visits every radio station in the state. A discussion is held with the program manager or other authority. At this time the mechanics of the project are made clear, a football press-kit is left with the station, and a followup is made later. Each station is assured of a weekly three-minute taped interview with the head football coach, covering the past and forthcoming games; each station receives two complimentary tickets plus the option of purchasing additional ones; each station receives copies of all releases and publications. This network of broadcasting stations has increased the listening audience and made people aware of the program not only by means of the broadcast but by a continuous use of spot announcements regarding the next game.

An unusual program was started in 1975 by the Arizona State University at Tempe. Business and community leaders were motivated to provide transportation to home football games for underprivileged children. Each adult would bring from one to five children to the campus where they would have one meal and spend the day. In the evening the children were guests of the university at a football game. Following the game, the adult transported the children to their homes. Dividends in general good will, developing future fans, and helping adults to be directly involved in aiding underprivileged children and in the university football program are apparent.

Washington State University at Pullman, Washington, has sponsored a breakfast on campus for all members of the "Cougar Club" and other interested sports fans. These breakfasts are held prior to each home football game; a luncheon is held before each home basketball game. Both the home and visiting coach are present; each gives a brief estimate of the upcoming contest. The university president is present. There is an informal atmosphere; a great deal of socializing takes place at these events. In addition to removing any concern about personal antagonistic feelings among coaches, this event does much to bring together interested and prospective fans.

The "Rutgers Athletic Caravan" was started in 1973. The University of Rutgers planned six stops at key cities in the state of New Jersey. The football coach, basketball coach, the department business manager, and a representative of the "Scarlet R Club" (the department fund-raising organization) comprised the travel team. Meetings were held at well-known hotels. Members of the media were invited by telephone. No promotional materials were used prior to the meetings. At these meetings each member of the team gave a brief summary of his particular interest area. Media representatives asked questions. The outcome of the meetings was a better and closer understanding between the university and the media.

Mt. Hood Community College at Gresham, Oregon, started an "Athletic Roundtable." Luncheon meetings are held each Thursday. As sports seasons change, the coaches attending change also. Two local high school coaches and their outstanding performer for the past week are invited. The luncheon is open to all. Guests are compliments of the community college. Coaches and athletes are given an opportunity to discuss timely topics, and townspeople are given a chance to ask questions of hosts and guests on the speaker's platform. This event is well-received by all. The next stage of development will be the addition of women coaches and athletes.

As stated previously, public relations activities are the fruits of imagination, experimentation, and adaptation. The foregoing examples make it clear that there is no best way to conduct public relations. Public relations are used by institutions of all sizes and athletic programs. If nationally recognized leaders in athletics utilize public relations activities, shouldn't every institution consider doing the same?

SPECIAL PUBLIC RELATIONS ACTIVITIES
FOR HIGH SCHOOL ATHLETICS

Various activities suggested for college public relations athletic programs and high school physical education programs can be used for the high school athletics public relations program. Some of the possible activities that are especially available and practical for school athletic programs are identified below.

1 Hold banquets for various athletic teams at appropriate times. (See Appendix B for detailed checklist.)
2 Use tournaments for different sports and classifications to stimulate added interest.
3 Hold team reunions in conjunction with a reception, dinner, and game.
4 Invite senior citizens, handicapped persons, disadvantaged youth, Boy Scouts, Girl Scouts, and other groups to attend games as guests. Often these programs are enhanced by coordinating the event with a civic or service club; in this case the members of the club provide transportation and supervision.
5 Stage clinics in all popular sports; clinics can be held for various age groups. Use own staff as much as possible. (See Appendix A for a detailed checklist.)

6 Demonstrate various sports and skills to different groups, particularly to junior high school and elementary students.

7 Sponsor father–son night at which time contests are held between students and parents. This program can be expanded to include refreshments and brief talks by faculty and students.

8 Hold a sports jamboree in which sports for the forthcoming season are conducted; demonstrations by students of all sports occur at the same time. Additional touches can include refreshments and talks.

9 Give prevention and care of injury clinics for parents that feature talks by a physician, nurse, coach, and trainer. Exhibits of protective gear are shown. Taping methods for preventative and rehabilitative purposes are demonstrated. Discussions on nutrition, rest, illness, use of ergogenic aids, and drugs are conducted.

10 Realize that a good public relations project is one where all the coaching staff and team members of all sports purposively seek to become directly engaged in some public project. For example, volunteering to collect funds for the March of Dimes, United Fund, Disadvantaged Youth, Community Recreation Program, and other organizations are conducive to earning public support. On-campus activities for which these groups may volunteer services include ushering at drama, music, and art programs, beautification of the campus, and distributing fliers for other departments and programs.

11 Conduct fund-raising and public relations projects that might include a hole-in-one contest, a flea market sale, car wash, and special sports nights.

12 Attempt promotion of ticket sales by obtaining schedules printed on shopping bags, on napkins at publich restaurants, "hitch-hiking" on advertisements, and T-shirts.

CHAPTER EIGHTEEN
PHYSICAL EDUCATION
PUBLIC RELATIONS
ACTIVITIES FOR
COLLEGES AND
SCHOOLS

Basic ingredients for public relations differ little between those used for athletics and for physical education. Most of the differences are found in the type of public relations activities each conducts. Physical education public relations activities are essential in order to obtain the support of parents and other community citizens. This support is required in order to supply the necessary financial base for providing adequate teaching staff, facilities, equipment, and time. Physical education is a subject area prey to many interpretations and criticisms. Emphasis given by physical education to its major objectives has changed from time to time, making it even more difficult to interpret to the lay-person. Who does not remember the heavy stress placed upon sports skills, then fitness, then movement, then lifetime sports, just to name a few? These changes have much merit, but the shifting of emphasis does create confusion among students and lay-persons. To offset this negative reaction, a perpetual program of public relations must be carried on by all concerned. Some experts are of the opinion that the root cause for physical education being threatened with extinction or reduction is due to a lack of understanding concerning the major objectives of physical education. A survey in a medium size community revealed that 92 per cent of the lay-persons did not understand the objectives of physical education. This same survey then identified three physical education objectives and asked if these were being realized at the local high schools; the results showed that only 45 per cent believed that the physical fitness objective was reached, knowledge of game skills satisfied only 45 per cent, and use of leisure time showed only 40 per cent approval.

CURRENT TRENDS IN PHYSICAL
EDUCATION REQUIREMENTS

Current trends show a movement away from compulsory physical education requirements. Some states have removed all requirements at the secondary level; others have assigned the prerogative of requiring physical education the last two years of high school and the two years at community colleges to the local district. These easements of required physical education should be warning flags to all concerned physical educators. The issue is simple; unless a good physical education program is offered to students and unless a good public relations program is conducted, physical education participation may be drastically reduced or totally eliminated at a particular district or in any one state.

PUBLIC RELATIONS FOR PHYSICAL
EDUCATION PROGRAMS

As explained previously few, if any, high schools or colleges have a full-time or part-time public relations specialist for their physical education programs. If this is the situation, and public relations is considered vital, then what can be done about it? Certainly it would be wishful thinking to believe that monies will be appropriated to employ a public relations practitioner. The most feasible solution is for all physical education staff members to voluntarily agree to absorb a teaching overload, relieving at least one staff person to devote full or part time to public relations activities.

PUBLIC RELATIONS PROGRAMS
THAT WORK

The number and types of public relations activities that can be used to enhance physical education is limited only by imagination and creativity. A partial list of activities is given below; any one of these may be used as noted or may be modified to meet peculiar circumstances.

1 Develop a pamphlet or handbook explaining the objectives, programs, and facilities for students and community uses.

2 Distribute this pamphlet or handbook to incoming students prior to their registration.

3 Develop community programs that use school facilities.

4 Sponsor special events that can involve an unlimited number of persons, such as bicycle tours, marathons, hiking tours, and others.

5 After Parent–Teacher Association meetings or other meetings involving school patrons, offer various activities such as horseback riding, bowling, karate, fencing, swimming, cycling, and so on.

6 Investigate the attitudes of parents by means of a standardized attitude scale before and after a program of education, including demonstrations, films, and participation.

7 Develop ways to have parents become involved in the physical education program; suggest ways for parents with high levels of skills to demonstrate by performance. Some of the activities that lend themselves to this program are tennis, golf, diving, swimming, resistive exercises, dance, and volleyball.

8 Initiate an information return center. Seek volunteers from among parents to canvass certain geographical areas. Learn what people like, dislike, or do not understand. This is productive in that the volunteer workers are brought closer into the school's sphere and those questioned feel that they have had an opportunity to voice their opinion.

9 Prepare "glad notes" so that physical education instructors can quickly indicate some pleasant news regarding a student and send this to parents.

10 Develop a physical education "Honor Roll"; base membership on objective measurements. Post this honor roll in a conspicuous place on campus where all students, faculty, and others can see it frequently.

11 Prepare timely news releases for the community newspaper and radio station; typical subjects include new curricula, outstanding individual and group results, and related types of materials.

12 Distribute a district or school newsletter as often as possible and/or desirable. Include vital news pertaining to physical education, especially toward realization of stated goals.

13 Initiate special physical education programs for senior citizens; possible activities include swimming, resistive exercise, dancing, bowling, golf, shuffleboard, and other suitable types.

14 Plan an organized parent–teacher conference calendar.

15 Initiate a speaker's bureau; solicit speaking engagements.

16 Develop a series of spot announcements for the local radio stations.

17 Plan special programs of visitation, demonstration, publications, interviews, motion pictures, and other means of communication for school board members.

18 Conduct periodical surveys among students to determine interests, needs, likes and dislikes, and other pertinent information.

19 Plan a program for after-school participation for all students; seek funds from local community leaders and organizations; purposes are basic plus the reduction of juvenile delinquency.

20 Develop a series of motion pictures, video tapes, and slides of all the activities conducted by physical education; these are shown in conjunction with public talks or are made available to interested groups or to television stations.

21 Arrange for a stimulating bulletin board display at a strategic location on campus; also, utilize the same materials, plus others, for displays in the community. One simple method is to move displays according to a pre-planned calendar showing them at business, commercial and industrial firms, city offices, and other key locations.

22 Seek to obtain appearances on the local radio program; this can be in the form of a panel, question and answer, or straightforward presentation.

23 Develop some phase of physical education, such as perceptual-motor training, movement education, lifetime sports, and activities for the handicapped; arrange to present these programs to elementary schools, civic clubs, and other community organizations.

24 Develop a program to establish rapport with the adult members of off-campus youth baseball, football, basketball, soccer, swimming, and other sports groups.

25 Seek to develop a year-round use of facilities; plan programs for various publics, arrange use of facilities, and lend leadership.

26 Plan conferences with teaching staff at your school; explain objectives and methods to teachers; hold question and answer periods.

27 Approach parents to learn if they are interested in having their children participate in supervised activities during the summer period, such as bowling, swimming, golf, and tennis. Arrange with commercial enterprises to make their facilities available free or at a minimum cost during their off hours.

28 Initiate a parents' advisory committee to meet and discuss program, philosophy, policies, and procedures for physical education; this involvement pays good dividends. Committee members should represent the opinion leaders, if possible. Include representation from the students on the committee.

29 The development and use of posters for use throughout the local school system and community should be considered; sponsorship of posters can be obtained from some reputable organization. Be careful to avoid any commercialized interpretation.

30 Initiate a letter writing campaign. Personalize letters, mail them to opinion leaders in the community, express the objectives and program of physical education at your school.

31 Hold a special "open house" for media representatives. Plan a demonstration program; have materials prepared for distribution. Combine this event with a breakfast or luncheon.

32 Hold a special "open house" for various civic and service clubs. Arrange for the club to have a breakfast or luncheon at the school cafeteria and their regular business meeting; thereafter provide the club members with a demonstration of physical education activities; have materials prepared for distribution and to take with them.

33 Arrange to have demonstrations presented at school assemblies, half-time at football and basketball games, parent–teacher meetings, county fairs, and other sites where large numbers of people meet.

34 Develop exhibits for use on campus and off. Exhibits should be of quality in order to be helpful.

35 Plan a parents' day for sports activities with students; activities such as horseshoes, putting contests, skating, swimming, and others can be used.

36 Plan a physical education festival, including a luncheon or dinner. Award physical education recognition in form of certificate, medallion, or other item.

37 Hold an interservice club recreation night involving competition between members of civic and service clubs.

38 Stage clinics for lifetime sports; have separate clinics for different school age groups and parents.

39 Physical education instructors should seek, not avoid, faculty meetings, committee appointments, and special assignments. By interacting with other faculty, opportunities are made to espouse the merits, objectives, and programs of physical education.

40 Combine a style show with sports activities. Obtain one or more of the local sporting goods firms to provide clothing. While emphasis is originally on the clothing, attention is subtly shifted to the types of instruction and participation in the physical education program.

41 Hold an annual physical education show. Involve every student. Program events so that all the activities in the curriculum are demonstrated briefly.

42 Conduct essay contests in conjunction with the school paper journalism, or English departments pertaining to certain aspects of physical education.

43 Conduct a quiz show at a school assembly. Organize teams consisting of a male student, a female student, a faculty member outside the physical education department, and a member of the media. Questions are prepared by the physical education staff and modest prizes are awarded to winners.

44 Plan and develop a physical fitness program for the general faculty, men and women. Require medical approval. Take measurements at start of program involving weight, cholesterol level, resting heart rate, blood pressure, and body fat by skinfold tests. Repeat tests at appropriate time intervals.

45 Prepare and disseminate a newsletter to parents from four to nine times a year. Include information about program as it pertains to the student. Do not make the letter more than one or two pages.

46 Seek to obtain a "Physical Education Week" for your community. During the week hold open-house programs, utilize radio spot announcements, prepare news releases and photographs, have a "quiz" appear in each day's newspaper pertaining to some basic concepts and misconceptions regarding physical education, and other activities.

47 Design bumper stickers extolling physical education; use a slogan that calls attention to it; seek to find a donor of these.

48 Install a suggestion box for students' use.

49 Determine advisability of preparing bulletins or newsletters in a foreign language for use in your community.

50 Plan a "physical fitness" night for everyone. Have a panel of speakers consisting of a physician, physical educator, nutritionist, and psychologist. Discuss pros and cons of physical fitness for adults. Have slides, films, and other visual materials prepared. Plan to hand out a pamphlet. Have a question-and-answer period.

PART TWO
PROMOTIONS

CHAPTER NINETEEN
UNIQUE PROMOTIONAL
ACTIVITIES FOR
ATHLETICS BY
COLLEGES AND
UNIVERSITIES

School and college athletics programs are confronted with the necessity to sponsor promotional activities in order to survive, maintain their present status, or to improve their status. Most other enterprises find it necessary to promote their programs, products, or purposes. Intercollegiate athletics, in general, and to some degree interscholastic sports, must likewise engage in promotional activities. From a philosophical viewpoint, it is believed that the vast majority of persons engaged in athletics programs would prefer to be exempted from promotional activities so that they might devote more of their creativity, time, and energy to the actual conduct of athletics. But this is not the case, nor does it appear that there will be any drastic changes in the future. Promotional activities are necessary for survival.

In the succeeding pages of this chapter, actual accounts of promotional activities conducted or sponsored by colleges and universities are related in order to demonstrate the wide scope of the activities used and to stimulate the creation of new ideas.

A "trade-out" was arranged by the University of California at Irvine, California, with the local newspaper of some 60,000 circulation (Figure 1). In exchange for 200 free tickets, the newspaper carried a 4 by 8 inch advertisement for 12 days. Names of subscribers were inserted in the classified advertisement section. Winners had to telephone the newspaper office to find out where to go for free tickets. The outcome of this program was that more people showed up for basketball games than before free tickets were offered.

The University of Illinois representatives met with the Chamber of Commerce in each large city with the intention of promoting game attendance of that city to football games. The Chamber of Commerce operated ticket agencies in their cities. Emphasis was upon "Family Day" whereby a regular ticket would entitle the purchase of an adjoining seat for less than one-third the regular price. These "City" days were announced through the media. Special bus parking was provided for each city. Half-time ceremonies honored the visting cities and the major was introduced and presented a souvenir. Results of this project have stimulated a new audience to attend. It is believed that once this new clientele is exposed to the caliber of entertainment available, they will return on their own impetus.

The University of Illinois has also conducted a successful Christmas Gift program. Season ticketholders in football and basketball are assumed to be convinced that attendance at games is most satisfying. On this assumption, mail gift certificate applications were sent to all current season ticketholders for use as gifts to others (Figure 2). This program has every indication of becoming a major source of ticket sales.

Northeast Louisiana University at Monroe, Louisiana, has a "package" for major donors to their booster club. Members are recipients of windbreakers with appropriate insignia, a set of eight glasses with insignia, a coach's cap in school colors, an associate coaching card that grants them certain privileges, a personal letter weekly to each member updating them on "inside" information, special parking privileges, special ticket privileges, guests on football trips, auxiliary sideline coaches during games, invitations to banquets, and complimentary tickets for prospective donors.

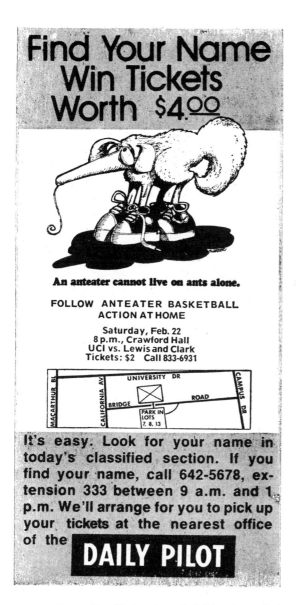

Figure 1.   University of California at Irvine Advertising Plan.

THIS WINNING CHRISTMAS GIFT IS
MORE THAN JUST FOOTBALL!

Besides action on the field, you and your friends
will enjoy fun-filled sideline events. The Fighting
Illini Pork Barbecue cook-out kicked off this season's activities, for example. But there's more . . .
Inside Tailgate brunch parties set the stage for
all home games, honoring special guests at the
Ramada Inn. Joining you for these and other
activities will be Chief Illiniwek, the Fighting Illini
pep band, cheerleaders, and pom-pon girls. At
the games you will be entertained by the great
Marching Illini and visiting personalities.

THIS YEAR'S SCHEDULE MATCHES GRIDIRON
ACTION AND GRIDIRON MEMORIES

The 1974 Fighting Illini schedule not only brings
football powerhouses to Zuppke field but nostal-
gic glimpses of the past. It will mark the fiftieth
anniversary of the Memorial Stadium's dedication game in which Red Grange galloped to five
touchdowns against Michigan. There'll be I-Men's
Day, Family Days, Homecoming, and Dad's Day.
Something for everyone, with guaranteed football thrills from your Christmas gift.

1974 Fighting Illini Home Schedule

Sept. 14	INDIANA ('I' Men's Day)
Sept. 28	WASHINGTON STATE
Oct. 5	CALIFORNIA (Dad's Day)
Oct. 19	MICHIGAN STATE
	(Red Grange Day)
Nov. 9	MICHIGAN (Homecoming)
Nov. 23	NORTHWESTERN

FOOTBALL TICKET OFFICE
100 Assembly Hall
University of Illinois
Champaign, Ill. 61820

Figure 2.   University of Illinois Christmas Package.

Drake University features a different major industry, business, professional group, or other local enterprise on the covers of its football and
basketball game programs. Additionally, a representative of the athletics
department calls on the key members of the activity being honored. At
this time attempts are made to sell blocks of tickets for use by employees
of this activity. At half-time this activity is honored, as are the leaders in
the field. This combination has produced good results.

Fighting Illini Football for Christmas!

LET SANTA CALL THE PLAYS THIS CHRISTMAS!

He'll pass on a gift idea for the man or woman you think has everything. Give season tickets for the excitement of 1974 Illinois football games in beautiful Memorial Stadium and an August professional football pre-season game between the Chicago Bears and the St. Louis Cardinals. That's where the action will be!

Your friends, family and business associates will thank you for an Athletic Association gift certificate, followed by great seats to watch the Illini and the pros in action.

IT'S THE TRIPLETHREAT GIFT OF THE YEAR!

Besides the Fighting Illini home games, your gift recipient will **also**

see the Chicago Bears-St. Louis Cardinals professional football pre-season game August 3, 1974, on Zuppke field in Memorial Stadium. And you can get tickets for these seven exciting football games yourself by completing the application below.

Here's all you do:

1) Fill out the coupon below and mail with check for the appropriate amount.
2) Your gift recipient will receive his gift certificate and be informed that you are the contributor.
3) Orders will be filled in the summer of 1974.
4) Deadline for Christmas gift orders is Monday, Dec. 10, 1973.
5) Certificate will be mailed prior to Christmas Day.

Clip and Mail

1. Season tickets (Six home games) Number of tickets _____ at $42.00 equals _____ plus .50 postage. Total remittance _____ .

2. The exciting Bears-Cardinal pro game Number of tickets _____ at $7.00 equals _____ plus .50 postage. Total remittance _____ .

Make remittance payable to: U. of I. Athletic Association. Mail coupon and checks to Football Ticket Office, 100 Assembly Hall, Champaign, Illinois 61820.

GIFT CERTIFICATE(S) FROM:

LAST NAME	FIRST NAME	INITIAL
STREET ADDRESS		
CITY	STATE	ZIP CODE

THE ENTIRE FIGHTING ILLINI FAMILY

CECIL COLEMAN
Director

BOB BLACKMAN
Head Coach

WISHES YOU A VERY MERRY CHRISTMAS

Mail with check before December 10 so that gift certificates may be sent in time for the Christmas tree ! ! !

MAIL GIFT CERTIFICATE(S) TO:

NAME

STREET ADDRESS

| CITY | STATE | ZIP CODE |

NAME

STREET ADDRESS

| CITY | STATE | ZIP CODE |

List additional names on separate sheet and attach to order.

Figure 2.—(Continued)

Kent State University has produced a color–sound motion picture covering all sports in their athletics program. The film is action-packed, with scenes changing every few seconds, backed with appropriate music and minimum narration. It is used to show to the various publics in the area. A roster of those present at a showing is obtained, indicating their business affiliation. Then, representatives of the booster club call on those in attendance a day or two after their viewing of the film for the purpose of soliciting ticket sales and membership into the booster club. The film is a "door-opener" for these purposes, as well as being a good public relations tool to inform the public of the nature of the athletics program.

East Carolina State University created a "Port Hole Gang" in 1974. This group is limited to youngsters age 12 and under. To join the club it was necessary to buy a season football ticket for $7; this price also included a special T-shirt in university colors with the club name spelled across the front of it. Seating was in a special section under adult supervision. The club was carried over into basketball. If the youngster was already a football ticketholder, then the price was $5; otherwise it was $7.50. The purposes of this club were to generate interest and enthusiasm among the youngsters, relieve parents of "baby-sitting" obligations during the game, and to develop future fans.

Wake Forest University athletic officials showed what can be done with some imagination in obtaining facilities (Figure 3). A citizen was located who would underwrite the cost of four indoor tennis courts. The

Figure 3.   Wake Forest University Indoor Tennis Club.

WAKE FOREST

INDOOR TENNIS CLUB

WAKE FOREST INDOOR TENNIS CLUB
At long last!

For your tennis pleasure in Winston-Salem — four beautiful Indoor Courts located on the Wake Forest campus, adjoining the large parking lot across from the varsity tennis courts.

Join now and choose permanent play time while the memberships last, or while there is still open time, to assure yourself of the following advantages:

1. The lowest Indoor Court rates in the country
2. Complete climate control winter and summer (you may never play outdoors again!)
3. Indirect championship quality lighting
4. Synthetic cushioned surface
5. Ceilings high enough for your defensive lobs
6. Fully carpeted lounge area with unrestricted view of the courts
7. Attractive locker rooms for men and women
8. Courts will be open from 7:00 a.m. to 11:00 p.m. for members only (and their occasional guests)
9. Wake Forest tennis coach Jim Leighton will head a staff of teachers available for individual or group instruction for all ages.

There are three basic membership categories to choose from:

1. Family $ 250.00
2. Adult/Child   200.00
3. Individual   150.00

courts were completed, and open to the public for use. On the basis of use-fees it appears that not only will the original cost be repaid but thereafter all profits will be assigned to the athletics program. Not only have modern facilities been obtained for the use of the campus community and the general public at no cost to the university, but a tremendous amount of goodwill and loyalty has been generated, which is reflected in ticket sales to athletic events and to contributions to the booster club.

The University of Utah has announced a program entitled "Challenge the Utes." In this instance the head basketball coach and two of

Figure 3.—(*Continued*)

Annual memberships are payable October 1 to Wake Forest University (mark your check for **Tennis**) and send to:

    Wake Forest University

    c/o Mr. Zeno Martin

    Athletic Office

    P. O. Box 7265

    Winston-Salem, N. C. 27109

There will be two seasons:

    Winter — Approximately October 15 - April 15

    Summer — Approximately April 15 - October 15

Courts may be reserved on a permanent time **basis by** groups or individuals **during the Winter Season** only. Open courts (non-permanent time) may be reserved as desired by members on a first come first-served basis. During the summer season all courts will be reserved on a first come basis.

COST PER COURT

Courts 1 and 2 are divided into hourly periods from 7:00 a.m. to 11:00 p.m. Courts 3 and 4 are divided into 1½ hourly periods, except from 7:00 a.m. to 9:00 a.m.

Courts 1 & 2

    7:00 a.m. - 9:00 a.m.
    $4.00 per hour

    9:00 a.m. - 1:00 p.m.
    $5.00 per hour

    5:00 p.m. - 11:00 p.m.
    $6.00 per hour

Courts 3 & 4

    7:00 a.m. - 9:00 a.m.
    $4.00 per hour

    9:00 a.m. - 1:30 p.m.
    $6.00 per 1½ hours

    5:00 p.m. - 11:00 p.m.
    $8.00 per 1½ hours

All above rates prevail for weekend play! Members will not pay at the club but will be billed monthly.

Guests may play at an additional cost to the member of $2.00 per hour; $3.00 per hour and a half. The same guest may be invited only twice a month.

The Wake Forest tennis team will use the courts weekdays during the winter from 1:00 p.m. to 4:00 p.m.

All courts are open with air-conditioned play during the summer season at the low rate of $4.00 per hour. However, occasional weekly summer camps will be given for children, adults, and teachers during this period.

Jim Leighton is in charge of memberships and court reservations. Call him at 725-9711, Ext. 419 or leave word at the Athletic Office for him to contact you!

the varsity basketball players visit each junior high school in the state. Prior to their visit, the physical education teachers at the school conduct a basketball foul-shooting contest for boys and girls. The top two girls and two boys are then matched against the varsity players from the university. The university contingent brings a portable basketball standard with them. The head coach is the master of ceremonies. In addition to providing excitement and entertainment with the contest, the head coach makes appropriate remarks about the basketball team and forthcoming season. The purpose of this program is to create interest among the young students so that they and their parents may wish to attend the university games. Aside from sales, a great deal of goodwill is formed.

Boise State University in Idaho turned the promotion of their 1974 spring football game over to the university Alumni Association. The agreement was to divide the receipts and over 10,000 tickets were sold. The Alumni Association was responsible for organizing and coaching the alumni team. The experiment was termed a rousing success, with an all-time high in the sale of season football tickets attributed to this program. The following year the Alumni Association also put on the half-time show at the spring game.

Purdue University printed an eight-page newspaper tabloid, *The Boilermaker Special,* and it was inserted in the leading two newspapers, one with a circulation of 50,000 and the other with 389,000. An additional 1000 copies were printed for athletic department use. Printing costs were $4500 and insertion rates were standard. Additionally, 180,000 copies were inserted in the university-produced tabloid. This heavy concentration of information is believed to be responsible for an upsurge of ticket sales; a study is underway at present to evaluate objectively the results of the program.

McNeese State University has a "trade-out" plan with advertisers in game programs. Depending upon the size of the advertisement taken, the advertiser receives a certain number of complimentary tickets to football and basketball games. This plan is used to encourage advertisers who might otherwise reject an appeal.

Princeton University selected three football games as "Family Days." Motivation was due largely to advertisements placed in the two daily newspapers in the area. Advertisements were placed on Sunday and Friday preceding each game. Tickets were exchanged with commercial radio stations for promotional announcements. During the two years, 1973 and 1974, that the program was operative, there was a return of over $8 for every $1 invested. The long-range expectation is that new fans will be created who will attend without any special promotion.

Temple University evolved a cooperative ticket sales program with a major grocery retail chain. Each of its 206 retail stores carried window signs. Advertisements stated that the stores would grant a coupon worth $1 on the purchase of any Temple University football game. There were 49 redemption centers where tickets were available, or they could be mailed to the university football ticket office. The store chain developed a solid radio advertisement package; the university paid one-third of the cost of the original advertisements, but after the first game the chain store assumed all the costs. The results were evident in that the largest crowd in history witnessed the Temple–Delaware game with an attendance of 37,265. The program was satisfying to both parties and proposals are now underway to continue the agreement.

Lehigh University videotapes all of its home wrestling meets. These tapes are then shown over the local educational television channel the next day. Thereafter, the tape is shown on as many as 41 different channels. The cost of the program is negligible. Considerable interest has been developed through the use of this tool.

Kansas State University launched several promotional plans in 1974. One was a coupon book given to students and faculty with their purchase of season football tickets. The coupons are worth approximately $50 from participating merchants. Another program involved the sale of backrest stadium seats to ticketholders; once purchased, the purchaser was assured of backrest seats so long as he or she continued to purchase season tickets. Another program was the "Measure Your Pride B(u)y the Yard" that was used to obtain pledges for the cost of artificial playing turf. A similar program was responsible for obtaining a new running track and was termed "Measure Your Pride B(u)y the Stride."

The University of Wisconsin at Milwaukee uses a share-the-ticket program with various Fraternal Organizations, Service Clubs, and others. The basic concept is that the cosponsoring organization pays for the printing of 10,000 special football tickets. Members of the organization and the university ticket department each engaged in selling tickets at $3 each, whether for adult or child. Proceeds of these sales are divided equally, fifty per cent to the organization for their project (Aid to the Blind, Big Brother, Muscular Dystrophy, etc.) and an equal share to the university. This program uncapped a new market of fans. The long-range objective is to cultivate regular viewers and ticket buyers.

South Dakota State University has a "Beef Bowl." A certain football game is designated as such. This project is held in association with the Stockgrowers' Association. A beef barbecue is held before the game and a donated steer is auctioned off at half-time. In conjunction with this affair, the High School Relations Department holds an "Academic Fair" on campus. This is attended by hundreds of high school students. Each academic department provides their own program. Thereafter, each department purchases and gives each visiting student and counselor a complimentary ticket to the barbecue and the athletics department gives each a ticket to the game. South Dakota State University also features some other events. The Alumni Association sponsors a "fly-in" day, whereby alumni arrive at the game via their own aircraft. On other occasions the local Chamber of Commerce sponsors a "State Legislators' Day," when these persons are campus guests. Another event is the "Camporama Day," when everyone is encouraged to attend the game and stay the weekend in their campers, motor coaches, and trailers adjacent to the stadium. These activities exhibit much initiative and imagination.

Utah State University has a unique method of attracting attention attention to their season's football opening game. Starting one week prior to the game until midnight of the date of the game, the four area hospitals keep records of all children born during that interim. The children born during this time span are sent a football ticket, a special certificate of welcome, and pictures of the parents and child appear in local papers along with the head coach (Figure 4).

Vanderbilt University and the home of country music are located in Nashville, and the university has been successful in obtaining the active support of the Music City people. The National Commodore Club, the athletic department's booster group, has benefited from this. Club membership obtains preferred parking, newsletters, brochures of sports, chapter meetings, ticket allotment, social events; promotional items to stimulate interest includes bumper stickers, lapel buttons, candy trays, ash trays, luggage identification tags, letter openers, desk note pad holders, writing pens, coats, jackets, shirts, sweaters, and autographed pictures.

Clemson University's football stadium had a large unused grassy bank that was converted to seat high school ticket purchasers. A special ticket promotional campaign increased the number of these tickets sold from 12,385 for six games to 18,368 for the 1974 season. In addition to the gain of over 6000 tickets, it is expected that many will become regular viewers in years to come.

Figure 4.   Utah State University Welcome to New Baby.

Rice University sponsored a golf tournament, entitled the "Executive Club." Arrangements were made to use the area's outstanding golf facilities; the program included carts, jackets, trophies, and a cocktail reception. A substantial entry fee was charged to each organization that allowed four representatives to play. The success of bringing together community leaders has created new interest in the athletics program.

Texas Christian University employed a well-known baseball star as their basketball promotions coordinator. His salary was paid by a group of local business groups. His assignment called for arranging half-time entertainment, signing autographs, speaking at no cost to groups, and selling advertising in game programs. Advertisements increased at higher rate; circulation of programs increased from 25,000 to 125,000. A city edition was issued for placement in local businesses. Program revenue paid for additional promotional costs. "Trade-outs" with local firms provided 5000 pictures of the professional player with the playing schedule on the reverse side; another merchant paid $2000 for a T-shirt displaying the TCU "Fightin' Frog" on the front and the merchant's name on the back;

another merchant donated a wrist band along with a TCU picture; fan appreciation night had drawings for next year's season. Half-time entertainment usually involved children and women. Results showed an increase of 15 per cent in attendance. The total cost to the university was zero.

University of the Pacific obtained a $250,000 gift to construct a stadium club. Containing 4000 square feet, the facility is fully equipped to serve meals to as many as 300 persons. The club is used by the "Tiger Club" members before and after football and basketball games; it is also made available to recognized campus groups and community organizations. The club has stimulated a greater feeling of "oneness" that has been reflected in higher ticket sales and contributions to the booster organization.

The University of the Pacific also shows appreciation to automobile dealers who provide transportation to its staff and team on a "trade-out" basis. At a home football game, the participating automobile dealers enter a new model of their product for a parade around the perimeter of the field.

University of Arkansas faced the problem of overcoming rumors that tickets to their home football games were impossible to obtain. To counteract this rumor, posters and ticket order pads were distributed in outlying areas.

At the University of Iowa it was decided to feature athletes in other sports. A special drive was started to publicize half-time events. Wrestlers, gymnasts, track and field performers, football players, tennis players, and other sports performers were utilized. This extra entertainment has been well-received by fans and media.

The University of Minnesota evolved a plan with local merchants. Student football season ticket purchasers were presented with a special card. The card entitled students to discounts at specified retail outlets. Billboards were placed at strategic locations on campus telling about the plan; advertisements were placed in the student newspaper; a special mailing was sent to all incoming and returning students. The plan has been operating for the past two years with success.

The University of Miami in Florida decided to add another dimension to its football program. An after-the-game cocktail party is held in their press box for V.I.P. members and their spouses; chartered flights to away games are used; photographs are taken of the activities and made available to participants; photographs are sent to friends of the travelers in order to show others the enjoyment and experiences that are available.

A social column has been included in the sports newsletter, mentioning people, places, and happenings.

Ohio University at Athens, Ohio, used a tabloid newspaper to motivate ticket sales. The newspaper contained pictures of coaches and players in all sports, player profiles, facility information, sales pitches for tickets, and application forms. In addition to using the newspaper to generate fan interest, the coaches have used the publication as a recruiting device. The costs of this publication are less than any previous type of materials used.

The University of Virginia launched a ticket sales program in 1974 that resulted in a 23 per cent increase in football season tickets sold. With the employment of a new head football coach, a thirteen-point sales program was started. (1) Supporters were organized into sales team, each with a captain. Eight teams were formed in the local university community and six others in leading cities in the state. A kick-off dinner was held in early May. Announcements of weekly results are mailed each week; prizes are awarded to leaders; (2) a special newsletter was mailed to all past season ticket holders, alumni, faculty, and booster club members; (3) a four-page season ticket application and brochure was mailed to each of the above on May 1; (4) color schedule cards and bumper stickers were distributed throughout the state with promotional posters; these items were donated by business firms; (5) a radio campaign was conducted; radio time was exchanged for tickets; (6) season ticket prices were $30 before July 4 and $35 thereafter; by July 4 the previous year's total had been surpassed; (7) a three-month newspaper advertising campaign was used, stressing the new coach and prospects; (8) a 15-minute promotional film on the new coach and spring practice was developed; this film was shown throughout the state; (9) a special ticket program was designed for industries and companies; these persons were invited to a luncheon preceding the spring practice game at which time the entire football program concept was made known to them; any purchaser of 25 or more tickets was required to pay only $25 per season ticket; (10) a faculty–staff mixer was held to improve internal relations; (11) billboards were obtained on a complimentary basis; (12) in mid-July, a 12-page tabloid newspaper was mailed to over 65,000; and, (13) in mid-August radio spots were intensified, mailings were sent to those former ticket holders who had not renewed, a special advertising campaign was initiated to sell tickets to spouses of students, and arrangements were made for special game days honoring youth, employees, industries, bands, and Commonwealth.

Arizona State University at Tempe prepares ten copies of the football highlight film and six copies of the basketball highlight film. The cost for the films is underwritten by a local bank, which receives a brief advertisement at the end of each film. These films are shown throughout the state to various publics. The purposes are to generate interest and participation in the university's football and basketball programs, expressed by purchasing game tickets and joining the boosters' club.

Washington State University each year promotes the plan of having members of their booster organization accompany the football team on chartered flights. Care is taken to arrange for players to be seated with patrons. Upon arrival at the destination, boosters are guests at a social hour. This travel plan has created greater interest in the sports program, and it has been responsible for attracting new booster club members.

Rutgers University used a "trade-out" plan to motivate season football ticket sales. Tickets were exchanged for advertising space and time. Newspaper advertisements, radio spots, and placards on buses were used. Some twenty-two business firms acted as ticket outlets.

Mt. Hood Community College at Gresham, Oregon, arranges with a civic or service club to co-sponsor ticket sales for a particular game. Special tickets are printed, advertising is designed accordingly, and prizes are awarded for leading sales. Proceeds of these ticket sales are divided. Those of the club are used for charitable causes.

Boston College capitalized upon the scheduling of a home football game against one of the nation's perennial powers. A special promotions program was planned to have tickets to the game as Christmas gifts (Figure 5). Appropriate selection of holiday colors and artwork enhanced the gift package.

At Bellevue Community College in the State of Washington, an annual baseball clinic is held for one day. Famous professional baseball players are featured instructors. Invitations are extended to all school coaches, team members, youth groups, parents, and the general public. Attendance has been most satisfying. At the proper time, during the clinic, the needs of the local program are explained and methods of assisting are suggested.

Promotions have no boundaries except good taste and reasonable judgment. As the various promotional activities described in this chapter indicate, there is no single approach that suits every situation. One must carefully analyze a particular setting, become knowledgeable about ideas tried by others, and then fashion a promotional program that is specifically designed for a specific situation.

NON PROFIT ORG.
U.S. POSTAGE PAID
PERMIT NO. 55294
BOSTON, MASS.

Boston College A.A.
Roberts Center
Chestnut Hill
Mass. 02167

GIVE NOTRE DAME FOR CHRISTMAS   *The Irish are coming!*

On September 13, 1975 the Boston College Eagles will host the legendary Fighting Irish of Notre Dame at Schaefer Stadium in Foxboro, in special kickoff to Boston's Bicentennial Celebration. And now, the Boston College Athletic Association is offering you an opportunity to purchase B.C.-Notre Dame tickets as Christmas gifts for your family and friends. —You can be sure that this will be a holiday gift well received and long remembered. —Upon receiving your order on the attached card, the B.C.A.A. will send out an attractive gift acknowledgement to the persons you have selected to receive the tickets. — Of course, we'll sign your name to the specially-designed holiday card. — Then, during the summer, we'll mail out the tickets to the gift recipients. — Or, you may choose to give tickets for the entire 1975 Boston College season which would include Notre Dame and the Traditional B.C. - Holy Cross game to be played in Worcester next season. To order your gift tickets simply fill out the attached order form — AND BE SURE TO FILL OUT THE SIGNATURE CARD — so that you'll be properly identified on the gift certificate.

And last but not least, we send our best wishes to you and your family for a happy and peaceful Christmas season. Wishes all the way from Chestnut Hill . . . even to South Bend.

1975 FOOTBALL SCHEDULE

Sept. 13	NOTRE DAME
Sept. 20	at Temple
Sept. 27	at West Virginia
Oct. 4	VILLANOVA
Oct. 11	TULANE
Oct. 18	NAVY
Oct. 25	at Syracuse
Nov. 1	MIAMI
Nov. 8	at Army
Nov. 22	MASSACHUSETTS
Nov. 30	at Holy Cross

Figure 5.   Boston College Christmas Gift List.

GIFT SIGNATURE CARD

I would like my Boston College football tickets gift certificate to read from:

Name _____

Street _____

City _____ State _____ Zip _____

Fill in the name of the person you
wish to receive the tickets on the appropriate form(s) below:

_____

1975   NOTRE DAME GAME   1975
APPLICATION

NAME_____ | OFFICE RECORD

STREET_____TEL. NO._____

CITY_____STATE_____ZIP_____ | SECTION

I APPLY FOR_____NOTRE DAME TICKETS @ $8.00 | ROW

POSTAGE AND HANDLING | .50 | SEATS
DUE

THE NOTRE DAME GAME WILL BE PLAYED AT SCHAEFER STADIUM
ON SEPTEMBER 13, 1975.

1975 FOOTBALL SEASON TICKET APPLICATION

NAME_____ | OFFICE RECORD
Do not write
STREET_____ TEL. NO. _____ | in this
column
CITY_____ STATE_____ ZIP_____ |

I apply for ___ Turf Club Tickets	@ $50.00		Sec.
I apply for ___ Sideline Season Tickets	@ $38.00		
(Plan A-does not include Holy Cross game)			
I apply for ___ Sideline Season Tickets	@ $44.00		Row
(Plan B-includes Holy Cross game in Worcester)			
I apply for ___ Faculty Sideline Season Tickets	@ $23.00		
(does not include Holy Cross game)			
I apply for ___ Adult End Zone Season Tickets	@ $28.00		Seats
I apply for ___ Children End Zone Season Tickets	@ $18.00		
Postage & Handling		.50	
Total Due			
Enclosed			
Balance Due			

$15 deposit required on each season ticket.   Make Remittance payable to:
Faculty priced season tickets are for home games only.   Boston College Athletic Association.
Children's price applies to anyone of high school age or under.   No acknowledgement will be made —
                                                            your cancelled check is your receipt.

Figure 5.—(Continued)

𝔐𝔢𝔯𝔯𝔶 𝔆𝔥𝔯𝔦𝔰𝔱𝔪𝔞𝔰!

The Boston College Athletic Association is happy to inform you that ____ tickets for the BOSTON COLLEGE - NOTRE DAME football game have been reserved in your name. The game will be played next September 13 at Schaefer Stadium, and the tickets will be mailed to you during the summer.

Your BC-NOTRE DAME tickets are a gift from:

Figure 5.—(*Continued*)

PART THREE
FUND-RAISING

CHAPTER TWENTY
CONCEPTS OF
FUND-RAISING

The United States is unique in many ways. Its political system, free-enterprise, and educational programs are just a few of the peculiar and successful attempts that make this society different. A special feature, in addition to those named and more that exist, is philanthropy. No where else in the world do the citizens of a nation give more voluntarily to various causes than in the United States. Philanthropy is truly big business in America.

FUND-RAISING AND EDUCATIONAL
INSTITUTIONS
Educational institutions have relied heavily in the past decades on voluntary fund giving; as the nation enters the late-1970s, there has been a

steady decline in the financial support of educational institutions by state and federal agencies. In order to maintain an acceptable quality of education for all citizens, young and aged, it is clear that educational institutions will need to rely even more than in the past on voluntary financial support.

FUND-RAISING AND SURVIVAL OF ATHLETIC PROGRAMS

Anyone familiar with the administration of an intercollegiate or inter-scholastic athletic program recognizes that it is often the first victim of any curtailment of public funds. In most cases, the athletic programs are either fully or partially self-sustaining, which, in itself, is unique among institutionally sponsored activities. Where programs depend upon appropriated funds for their operations, and when this level of support is minimal to begin with but reduced to even a lower amount, then fund-raising becomes absolutely necessary if the program is to be maintained at previous standards. There have been many directors of athletics who have resisted fund-raising campaigns on various grounds. For example, some believed that fund-raising was the antipathy of an educational program; others have associated fund-raising with a form of prostitution of an educational program; others have steadfastly believed that if an institution sponsors an athletic program then it should fund it in the same manner and to the same level as enjoyed by other campus activities.

CHOICES FACING ATHLETIC PROGRAMS

Faced with ever spiraling costs, limited income, and a change in attitude toward the concept of fund-raising, there seem to be several alternatives open to administrators of athletic programs. First, the intensity of the athletics program can be reduced. In other words, in place of striving for success in terms of won–loss records at high-level competition, actions can be taken to compete at a lesser cost level. This decision usually means a curtailment in the number of coaches and support staff, fewer grant-in-aids issued, reducing the dollar value of any grant-in-aid, limiting recruitment expenses, altering playing schedules for financial reasons, and other economy measures. Such a decision is not as easy or simple as it may appear. There are vested interests that will overtly resist such attempts. These are manifested by a segment of ardent alumni, students, fans, and members of a booster organization; others may include community commercial enterprises that are directly affected by what occurs in the athletics program.

Another choice is to totally eliminate the competitive athletic program. Few institutions have selected this alternative; it is unlikely that very many others would consider such an extreme action.

The third alternative is selected by most institutions, that is, to attempt to maintain or even improve the caliber of its competitive athletics program by soliciting voluntary funds. Probably the majority of institutions that have opted for this alternative do so not out of genuine enthusiasm and endorsement, but because they believe that maintaining the prescribed athletic program has a higher priority. Consequently, they are willing to forfeit some degree of autonomy, engage in the pressure of fund-raising, and depend upon outside sources for their financial well-being.

The major part of this section is directed to those institutions that have selected the latter option.

INTERRELATIONSHIPS OF PUBLIC RELATION, PROMOTIONS, AND FUND-RAISING

Fund-raising must be approached as a sophisticated art if it is to be successful. Essential ingredients are publicity, promotion, organization, people, and a viable cause. Public relations is vital to fund-raising. Without a climate that is created by good public relations, fund-raising will fail or be severely limited. A more accepted public relations climate is necessary in order to encourage a person to give a certain number of dollars than to spend them. Public philanthropy is based upon public relations. It should be clear that an educational institution and its athletic department should conduct its public relations program on a year-round basis; ignoring the importance of public relations until the eve of a fund-raising campaign usually assures total failure.

PROFESSIONAL VERSUS VOLUNTEER FUND-RAISING

There are professional fund-raising firms that will contract with nearly any public or private enterprise. Generally, the use of professional fund-raisers by educational institutions or athletic departments is not advised. In some cases, specific advice of professional fund-raisers may be used advantageously. In nearly every case, the athletic department should sponsor and supervise its own fund-raising programs. There are many benefits derived from the use of a volunteer fund-raising campaign. Foremost is the broadening of the base of persons who are directly involved in the campaign, and because of this they are likely to remain as active participants in other phases of the athletics program. The probabilities of forming a solid foundation for general good will are increased. Additionally, the use of a volunteer group results in having large numbers of persons directly engaged in fund-raising activities. There is a simple formula for raising money: a great number of people must ask a greater number of other people for money. Of course, organizing these solicitors in such ways as to maximize their effectiveness is necessary; these methods and techniques are discussed in the latter portions of this section.

PRINCIPLES OF FUND-RAISING

The principles of fund-raising are simple, few in number, and easy to apply. Approximately half of all the time and effort given to a fund-raising campaign is in public relations. Public relations should be a never-ending process. As the campaign is prepared to launch and during the stage of heightened activity, public relations are vital not only to encourage gifts but to motivate the volunteer workers.

A successful fund-raising campaign is the sum of a good cause, detailed fact-finding, careful planning, and skillful communication. The cause must be worthy and acceptable; this must be transmitted to workers and to givers. Fact-finding should reveal potential contributors and the amount each should give; community opinion leaders must be identified. Workers need to be selected on the basis of their past performance and future potential.

The cause or the idea must be repeated over and over again. Strategy and tactics may change, but the basic cause or idea remains permanent.

Appeals for money should be individualized. The size of the contribution should be tailored to the individual giving. The methods and persons used to solicit money should be carefully planned for each potential donor.

Various classes of membership or contributions should be established so that any individual can be satisfied. Each contributor should experience a sense of "belonging" through participation.

STRATEGIES AND TACTICS OF FUND-RAISING

Fund-raising strategies and tactics are varied and adapted to meet specific circumstances. Regardless of the special approach used, there are some fundamental steps to be followed in conducting a fund drive; depending upon a given situation any one step may be emphasized more than others, or the sequence of steps may be arranged to meet a specific condition. A fund drive can be organized into the following three major activity areas.

1 The Planning Period
    a Choose campaign planning or steering committee
    b Select campaign chairperson (chosen by committee)
    c Review and analyze previous campaigns
    d Develop the overall plan for the campaign, the organization, publicity and promotion, and draw up a time schedule
    e Prepare a list of prospects, plan division tasks, set division quotas, organize advance gifts division as soon as possible
    f Plan the general public relations program; itemize and assign dates
    g Appoint division chairpersons
    h Identify prospective workers
    i Release preliminary publicity
    j Plan indoctrination meeting for workers

2 The Preparation Period
    a Form operating committee from chairpersons, division leaders, and other leaders
    b Schedule and hold meetings frequently to promote and check progress
    c Division leaders select captains
    d Captains select workers
    e Check campaign supplies and office requirements
    f Conduct speaking campaign before clubs, organizations, and informal groups
    g Follow through on obtaining advance gifts
    h Hold planning and instructional meetings for all workers; launch an intensive publicity campaign; climax the week with a "kick-off" luncheon or other event

3 The Solicitation Period
    a Start general solicitation on an assigned day

b   Keep publicity phase at high peak
c   Have campaign chairpersons and leaders check daily with workers by
    means of a pre-planned system of communication
d   Be alert for weak areas; be ready to administer aid
e   Hold report meetings as planned in advance; make reports in accord-
    ance with early directions
f   Employ pre-planned "clean-up' methods to assure full response
g   Submit all reports as planned
i   Stage a "victory" meeting; express appreciation to all workers and to
    contributors
j   Follow-up efforts of appreciation to mass media, the general public,
    and to the primary leaders

IMPORTANCE OF A GOOD CAUSE

Fund-raising is a technique of using large numbers of people to ask other
people for money. To justify this request, every cause should be worthy.
If a cause is worthy, people will support it; people are needed first, and
then funds will follow. Therefore, the initial objective is to derive a good
cause that will be embraced by people; don't merely launch a drive for
funds unless a good cause is attractive to people. If this is done, then
public attention, interest, confidence, support, service, and financial
contributions will follow.

PROSPECTS CAN BE CATEGORIZED

Fund-raisers have categorized people into three major groups plus a segment that will remain inactive. An awareness of these groups and their
characteristics are useful in the planning and timing of a fund drive, the
costs of conducting the drive, and the number and kinds of gifts likely
to be obtained.

The first group is the leaders. They seldom make up over five per
cent of the public. However, they are most valuable in their influence
over others by means of establishing standards of giving, creating confidence in the cause, promoting a conducive atmosphere, and motivating
others.

The second sub-group is described as responsible. This group represents about 20 to 30 per cent of the total population. Generally, one can
be assured that members of this group will be active in the support of
the campaign. They are receptive to requests for gifts and active work

in the drive. However, they require organization, leadership, and guidance. It is from this group that most of the campaign field workers are obtained.

The third group is the responsive. This group is free of any predetermined decision. They are a latent group, susceptible to ignition. The skills of the campaign director and the workers will determine whether or not this large segment of the population is persuaded to actively support the cause by their gifts.

The final group is the inert. This group represents about 20 per cent of the population. They are immune to any plea or tactic. They are stubborn or indifferent. Ironically, this same group is the most vocal in its criticism of the cause, the athletics program, or the institution. Although they seldom give to a campaign, they threaten to withdraw their support unless events are altered to suit their desires.

WHO ARE SOURCES OF FUNDS?

The typical university or college athletic program fund campaign receives its money as follows: about one-third of the total amount is obtained from the ten top gifts; the next one-third is derived from the next 100 top givers; and, the other one-third is obtained from the remainder of the gifts. In planning a fund campaign, careful attention should be given to the potential sources of funds, and thereafter time, effort, and expenses should be allocated accordingly.

WHO ARE THE PRODUCTIVE WORKERS?

Workers in a fund campaign have also been categorized by experienced fund-raisers. About one-third will do nearly all that is asked of them, another one-third will respond to pressure and urging, and the other one-third will rarely contribute. In planning, one should be prepared to identify members of the latter group. Once this is done, means for shifting their responsibilities to the other groups should be employed. There is no point in compounding an original error of judgment by allowing these persons to retain their responsibilities.

PSYCHOLOGICAL BASES FOR INVOLVEMENT

It has been stated repeatedly that people are necessary for any sustained fund drive. If this premise is accepted, then it is important to review a few of the psychological bases for getting people involved. Some of these include the following.

1 Most people want "to be sought." This is an important principle for fund drive leaders. People should be asked to serve the cause; do not wait for them to volunteer their services.

2 Most people have the need to be a "worthwhile member of a worthwhile group."

3 Most people derive a sense of pride by associating with known leaders or worthy causes.

4 Actual participation and accomplishment are satisfying to most people; pride can be nurtured by communications from esteemed individuals, by ceremonials, and other forms of recognition.

5 When people participate in activities, their attendance is virtually assured; attention should be given to this fact. This is the prelude to accepting responsibility that then leads to vigorous and enthusiastic support.

6 People prefer to be associated with a program that has continuity; they are most comfortable with programs that have a successful history, a currently ongoing program, and an implied or real promise for a bright future.

7 People tend to offer their support when leadership, causes and institutions are acceptable.

8 People respond to acknowledgements of achievements. A substitute form of "gold stars" should be considered for adults. Causes need quotas and measurable objectives. There should be a way for every worker and contributor to "win," based upon some good reason.

9 Use tangible means of rewarding accomplishments of workers or gifts of donors; utilize objects that are visible to others, such as certificates, plaques, publicity, diplomas, wearing apparel, and special seating at athletic events.

10 Establish various deadlines; people tend to act more decisively under these conditions. A sense of urgency should be created.

11 People tend to participate in those activities that are pleasant and fun. Although much work is required for a successful fund drive, there should be a determined effort to assure a full amount of fun and gaiety.

12 Some people will join in a campaign out of fear, avoidance of criticism, or prestige but will never attempt to contribute to the success of the campaign in any way. Make certain that these people are not rewarded for something they have not done. To do otherwise will destroy the enthusiasm of actual performers.

13 We are a highly mobile nation; the average family moves at least once every four or five years. An important reality is that the makeup of a community changes. Because of this, the traditional ties of community feeling and pride tend to be diluted. Special efforts should be made to offset this atmosphere.

14 People like to have their advice or opinion requested; preferably people want to be recognized before a group or committee that has prestige.

15 Invite people to board meetings or to associated events. This tends to remove any barriers and allows for interaction.

16 Ask a person to make a speech, for permission to use his or her name or to use their picture.

HOW TO DEVELOP THE PROPER CAUSE

The identification of a worthy, acceptable, and meaningful cause is necessary for successful fund drives. Nearly all voluntary agencies and nonprofit agencies have the need to conduct a fund campaign for some cause. Some of these agencies will flourish, some barely survive, and some disappear; the cause they espouse is a dominant factor in determining their future. A cause should be totally compatible to advocates, supporters, and contributors. Every cause should show relevance, importance, and urgency. A cause should be relevant to some major need or problem that is meaningful to the personal interests, loyalties, or concerns of its own natural constituency. Once relevance is established, a cause should have a clear image of importance. A sense of urgency should be established and maintained. A cause can be both relevant and important and still fail if the obvious urgency is either obscure or merely temporary.

LENGTH OF TIME FOR A FUND CAMPAIGN

A fund campaign should be limited in length of time. Interest of workers and public can be sustained only for a relatively brief period. A fund-raising campaign should seldom exceed four or five weeks. Should a fund campaign fail to achieve its financial goals within the specified length of time, it is generally a serious mistake to extend the solicitation period. In most cases the cause, the overall plan, or some other aspect of the program is in need of change.

PUBLICITY AND FUND CAMPAIGNS

In issuing news releases, it is recommended that public messages be kept brief, vigorous, optimistic, and factual. Use of slogans or phrases is recommended. Repeat the message over and over. Use visual methods that help convey the message quickly and clearly. People tend to ignore or avoid information that is detailed and requires intellectual exercise to reach certain conclusions; people are more prone to react as desired to emotional appeals, leaders, testimonials, and concrete examples.

Publicity and public messages should create the mood that there is a willingness to tell all. However, everything is not exposed. In this way there is room for individual imagination. This allows one to evolve a rationale for their own support better than anyone else can do it.

Appeals for funds should be based upon a worthy cause. Do not use the deadly tactic that someone "owes" something to the athletic department or institution.

Any new idea or change threatens someone's security and position. When new ideas or changes are to be introduced, it is advisable to contact those who may be threatened and seek to remove any doubt or fear. Persons who may feel threatened can be found both on and off the campus.

The typical person likes a "winner." Financial support is easier to obtain for *promising* programs than for *needy* programs. The admonition is to refrain from basing your pleas for funds on needs or disadvantages; instead, assume a confident, positive approach that offers everyone an opportunity to be a part of something new, better, and more successful.

People like to hear and read their names. In issuing news releases, reports, and other publications, use as many names as feasible; radio and television programs should strive to incorporate as many names as possible. Whenever possible, use pictures of people who are active workers or primary contributors; in the latter case, obtain prior permission to use pictures.

TYPICAL EVENTS FOR NEWS RELEASES

Some of the typical events associated with a fund campaign that are worthy of news releases include the following.

1 Holding a pre-campaign press conference at which time the drive chairperson outlines the past achievements of the organization and goals of the current campaign, explains the various activities to be used in the present campaign, and stresses the urgency of the campaign.

2 Distribution of "press-kits" to all members of the media. This would include names and titles of the organization's personnel, history of the organization, previous achievements, campaign dates and goals, the cause of the campaign, and the aspirations of the organization.

3 Staging a press conference where community leaders are photographed and their statements are issued.

4 Release of names of campaign chairperson and volunteer leaders.

5 Release of past campaigns, purposes to which funds were used, and the values of these activities to all concerned.

6 Major release announcing the opening or "kick-off" of the campaign.

7 Releases for each phase of the campaign; use of photos whenever appropriate. These would include the launching of mass-mailing campaigns, prominent persons making contributions, and special events such as the "kick-off" luncheon, dinner-dance, and others.

8 Release of dollar amount received at mid-point through the campaign.

9 Use of feature stories on persons working on the campaign.

10 Release of stories or statements by prominent community leaders.

11 Major release on wrap-up of campaign and the featured activity such as a dinner and key speaker.

12 Post-campaign wrap-up, stressing individuals and their support, amount raised, and review of the purposes of the fund drive.

CONTRIBUTIONS AND TAX EXEMPTIONS

Few persons contribute to acceptable charitable, educational, and non-profit organizations as federal and state income tax regulations permit. Many do not make the full contributions to which they are entitled largely because no one has specifically asked them to do so. The typical fund-raising campaign conducted by an educational institution's athletic department meets the requirements necessary to qualify the contributor's contribution for tax exemption.

When all the persons in the nation are considered, the percentage of giving versus taxable income is still far below four per cent. Corporations are allowed up to five per cent of taxable income for such contributions, yet the average contributions are less than one and one-half per cent. On the basis of these facts, one can conclude that giving is not a popular and practiced phenomenon. However, because this disparity exists between what is given and what can be given under tax regulations, a well-organized and smartly conducted fund campaign can benefit.

DIFFERENCES BETWEEN COLLECTIONS
AND FUND DRIVES

A distinction between a collection and an organized fund drive should be clear. A collection usually has no quotas. It is based on a major cause but usually there are few specific programs planned or revealed. Appeals are made to nearly all persons at about the same level; there are few specific appeals to persons capable of giving a great deal or very little. Ordinarily a collection program has few volunteer workers. Some causes, particularly national ones, have no definable constituency. This lack of identity is the basis for indifference.

An organized fund-raising campaign proposes to finance stated programs; goals are sought by means of quota systems; there is a time schedule and sense of urgency; and volunteer solicitors, who are knowledgeable and dedicated, are utilized. Prospect lists are prepared; various amounts of contributions are expected from certain prospects. While everyone is invited to contribute, the majority of time, effort, and money expended in the campaign is funneled toward the most promising prospects; there is an awareness that the farther the prospect is removed from the cause, the more resources are required to obtain less amounts. Publicity is utilized; however, there is acknowledgement that publicity alone seldom brings in money. Supplemental information through publicity may aid workers in obtaining funds. Publicity is focused upon the proposed program; fund-raising is recognized as a means to an end.

Probably the greatest differences between collections and organized campaigns are thoughtful and proportionate giving according to ability to do so, conscious evaluation of the relative importance and urgency of the cause, the donor's own bond of interest and sense of responsibility, and the ability to give.

WHO ARE BEST PROSPECTS AS GIVERS?

The best prospects for giving are those who have already given in the past. Additionally, the more one has given, the more one is likely to give. Those persons who have been consistent givers are likely to continue to give, assuming they have not been antagonized in the meantime. Productive solicitors are found among workers who have given to the cause. The best solicitors are those who convinced themselves of the importance of the cause and have given to their maximum ability.

PEOPLE MUST BE ASKED TO GIVE

The typical person will seldom give large amounts of money unless a special request is made. Seemingly, there is a psychological block that prevents people from giving large amounts without being asked; this phenomenon may be due to an attempt to avoid being labeled an exhibitionist. People tend to give large amounts of money when they are directly asked by persons of similar financial standing or prestige. Those able and willing to make large contributions usually require a detailed explanation of the cause to which they are being asked to give. Solicitors should be knowledgeable about the cause and the specific programs to be undertaken. Furthermore, the solicitor should have made an equal or larger contribution than that being sought. The more personal the solicitation, usually the more successful it is. The more influential the solicitor is in the community, usually the more desirable are the results. Strangely, most people do not object to being listed among those expected to give the greatest amount. Another peculiar psychological phenomenon occurs when a person is asked to give a higher amount than one expects to receive; in many cases, the actual gift is larger than anticipated.

PSYCHOLOGICAL APPEALS FOR GIVING

In our modern society, funds are solicited nearly every day of every week for one cause or another. The typical person does not take the time, and often does not have factual material available, to scrutinize every request. In most cases, responses to requests are based upon emotional reactions rather than intellectual deductions. The fund campaign director and all the workers should be equipped with factual materials; however, their appeals should be based upon emotional grounds. Generally, the closer the prospect is to the cause (such as an alumnus to the athletic department), the more emphasis there ought to be on emotional appeals. Contrariwse, the farther the prospect is removed from the cause of the campaign, the more dependence should be placed upon intellectual rationale.

PATTERNS OF GIVING

When soliciting money, one should be aware of another psychological pattern. Most people tend to give in amounts ending in round numbers such as $100, $500, $1000, and so on. Also, solicitors should be cognizant that contributors tend to follow habits in giving. About half of the people give the same amount as they did the previous year; 15 per cent tend to give less; about 25 per cent will give more than previously; and about 10 per cent are new or returned givers. Efforts should be made to increase the amount of the gifts by citing past accomplishments and extolling future expectations and relating these to the individual's interest and responsibility.

WHEN TO USE THE TAX
DEDUCTIBLE APPROACH

The use of the tax deductible benefit should not be introduced into the conversation until the prospect has agreed to make a gift. Incidentally, it is usually advantageous to first solicit an agreement to give, and then request a specific amount. However, just before requesting a specific amount, bring to the attention of the prospect the tax deductible privileges.

THERE IS NO "RIGHT" TIME TO
SEEK FUNDS

Some solicitors adjust their efforts according to various financial barometers such as stock market conditions, newly enacted federal laws, and other actions. Experience has shown that there never is a "right" time to seek funds. Furthermore, on a national scale, people tend to give more during periods of recession or depression than during periods of affluency.

NEED TO DEVELOP A FINANCIAL PLAN
FOR FUND-RAISING

In the early stages of planning a fund drive, the number of gifts and their monetary size to be sought should be determined. Unless this step is taken there is the probability that solicitors and donors will revert to past habits. The expected total to be derived from the fund drive should be about 20 per cent more than publicly announced. When the announced goal is exceeded, the psychological impact is of immense importance to both present and future campaigns.

ATTITUDE IS IMPORTANT

Everyone connected with the fund drive should develop an air of optimism. In discussions with prospects, project the attitude that the prospect is considered a worthwhile candidate for a worthwhile group, and that there will be mutual pride in the association to be made.

CATALOGUE PROSPECTS

Persons who actually give money to fund drives can be catalogued. One of these groups is comprised of the conscientious minority who are activated by social conscience and propelled by heart and mind. Ordinarily these persons are along in years, are no longer primarily concerned with accumulating material possessions, and have the inner need to share their wealth with a worthy cause. This group comprises about five to ten per cent of the constituency, and in big money campaigns, they contribute all but from five to ten per cent of the total amount of money raised. A secondary contribution of considerable importance is their leadership.

The next group is comprised of individuals who are sympathetic to the cause and who will react according to the leadership and the levels of expectation set for them.

The following group is the conformers who give when it is an accepted part of the social pattern to which they adhere.

The next group are those who give because of fear or personal advantage.

The last group are the inflexible nongivers.

PREPARE A GIFT TABLE

As noted earlier, a gift table of expected gifts should be constructed before a campaign is started. In all cases one should remain aware of the fact that about one-third of all monies received is derived from the top ten givers, another third of the amount received is given by the next 100 givers, and the final third of the total amount comes from all the other givers. In a typical fund-raising campaign, about one per cent of the prospective list can be expected to lead to success or failure.

CAUSES FOR FAILURES IN
FUND-RAISING CAMPAIGNS

Before discussing the techniques and procedures essential to the success of a fund-raising effort, one may benefit from knowing the major causes for failure.

Selecting a poor cause is a major error. Even though the proposed cause is acceptable to persons closely associated with the mechanics of the drive unless it is perceived as such by the constituency hope is then dim. A cause may be weak due to several specific factors.

One of these is that the cause is too institutional and has little relevance to prospective donors. Donors should readily recognize the relevance of the proposed program to be supported with their own interests, whether psychological, social, material, or otherwise.

Another common failing is to place excessive emphasis on need rather than opportunity. People tend to close their minds to appeals based on need. Perhaps there is the implied connotation that the program has failed up to this point, and people do not like to get aboard a loser.

There is often a failure to stress the urgency and importance of the fund campaign. Specific programs should be identified along with the pressure of time to initiate them.

When it is apparent that the fund campaign has been poorly planned, persons involved are less than competent, and chances of it succeeding are minimal, potential givers will then tend to withdraw.

Often, those close to the fund campaign understand its importance, goals, and programs. However, those removed from the actual scene may lack this understanding—perhaps because of a one-time explanation of the fund-raising purpose. Repetition of the purpose or cause must be done frequently.

Another breakdown occurs when those involved with the actual operation of the fund-raising campaign expend too much of their time, effort, and concentration upon impressing their fellow colleagues instead of the prospects.

The second major area that determines the success or failure of a fund-raising campaign is its leadership. Good leadership is essential at both the professional and lay levels. A common error is to accumulate many names to associate with the fund-raising campaign but to minimize the selection of workers. Very frequently persons are appointed to leadership roles in the campaign for reasons other than enthusiasm and past productive efforts. Merely naming persons with prestige and power in the community is no assurance they will or can be leaders. Getting people involved is necessary if one wishes to receive a maximum of effort and support. One typical method of increasing involvement is through the use of committees. Committees can be productive if given specific charges, if they receive good leadership, and if their efforts are recognized and accepted. Avoiding the appointment of committees or nullifying their efforts are certain to lead to disappointment.

The third significant category that can lead to failure is that of pro-cedures. One of the common pitfalls is to "overorganize." When this occurs much time, effort, and expense are directed at the "organization" instead of the main target. Overorganization usually leads to the lack of involvement by large numbers of volunteer workers because there is too little attention paid to areas other than internal affairs. An additional failing is that of placing emphasis upon minor motivations and side issues. In some cases this imbalance reaches the point where most of the concerns are on these matters rather than the main target. When organization predominates it is expected that "busy" activities, rather than accomplishments leading to the realization of the main target, are spotlighted. Other symptoms of poor leadership can be found in the lack of enthusiasm on the part of all the workers, too little dramatization and excessive boredom, a provincial approach to fund-raising, absence of due recognition for those who deserve it, and lack of conviction about the importance of the cause.

RECOMMENDED PRACTICES AND PRINCIPLES FOR FUND CAMPAIGNS

Previous sections identified many of the causes for failure and are presented as precautions or warning signals. Knowing what constitutes good techniques in conducting fund-raising campaigns is equally important. Some of these essential techniques are now considered.

Campaign Office

A fund-raising campaign should have a suitable headquarters. The office should be in close proximity to that of the director of athletics. This facility should be located so that all workers can easily find it; adequate parking should be considered. The office area should provide ample space for the director or chairperson and for all the office personnel required. In many cases the amounts of monies to be received are sizeable; efficient handling of all monies is essential. For this reason, among others, the office should be equipped with modern devices. Expert advice should be obtained to install proper accounting procedures. Office personnel should be instructed on public relations, including methods of answering or placing telephone calls, preparing letters, avoiding errors in spelling names, addresses, titles, and financial details, displaying general courtesy to everyone, following up immediately on matters that require a reply or information, and being made aware that the fund director or chairperson is never "in conference" to callers.

Prospects

A well-designed fund-raising campaign utilizes a prospect list; it is absolutely essential and should receive attention all year round. Not only names of prospects should be noted, but an evaluation of their financial capability should be made as well. A master card file arranged in alphabetical order is highly useful; this is generally referred to as the "locator" file. Separate files, compiled from the master file, may be useful and needed. So-called "flat" lists or rosters of prospects are provided to volunteer solicitors for easy reference on keeping track of assignments completed or planned. "Stop" cards are of a different color from the regular card file; these are used to indicate that the master card has been pulled for a particular reason, such as preparing a special prospect list. These cards also indicate that the prospect is assigned some special consideration concerning who will call on the prospect; this is to avoid having a little known worker calling on a donor of a potentially large gift. The fund director should review the top layer of prospects every day. The fund campaign director should know the current ten top prospects and precisely what is being done about them. Remember, the top ten givers will give about one-third of the total amount obtained; the top 100 donors will make up about two-thirds of the total amount collected. It is important to have the name, title, credit, address, and billing procedure exactly as the prospect wishes.

Campaign Materials

The fund-raising campaign requires certain materials and procedures; this is especially important when one considers that the number of volunteer workers may reach huge numbers. Campaign literature can facilitate the task of raising money. The literature should be attractive and attention-getting, it must tell the story in clear, simple terms, use visual aids when appropriate, and be easy to carry. Subscription blanks or pledge cards should be provided to all workers. These cards should contain pertinent information as to the cause, classifications of gifts, methods of paying the pledge, previous contributions, and, of course, the proper name, title, address, and related information. The card can aid in the solicitation. It should have a signature line, preceded by a simple pledge statement. A copy of the card should be given to the donor. The information on this card should contain the purpose of the campaign, proposed programs to be continued, initiated, or amplified, a list of influential community leaders who endorse the campaign, and a statement of assurance about the virtues of having given. The prospect's card should be prepared in typewritten form prior to the contact so that the prospect realizes that this is his or her own "personal" card.

Visual Aids

Various visual aids can be helpful. Some are prepared for the purpose of informing the prospects and donors of various facts. Others are useful in the actual operation of the fund-raising campaign. For example, a master checklist can help determine the status of any one item or overall plan at a glance. Individual check lists for workers and leaders can be of valuable assistance in directing efforts, timing, and procedures. A favorite visual aid for workers is a desk and wallet calendar showing the schedule of meetings and events associated with the campaign. Another visual aid of great importance is the campaign "progress chart." This chart shows the week-by-week total dollars pledged, the total number of gifts, the monetary value of all gifts, the number of new pledges, and the number of donors obtained by individual leaders or teams. Having a quick and accurate summary of these items is critical, especially when one realizes that in a typical fund-raising campaign about one-half of the total amount to be raised is obtained when the campaign is only one-fourth completed, and at the halfway point of the campaign more than 90 per cent of the total to be obtained is received. Good pre-planning and a quick, accurate evaluation of the status of the campaign at any time are essential to success.

Leadership

A campaign will never exceed the quality of its top personnel. In addition to the fund campaign chairperson and the director of development or foundation, the volunteer personnel who directs the program should be carefully selected. This group or committee should represent the major elements of a given constituency. Community opinion leaders, political leaders, power leaders, varying age brackets, men and women, different social levels, commercial and industrial representatives, alumni, and other major segments should be involved. The power structure should be involved in the actual campaign and not serve as a front. The power block is usually comprised of persons who have inherited wealth or a tradition of public service, the newly rich and powerful, the top managers of key corporations, and persons of high public standing. These power block members usually know each other. If possible, select your leaders and executive members from among these. They have influence, and with good management they can be encouraged to produce results. As a general guide, the governing board or committee should contribute at least 15 per cent of the total sum sought. One warning—do not stick with anyone who fails to produce. Do not elect leaders; appoint them instead on the basis of merit and expectation.

Workers

No fund-raising campaign can succeed without workers. It takes workers to contact people. Usually the more productive workers that are involved in a campaign, the more successful are the final results. In selecting

workers, attempt to locate those who will work without urging. This
group represents about one-third of the candidates. The next one-third
requires leadership and motivation. The bottom one-third is hopeless.
One should be alert as to which category any individual may be assigned. "Back-up" procedures should be ready for others to assume the
responsibilities of those workers who fall into the hopeless classification.
There is a psychological phenomenon that must be observed in obtaining
workers. Workers should not be asked to serve; instead they should be
invited to participate in the solving of some relevant and urgent problem.
Their potential in achieving this end should be stressed. After one has
emphasized the planned program and its major objectives, then the willingness, and even enthusiasm, to serve becomes a topic for discussion.
Sufficient time should be allowed to cultivate and secure a worker. It is
a mistake to send an invitation by letter or to call a general meeting of
potential workers, and, in either case, to barrage them with all the duties
and details the position requires. Instead, schedule your program so that
there is an acceptance of the cause plus a realization of the urgency for
immediate action, and then relate the specifics connected with their
duties. Emphasis should be placed upon the role the worker will fulfill
in the power structure and the organization. As a general rule, there are
about ten workers to every leader or captain. However, better results are
obtained by having five workers to every captain and one worker to
every five prospects. It has been consistently shown that there is a direct
relationship between the number of competent and dedicated workers
and the total amount of funds received. Some persons have a distaste for
the use of the word "committee"; consider the use of the term "commission" or a substitute. Do not expect workers to maintain a high level of enthusiasm for an extended length of time; arrange preliminary meetings and
fix the length of the fund-raising campaign to end before interest wanes.

Meetings

Most people are reluctant to attend meetings. Their past experiences
have resulted in boredom, repetition, and a feeling of wasted time.
However, meetings need not be of this nature. They can and should be
pleasant, fun, and end with a sense of achievement. Because most people
have had bad experiences with meetings they may seek to avoid having
them in connection with the fund-raising campaign. This should not be
allowed to happen; hold out for established meeting dates, times, places,
and purposes. Meetings are useful for many reasons, if properly conceived. One of the main reasons for planned meetings is that they serve

as deadlines; they also serve to motivate workers to attain various levels of performance. Fund-raising campaign meetings should be structured as much as necessary in order to accomplish the business at hand. However, care should be used to encourage free discussion and exchange of ideas. By following this format, everyone either participates in the discussion or at least has the feeling that they may do so. Another chief reason for holding meetings is to allow workers to make oral presentations to the entire group. By arranging for this action, the worker receives attention, satisfaction, and additional motivation. By such reporting, there is a competitive mood, resulting in greater efforts by all workers. Then, too the organization tends to develop a feeling of togetherness and accomplishment. Meetings are also the basis for news releases. This type of publicity is valuable in motivating workers, and it aids in solicitations yet to be conducted. Meetings and related publicity not only serve useful means for a current campaign, but also provide residual value in obtaining good workers for future drives. Serious efforts should be employed to energize all meetings. Use of music, signs, place-cards, novelty prizes, trophies, games, surprise speakers, humorous stories, and other variations should be considered.

Agenda
The agenda for meetings should receive careful attention. Improperly timed meetings can result in failure. Giving too much time to one particular segment may create a psychological setting that affects the remainder of the program, regardless of how important these items may be. Allowing "lag" moments between events or items on the agenda tends to create a feeling of disorganization, uncertainty, and lack of urgency. An agendum should be planned minute-by-minute. All participants in the "formal" phases of the program should have a copy of the agendum, and they should be advised of the importance to remain within the time allotted. All participants in the "formal" portions of the program should convene several minutes before the start of the actual program. Arranging such a meeting 15 to 30 minutes ahead of the general meeting provides time to review the importance and sequence of timing, and this is an ideal period to coordinate the topic or material to be presented. It goes without saying that meetings should start and end exactly as announced; allow no variations. There are times when there will be unfinished business, or there will be a desire to extend the meeting time because of enthusiasm. Do not waver on the principle of opening and closing on set times.

Meeting Schedule

Meetings during a fund-raising campaign should be scheduled as often as necessary, not less or more frequently. The purpose of meetings help to determine their number and schedule. Sufficient time should elapse between meetings so that significant work can be accomplished. Yet, the time lapse should not be so great as to curtail momentum or to weaken the motivation of workers.

Conduct of Meetings

Those conducting the meetings should be mindful of the basic psychological principle that participation increases interest, and interest improves efforts. Before the meeting is held, leaders should decide upon issues, problems, or procedures that will stimulate discussion, questions, and answers. Leaders should be aware of those individuals who may have real contributions to make but may be reluctant to speak out unless asked. Leaders must also seek to tactfully draw from workers their ideas and solutions. When a topic has been discussed, the alert leader will summarize the problem and solution before moving on to another area. This action tends to give everyone a sense of progress.

Visual Aids for Meetings

In most meetings and particularly for those attached to a fund-raising campaign there should be liberal use of visual materials. Visual materials have the capability, if prepared correctly, of conveying information and facts in a specific, concise, and brief way. Where many names of individuals, teams, and localities may be used along with numerous figures pertaining to dollars, numbers, new and old memberships, percentages, and financial status, visual materials are especially advantageous. Furthermore, there is a motivational factor involved in seeing names and accomplishments in writing displayed before a group.

Meeting Follow-up

As soon as a meeting is concluded, full effort should be made to mail a summary of the meeting. Envelopes should be prepared in advance. Mailing should be at least first-class; in many cases special delivery is recommended. The immediate receipt of a summary of a meeting tends to underline its importance and the reports made at it. Should any member of the fund-raising campaign be absent, attach a personal note to the summary; mention the loss to the group by the member's absence.

Successful Attendance

Meeting dates, times, and places should be widely known and should appear on a master calendar provided to everyone connected with the fund-raising campaign. Assign every member a "buddy." The responsibility of each member is to telephone his or her buddy the day before the scheduled meeting as a reminder. Meeting places should be selected with care. Holding a meeting where lighting is poor, acoustics are bad, noise is more than minimal, service of meals is slow, parking is absent, and other requirements are lacking can contribute to lack of attendance, poor results, and eventual failure of the fund-raising campaign. In arranging the meeting place, whether or not food or refreshments will be served, always plan for fewer seats or settings than will be needed. A fully occupied room or table setting contributes to the psychological reaction that one is attending a popular and exclusive function.

Briefing Workers

Before actual solicitation of money begins, all workers should be briefed on the strategy and tactics of "selling" the program. This briefing should utilize previously successful fund-raisers who can explain those points to be included in soliciting and those to be avoided. Their remarks should be supported by a brief pamphlet or guidebook for each worker that can be used to reinforce the presentations. Some of the basic principles in soliciting funds for a worthy cause include the following. The focal point of discussion with a prospect should be on the plans and aims of the program to be supported by the fund-raising campaign; do not talk about contributions or total costs of the program. Emphasize the hopes, aspirations, and opportunities that can be satisfied. Instead of asking for money at the outset of a contact, direct the prospect's attention to what can be accomplished by the campaign. Speak in terms of added improvements, such as additional grant-in-aid funds, intensified recruiting, attraction of better student–athletes, improved coaching, improved coaching devices such as videotape, films, resistive exercise machines, and better medical care, better academic counseling and supervision, improved scheduling, and other items.

Solicitation Methods

After the plans, hopes, aspirations, and opportunities have been presented, then attention should be directed toward asking for money. Have in mind the amount that will be requested from each prospect. Suggest that the prospect offer to make known how much will be given. Regardless of the amount of prospect offers, attempt to have him or her consider a larger amount or a commitment for an extended period of years. One should realize that the typical person will seldom offer to give the maximum amount according to his or her ability. Most fund-raising campaigns have various classifications established according to the amount of money given. Seek to have the prospect participate in a higher classification than offered. Of course, these suggestions should be made in a tactful, courteous manner. Solicitations should first be directed toward the prospects who are capable of giving the largest amounts. Contributions should be obtained from major contributors before the formal launching of the fund-raising campaign. This "priming" has a positive effect upon others, particularly those who have the same financial capabilities. Solicitations should be first requested of the primary constituents of the institution, such as faculty, administration, alumni, students, parents of students, and staff. Emphasis should be directed toward those prospects who have been identified as such. In fund-raising, it is commonly known that the farther removed prospects are from the mainstream of the institution, the greater the effort required, the higher the cost, and the smaller the gift.

Assigning Solicitors

A basic principle in fund-raising is to assign solicitors to prospects on the basis of similar prestige, financial status, power, leadership, and social standing. Solicitors should first contribute the amount expected of them before they contact prospects. A prospect who is contacted by a solicitor who has either failed to make a contribution or has made a contribution below that sought is subject to embarrassment and defeat. As a general rule, permit workers to contact those individuals they request. The best prospects are those who gave in the previous campaign. However, efforts should be made to have the amount of the gift increased, based upon the prospect's psychological investment in the total program and on increased operation costs.

Personal Contact

There is an axiom in soliciting money for a worthy cause that has held true for as long as fund-raising has existed, namely: "you can't milk a cow by mail." Mass mailings should be used only as a supplemental and final act. Successful fund-raising campaigns are accomplished by personal, face-to-face contact. Because of this fact, a great number of workers should be used so they can, in turn, contact an even greater number of prospects.

Soliciting Large Gifts

In soliciting a large sum of money from a prospect, sufficient time should be allowed. Do not expect to barge into a corporation chairperson's office and walk out with a five or six figure check. In making these contacts, have solicitors of equal stature set an appointment time and place. If necessary, the solicitor should be accompanied by someone fully familiar with all the facts of the current and proposed program. Do not expect to close the contract at the first meeting; usually a follow-up session is necessary. Incidentally, do not circumvent local executives in favor of contacting national officers; if necessary, operate through the firm's channels.

Alibis

Solicitors can rationalize for their failure to contact prospects. The most common alibis are that either the solicitor or the prospect does not have the time. Workers should be impressed that there is no "right" time. Time must be created and used. Another alibi is that contact was attempted but the prospect was too busy, not available, or not interested. The solicitor should not be satisfied with this situation and must make persistent efforts. Solicitors should be reminded that the number of persons who were to be contacted is not the same as dollars received. The fund-raising campaign is only as successful as dollars received.

Meeting Atmosphere

During meetings, the leaders should exude confidence, optimism, and enthusiasm for a good cause. When this is done consistently, there is a tendency for this attitude to rub off on others. It is most important that any setbacks or failures be minimized during meetings and that the gains and successes be stressed over and over.

Publicity

Publicity will not raise funds—it can help to raise funds. In order to help raise funds, publicity should be timely, consistent, interesting, clear, factual, brief, positive, and planned to include as many names as feasible. Publicity is of special value in making announcements, providing background information, reporting on campaign progress, citing special meetings and events, and for providing the basis for discussion and conversation.

Literature

The amount of campaign literature does not necessarily correlate with the amount of money obtained during a fund-drive. At no time should campaign literature be used to substitute for personal contact. The purpose of campaign literature is to help solicit funds, assist the solicitor in presenting his or her case, and aid the prospect to understand and endorse the cause. A campaign booklet or pamphlet is a useful tool. This publication should be done in good taste, not too extravagant in color, makeup, or print; it should also avoid the appearance of a drab, lifeless, and perfunctory publication. The content of the pamphlet should cover the history of the institution or program, current program, past support of the program, the proposed program, and the names of influential persons. This should be done in short, simple sentences that are easy to read. A slogan or theme should appear on all publications and in all news releases.

An "in-house" publication should be a bulletin that is provided to all workers on the fund-raising campaign. This may be a four-page, letter-size reproduction. The predominant mood of this bulletin should be one of optimism. Content includes all the names of persons who have been given responsibility, attained various successes, earned prizes, and other information relative to the fund-raising campaign. Names of leaders and workers for each division or team are listed, as well as individual and team quotas. A comparison with leading institutions should be included. Statements by administrative personnel can also be used.

Every worker should be provided with a "facts-sheet." This reference is to be used in making personal contacts and in presenting talks to various groups.

A weekly "report" should be prepared for all workers. This is a condensation of written reports submitted by workers and team leaders. The report should contain such information as to who was contacted by whom, results of each contact, proposed method of follow-up on certain prospects, summary of amount received, number of new members, a breakdown by classification of gifts, and other pertinent details. This "report" eliminates total reliance upon verbal appraisals; it becomes a part of the recorded results.

Mass Mailing

Reliance upon mass mailings for the solicitation of money is foolhardy. Nonetheless, letters can serve as a supplemental source of revenue for the moment and as a bridge to better understanding and possible future support. In preparing a letter of solicitation, emphasize that the institution and the department of athletics hold the individual in high regard in any case. Simultaneously, make it clear that you hope the feeling is reciprocal. Personalize letters in every way. Try to use personal salutations, personal signatures (using first name or nickname), and a personal P.S.; avoid multiple signatures. For a special prospect, the use of personal stationery is helpful. The content of the letter should resemble and read like a personal letter and not an editorial or magazine article. If a modern electronic typewriter is used to prepare each letter, allow for some personal notation, but do not try to conceal the manner of producing the letter. It is usually a better practice to explain the necessity for the mass preparation of letters and in some cases it is helpful to note that the method was used in order to reach all of the person's classmates, colleagues, club members, or other groups, and that concern for expense conservation motivated its use.

The makeup of the letter should be directed toward getting attention of the reader, maintaining interest, exuding confidence, detailing what you wish from the reader, and describing a method to accommodate immediate action. A P.S. is an ideal place to mention what the writer has done to assist the cause. If enclosures are used, keep them to a minimum. Ordinarily a pledge card, self-addressed, stamped envelope, and a pocket-size leaflet should be enclosed. The latter should re-state the cause for the campaign, the specific programs to be aided, persons who have endorsed the cause through their own contributions and effort, and a summation of the importance of the gifts made by each donor.

All mass mailings should plan on one follow-up. This follow-up should not berate or belittle the prospect for failing to reply to the first mailing. Instead, the second letter should include a summary of good news that has occurred since the original mailing, such as the number of new members, the amount of money collected, rate of progress, as well as generate an air of confidence. Stress the urgency of the cause and the time limits of the campaign. Review the personal satisfaction and benefits that will accrue to each donor through the realization of the programs planned. Envelopes for both mailings should be addressed in advance of the campaign.

Add reader attention and interest in the makeup of the letter. The use of underlined words, capitalized words, variable indented paragraphs, and blocked areas makes the letter more readable and different. The urgency of the drive and the cut-off dates should be clearly presented. End the letter by asking for specific action to aid the program or cause. Letters should be mailed to arrive at home addresses on Tues-

days, Wednesdays, or Thursdays. The arrival date of letters should be
coordinated with news releases. This tactic tends to add impetus to the
letter.

Membership Year

The membership year should be clearly spelled out for everyone. Some
institutions prefer a calendar year from January 1 to January 1. Others
prefer the membership year to be from July 1 to July 1. There are various
factors that should be considered in establishing a membership year. One
of the most important considerations is the date of the annual fund-
raising campaign. As suggested, if the month of May is the most successful for most institutions, then either of the two membership years
noted above are awkward, particularly in regard to relating the cause to
the ensuing academic year. Some institutions have found it desirable to
define the membership year from May 1 to May 1; others place their
membership year from May 1 to December 1. The purpose of limiting
the membership year is to avoid the confusion in the minds of some
prospects who erroneously believe they have contributed to two calendar
years. In other words, if a prospect gives a gift of money on May 1 in
x year, he may wrongly believe that he is a fully paid member for x year
and for the y year that follows.

Fund Accounting

A professional accountant should be obtained to set up the model for all
accounting methods and procedures in the office of the fund-raising campaign. Establishing a system that expedites the acknowledgement of gifts
is most essential. As much preliminary work as possible in this area
should be completed before the drive commences.

Post-Campaign Planning

Every major fund-raising project has some unfinished business at the end
of the campaign. In planning the entire campaign, the schedule, methods,
and responsibilities for cleaning up details should be included. There is
a tendency for workers and leaders to let-down after the close of an
intensive fund-raising effort. Because this reaction is expected, planning
and follow-through of clean-up procedures must be reinforced.

Panacea Substitutions

The director of athletics, the director of the support organization or
foundation, and the leaders of the organization should be aware of the
most common mistakes or temptations associated with fund-raising cam-

paigns. Because fund-raising appears to be a monumental and complicated task (to the novice), there will be some who want to assign the project to the professional fund-raiser. Unless most unusual circumstances exist, do not use a professional fund-raiser.

Some persons assume that a "get rich quick" scheme is better than a bona fide fund-raising campaign. Suggestions will often be made for a lottery or some other gaming program. Avoid these solutions for a long-term problem.

Another favorite approach is to mail merchandise, such as game tickets, membership cards, or other gimmicks with the expectation of a remittance under threat. Any reputable institution or department of athletics will never associate themselves with such a ruse.

At some time, one can also expect to hear the suggestion of staging a benefit. While some benefits have been successful, it is strongly recommended that they be considered only on a supplementary basis to the regular fund-raising campaign. Generally, these special benefits are financial failures, even though they may be artistic successes.

Fund-Drive Period

The typical fund-raising campaign has a definite date on which it starts and ends. As a general policy it is best to adhere to these dates, regardless of the outcome of the drive. In announcing the campaign results, it is beneficial to include those gifts still to be received but for which there is every reason to believe they will be given within a certain time. Funds that arrive after the closing date, and for which no previous use was made in computing results, should be assigned to the next campaign. These can be used for the "priming" process.

Failure

Should the fund-drive fall short of the goal, the result should be publicly announced with no reference to the original goal or with minimal attention. Emphasize plus factors that emerged, such as number of new members, largest gifts, leading fund-raisers, and other points of interest. In acclamation of workers and leaders reward on the basis of results, not on sacrifice or effort. If it is absolutely necessary to seek additional funds, then establish a completely new campaign; do not extend the old. If the old was acceptable by prospects, then there would not be the necessity of an additional effort. In seeking extra funds, the most reliable source is from among those persons who have already given in proportion to their capability.

Post-Campaign Actions

Assume that the annual fund drive is over. There are many details that need attention in order to close the event and to prepare for future drives. All solicitations that are still in doubt should receive a last effort; in many cases, changing the solicitor may bring good results.

All records should be brought to a close while information and personnel are present and still knowledgeable about details. An overall evaluation should be made of the campaign, in addition to an analysis of details such as meeting dates, times, places, procedures, and content, literature, workers, leaders, prospects, and every other important aspect.

There may be some hesitation on the part of workers and leaders to hold a summary evaluation. Their plea may be based upon fatigue, pressure of time, or any other reason. These should be resisted. All must be reminded that their extra efforts will be beneficial in years to come.

A formal, final report on the campaign should be prepared. This report should contain all the important facts, but with emphasis on goal attainment, overall results, and the forthcoming programs. Of course, the report should contain information regarding the number and sizes of gifts, leading workers and leaders, budget expense report, a chronology of main events and announcements, and a recapitulation of the goals sought, policies employed, and the efforts of all.

Workers and donors should receive a personal letter from the chairperson of the campaign, the director of athletics, and the president of the institution. These should be separate letters, each relating to some particular aspect or association. Most important is that workers and donors receive a second letter from each of these persons sometime later when the programs they supported have borne fruit. Letters should also be mailed to workers and donors when some significant project they supported has been started, completed, or sustained. The primary purpose of these letters is to let each individual know that his or her efforts were appreciated, valuable, and enduring. A small momento that can be seen by others is timely. This may be an office plaque, desk adornment, cufflinks, or similar token. These should be properly inscribed. Most people are not interested in material awards; they prefer receiving public esteem and honor.

One should be ever mindful that the manner in which a campaign is closed will have a direct bearing on the succeeding one. Workers who found satisfaction in their efforts, and who were recognized for them, are likely to be active the following year and also encourage others to become active. There should be a closing event, such as a victory dinner, at which time everyone deserving should be publicly acknowledged. However, the whole atmosphere should be one of fun.

Off-Season Actions

During the off-season a great deal of spadework can be completed in preparation for the next drive. Certainly a high priority should be assigned to developing a list of some 300, 500, or 1000 top prospects; each should be researched according to their capabilities to give. Analyze the power structure in the community; remember that this is a fluid situation. Start to identify the new leaders. Locate those persons who failed to live up to expectations; terminate their responsibilities in a tactful and friendly way.

Start to define the needs of the coming year. Programs may be curtailed or dropped, some may be expanded, new ones may appear. Priorities should be determined as early as possible. Avoid splintering your program in parts, such as football, track, and so on; present your requests as a whole, emphasizing the overall concept.

Some pledges are made on an installment payment basis. Accurate and reliable follow-up of these is essential.

PITFALLS IN FUND-RAISING STRATEGY

When determining the target amount of a fund-raising campaign, do not fall victim to the formula of multipling x number of dollars from y number of persons. For example, an institution with 10,000 alumni, each of whom gives $10 to the cause, can raise $100,000. This is a fantasy; it will not happen in real life.

When a renowned person associated with an institution or department of athletics dies, there will be those who immediately conceive the idea of a memorial fund drive. Generally speaking, these drives fall far below expectations. Care should be taken to evaluate emotional involvement with the individual in determining the practicality of this plan.

Some members of a board of directors tend to believe that expanding and emphasizing a publicity campaign will result in a successful fund drive. Publicity will not assure success in any fund drive.

The cause of the fund-raising campaign is unclear, argumentative, self-serving, or lacks universality. Defining the cause of the fund drive in clear terms is vital. Selecting a cause that will generate support and enthusiasm is necessary.

Failure of achieving goals in a fund-raising campaign can be due to one or more factors. Some of the most prevalent causes of failure are the following. Having no plan or a poorly planned program is usually a guarantee of failure. Simply employing a collection of money based upon need is deadly. Conducting the affairs of the fund-raising campaign on an impersonal basis leads to negativism. Failing to establish prospect lists and levels of giving will lead to minimal gifts. Presenting a program to prospects that is at best "second class" turns people away. A well-planned and well-conducted fund-raising campaign requires good personnel and good procedures, both of which should be funded sufficiently, otherwise neither is likely to be present.

Few fund-raising efforts have succeeded with poor leadership. When the cause is worthy and excellent leadership is present, most fund-raising campaigns are successful. Leadership involves the director of athletics, the director of the office of development, and the laypersons who are active in the campaign effort.

At one time not too many years ago, a fund-raiser was viewed with skepticism by many people. Today, fund-raising is an accepted and expected activity for all educational institutions and for most nonprofit, charitable, and educational organizations. The art of directing fund drives has achieved a sophisticated level, requiring the application of talent and training.

SELECTING A DIRECTOR

Selecting the director of development of the foundation is an important and critical responsibility. In addition to having sufficient knowledge of fund-raising, this person must understand the role of public relations on behalf of the institution and the department of athletics. The director should also have a grasp of modern and effective accounting procedures. Of course, it is desirable and essential that this individual possess all of the personality and character traits one would wish to find in any executive position that requires interaction with colleagues and the public.

MAJOR RESPONSIBILITY OF THE DIRECTOR

The primary role of the director in the actual fund-raising campaign is equivalent to that of the director and producer of a major motion picture. Seldom is this person "out front." Yet, the director must be involved in every minute detail, selecting all leaders and coordinating all activities. A director is seldom directly involved in face-to-face fund-raising activities; exceptions to this general approach are specific prospects that may be influenced by his or her presence.

In addition to the planning and management of the fund-raising campaign and the attention to a myriad of details, the director is responsible for selecting and developing leadership from among the volunteer workers. Perhaps no aspect of the job is more important. Campaigns fail or succeed in direct relationship to the proper selection and development of these leaders.

SELECTING AND DEVELOPING LEADERS

Before potential leaders can be attracted to commit themselves to a project, the proper cause must be identified. When the cause has merit, then the matter of inducing potential and proven leaders is much easier to accomplish. In selecting leaders, it is most important to eliminate from consideration those persons who are figureheads or ornamental fixtures. If the cause is worthy and of significant proportion, then genuine leadership is more likely to be available. However, good leaders must be sought just as major contributors must be solicited. Whatever time, effort, and expense is involved in obtaining good leadership, the investment will yield dividends. When good leaders are at the front of a fund-raising drive, it is easier and more likely that good assistants and workers will be obtained. Good leaders recognize the need and importance of committee activity; they will use it to advantage. Most importantly, the key leaders can by their own enthusiasm, words, deeds, and gifts set standards that will invoke similar action on the part of their assistants and workers. Although leaders may emerge from any walk of life, the most fruitful sources are the executives of banks, business managers or executives, professional representatives, and influential power blocks. The director should have an up-to-date analysis of the local power structure, including the opinion leaders. No person should be excluded from consideration as a leader merely on the basis of some arbitrary standard, such as a degree, title, or political affiliation. Instead, the analysis of the community and its leaders should be on an objective basis. Do not make the error of eliminating a person for consideration as a leader for the fund-raising campaign simply because that person is a "busy" man or women. Ordinarily, any community leader is a busy person. It would be foolish to believe that all that is necessary to marshal the consent of a true leader is to ask for their support. Leaders must be cultivated; it may take weeks, months, or even years. But, regardless of the time and effort, the results justify these costs. In seeking leadership, the search should be conducted in secret. Should one or more leaders refuse to accept the responsibility, word of this rejection can create additional difficulties.

OPERATING THE CORPORATION ON
APPROVED BUSINESS PRINCIPLES

As every private or public enterprise that seeks to remain solvent and to maintain public confidence, the office of development or the foundation should operate on sound business principles. One of the most important principles is to properly prepare and adhere to a budget. Depending upon a variety of factors, the budget for raising funds for a department of athletics program will vary. For example, at one institution the office of the foundation may be rent-free, while at others this is not the case. It is estimated that the cost of raising funds is from 10 to 15 per cent of the total obtained; most of the costs of a campaign are used to raise the last 10 per cent of the total. When the costs of a fund-raising campaign are added to year round expenses, the average expenses for the overall operation, including salaries, usually range from 17 to 25 per cent.

Many of the expenses for operating the foundation or development office can be "traded-out." For example, the costs of printing literature may be obtained from a printing firm in lieu of a cash contribution. The alert director of development or the foundation can locate other areas of trade-outs.

A typical budget contains items noted below; each institution will need to tailor its budget to meet specific demands.

Salaries and Fees
    Professional staff
    Clerical staff
    Federal and state deductions
    Auditor's fees, etc.
    Insurance, bonding, etc.

Organizational Expenses
    Entertainment of prospects
    Travel

Promotions and Publicity
    Printed materials
    Models and visualizations
    Art work
    Mailing costs
    Photographs, slides, etc.
    Television clips
    Promotional motion picture

Radio tapes
Television spots
Special presentations

General Expenses
Rent
Furniture
Office equipment
Office supplies
Postage
Telephone and telegraph
Freight
Messenger services
Utilities
Services and repairs
Insurance
Bank charges and interest

Fund-Raising Campaign Expenses
Research fees and materials
Literature
Letters
Postage
Meeting rooms, meals, refreshments, etc.
Entertainment, speakers, decorations, etc.
Prizes
Travel
Telephone

INITIATING A CORPORATION

Every precaution should be taken to avoid legal difficulties in setting up
an office of development or foundation, conducting a fund-raising campaign, and in the general operation of both. It is advisable to seek the
services of an attorney who is familiar with this area. Perhaps it is possible to utilize the services of one who is on the board of directors or is
an active leader in the fund drive. If such an individual is not available,
then it may be possible to consider a trade-out with an attorney.

Costs will vary from state to state and community to community.
The average attorney's fee for drawing up and filing incorporation papers
is $500. The average filing fee, required by the state, is $50.

The Internal Revenue Service recognizes two kinds of exempt organizations or foundations: public and private. Public organizations or foundations include major churches and religious denominations, organizations that receive substantial financial support from the general public, and/or organizations that provide charitable and educational services to the public at large. Public organizations have fewer restrictions and reporting requirements than private foundations, and so make much better sponsors than private foundations. Whenever possible, use a public foundation as the sponsoring agency.

To form a tax-exempt foundation or organization, the attorney should consult with the Secretary of State for the state involved. From this source one can learn the requirements regarding local incorporation procedures. There are four major steps required to satisfy most conditions.

Step 1 Determine if the purposes and activities of the proposed organization satisfy the requirements for tax exemption. To qualify as a tax-exempt organization so that donors can obtain tax deductions for their contributions, the organizations must qualify under section 501(c)(3) of the Internal Revenue Code of 1954. That particular section exempts: "Corporations, and any community chest, fund or foundations organized and operated exclusively for religious, charitable, scientific, testing for public safety, literary, or educational purposes, or for the prevention of cruelty to animals, no part of the net earnings of which inures to the benefit of any private shareholder or individual, no substantial part of the activities of which is carrying on propaganda, or otherwise attempting to influence legislation, and which does not participate in (including the publishing or distributing of statements), any political campaign on behalf of any candidate for public office."

Step 2 Most tax-exempt organizations are formed as nonprofit corporations. This entails: (1) selecting a name for the organization that is not held or used by any other corporation in your state; (2) drafting Articles of Incorporation, bylaws, and, if necessary, an application for exemption from state income tax; (3) holding the first meeting of the board where ordinarily bylaws are adopted, officers are elected, a corporate seal is adopted, and an officer is authorized to do all acts necessary to obtain state and federal tax exemptions.

Step 3 If your state has an income tax, you may find it necessary to apply for a separate state tax exemption. In California, for example, an application for state exemption (Form FTB 3500) is filed with the California Franchise Tax Board, and the Articles of Incorporation with the Secretary of State. Once the California Franchise Board grants the California tax exemption, the Secretary of State will file the Articles of Incorporation. At this time, the organization is officially a nonprofit corporation exempt from California franchise tax; a copy of the Articles of Incorporation should be filed with the Clerk of the county where the office is located.

Step 4 The application for a federal tax exemption (Form 1023) should now be completed and filed on behalf of the organization. If the application is approved, the District Director of the Internal Revenue Service will provide a letter that grants the exemption and explains the responsibilities of the organization under the law.

One should expect that the completion of all four steps will take from three to four months, if there are no particular problems.

Once the organization or foundation is formed and operating, there are several requirements imposed by governmental agencies. What is reported will depend upon whether the organization is considered a favored public nonprofit or private enterprise. This classification depends upon the sources of financial support. Most public foundations require that the organization obtain a certain percentage of its income from "the public"—that is, numerous small contributors or grants. The requirements for operating and reporting are much more complicated and restrictive for a private foundation than a public organization. If possible, seek to establish the former.

ACCOUNTING REQUIREMENTS
FOR THE CORPORATION

As indicated earlier, it is absolutely essential that the accounting procedures of the office of development or foundation be acceptable to the most demanding inquiry. In most cases it is advisable to obtain professional guidance. Also, it is recommended that arrangements be made with a professional accountant to review all procedures at least every three months. Satisfactory accounting procedures and practices are necessary for several reasons. Most important are the trust and confidence of donors; poor accounting procedures make future fund-raising campaigns suffer. Of course, good accounting procedures are necessary in order to prepare acceptable state and federal reports.

Good accounting practices do not necessarily need to be complicated. In fact, good practices are easy to understand and implement. Some of the practices that should be followed include these rudimentary guidelines: Funds pertaining to any other operation should be kept separate; do not mix profit and nonprofit accounts. A checking account should be opened; no payments should be made in money. A commercial-type checkbook is advisable that allows one to record the following information on the attached stub: date, payee, amount, and description. Do not make checks out to "cash"; these are hard to trace. The bank accounts should be balanced at least each month. A running balance should be maintained in the checkbook at all times. If petty cash is required, draw an initial check for the fund; thereafter, as money is withdrawn from the petty cash supply, submit a voucher and receipt that contains the date, payee, amount, and type of expense. When the petty cash fund is consumed, summarize the expenditures and draw a check for the difference. Thus, the money remaining in the fund plus the vouchers should always equal the starting amount. The director of the office of development or foundation should have the sole authority to authorize purchases, bill payment, and check writing. This same individual should also be responsible for depositing cash received by the organization.

FILING SYSTEM

A filing system is advantageous to the operations of the office. In most cases, the filing system should service the permanent records, such as separate folders for legal documents, tax records, grant documents, and the like; a separate section should be reserved for correspondence, filed on an A-to-Z basis in chronological order; files should be kept for program information such as working papers, memoranda, written reports, and the like; a separate filing unit should be assigned to accounts, both payable and paid bills. Bills should be filed separately. Unpaid bills should be reviewed regularly on the 1st and 15th day of the month and paid. For paid bills, set up an A-to-Z file. As a bill is paid, mark or stamp it "paid," write the check number, payment date, and the amount on the bill; this voids the bill and prevents double payment.

GOVERNMENT REGULATIONS

Each state has different regulations pertaining to payroll taxes. It is recommended that the office of the Internal Revenue Services and the state office (in California the authority is the Office of Human Resources Development), be consulted for guidance and proper forms to be filled.

Each employee is required to have an employee earnings card. This card should show the gross wages earned, net wages paid, the amount deducted for FICA (Social Security), federal withholding taxes, and SDI. If an independent accountant, attorney, certified public accountant, or other professional services are used, contracts for all such services should be in writing; all disbursements to these persons should be made only upon receipt of an approved bill or statement.

A daily log should be maintained. This log should provide quick information pertaining to expenditures, receipts, balances, and subtotals at the end of June and December. This log can provide information to prepare financial statements, foundation reports, and federal and state income tax returns.

MATCHING GRANTS AND BEQUESTS

Two special areas of fund-raising deserve full attention and effort. These are matching grants and bequests.

The area of bequests has been greatly overlooked in fund-raising campaigns. Many of the progressive institutions have placed stress on this type of program and have enjoyed great rewards. There are several explanations for the lack of concentration on bequests. Perhaps foremost is the false assumption that only the very wealthy should be approached, or that only those persons in twilight years or with terminal illnesses are prospects. In some cases failure to achieve any satisfactory response has been due to the type of solicitation used. Mailing out a letter, with or without a form to be completed, seldom produces any results.

Bequest requests require the same type of organization, leadership, and personal contact as typical fund-raising campaigns. A prospect list must be generated; information must be accumulated; specific amounts from individuals should be elicited. About half the adults in the United States and about 30 per cent of all lawyers have no wills at all. Furthermore, federal and state laws change rapidly so that provisions in a bequest must be updated continuously. The average lawyer will not suggest to his or her client that a portion of an estate be directed to a department of athletics through its development or foundation office. Special efforts must be made to acquaint the lawyers in the community of the advantages of considering your foundation; further, these lawyers should be apprised of your program and aspirations. If it is feasible to contact the prospective donor in person, then by all means this step should be undertaken. Institutions have used both specific and universal means of obtaining results. In the former instance, personal contact is made with a specific prospect; in the latter case, a broadly based campaign is conducted.

The office of development or the foundation should prepare an information and action pamphlet or booklet. This should contain the proposed programs of the department of athletics, the precedents of giving in this manner, the opportunities that are available to the institution when resources are sufficient, and names of influential persons who endorse the program. This should be accompanied by a cover letter. The mailing list should include lawyers, trust officers, specialists in estate planning, tax experts, and other in related fields. Ask them for questions and information, offer to send more information, agree to meet with them at their convenience, and keep everything simple and on-target.

The ideal person to utilize in contacting a prospect is one who is vitally concerned with the athletic program and who has made a bequest to it. This fundamental applies to all fund-raising activities, but it is crucial in seeking bequests. The place to start searching for bequests is from inside out. Contact the members of the foundation or support organization, the institution's administration and faculty, the board of trustees, the advisory board, and others closely associated with the institution and its department of athletics.

In recent years the "matching" grant has gained in popularity. Under certain provisions, the federal government allows commercial enterprises to provide amounts of money that must be matched by the receiving agency. The grant made by the commercial enterprise receives certain tax breaks. The development office director or director of the foundation should consult with the Internal Revenue Service about the regulations pertaining to this program. Thereafter, all the major commercial enterprises in the community and those outside the immediate service area who have administrative personnel vitally interested in your institution and department of athletics should be identified. Once this identification is made, then appropriate literature should be prepared and mailed to these individuals. Personal contact should then be used. Preferably those persons serving as solicitors should be managers of commercial enterprises who have adopted this program.

PREPARE STUDENTS FOR MEMBERSHIP

Often institutions of higher education tend to ignore their students in some way or another. This is particularly true when it comes to cultivating an early interest in the program, aspirations, and opportunities that pertain to the athletic department. This is a sad error. Students are the greatest potential future financial and moral supporters. Every feasible effort should be made to involve students in the athletic program. Some institutions have arranged for mailing of literature to seniors and graduate students. This material seeks to explain the purposes, values, program, and aspirations of the athletic department. Then, a complimentary membership is granted to each alumnus for the first year following the graduation or completion of the course of study. During this year the new alumnus or alumna receives all the literature, correspondence, and news mailed to regular members. Although many fund-raising campaigns have a minimal amount for membership, usually $10 or $15, special considerations are granted to recent graduates. Involvement is the key. The small givers among recent graduates will undoubtedly be your big givers in years to come. Time and care are needed to cultivate this vast potential.

THE TEAM CONCEPT FOR
FUND CAMPAIGNS

One of the more popular techniques of organizing volunteer workers for fund-raising is called the team concept. Essentially, this technique places emphasis upon competition both among individuals and teams. The formula employs the pyramid design to increase the number of leaders and workers. There are several variations of the use of the team concept of fund-raising. Basic principles remain somewhat consistent; only the design is altered to meet specific needs or desires.

Assuming that the concept has been in operation, the structure consists of the director of athletics, the executive director or director of the foundation, the campaign committee (comprised of top fund raisers, officials, coaches, and sports information director of the university) a commissioner for each of two leagues (usually American and National), a league secretary, plus the owner, coach, and players of each team.

The calendar of events for the team concept of fund-raising is explained, arbitrarily assuming that the campaign will operate from May 1 to May 30.

February 1   Breakfast meeting of the membership committee. Purpose: selection of campaign chairperson and league commissioners; campaign chairperson normally appoints commissioners.

February 7   Membership committee appoints team owners.

February 13   Team owners report on selection of team members; team members can be traded. Usually ten players or members to a team.

February 20   Team membership is finalized.

February 26   Meeting of commissioners and team owners. Director of Athletics and university official express needs, hopes, and programs.

March 1   First "scholarship level" luncheon (money equivalent to one full grant-in-aid at the institution). Ten to twelve people are asked to host the luncheon; they can invite as many guests as they choose who are potential donors of the equivalent of a full grant-in-aid. Brief, stimulating talks are given by the president of the institution, the director of athletics, the president of the foundation, and the campaign director. Hosts then submit their pledges or checks to the amount of a full grant-in-aid; guests are invited to sign a pledge card for the same amount.

March 12   First round of player draft.

March 19   Final player assignments; owners announce team membership.

April 1   Mailing to past donors of $15 (or minimal level).

April 2   Radio and television spots are prepared, using campaign leaders.

April 22   Assembly of all players. Players are given a complete fund-raising kit; included are responsibilities, pledge cards, brochures, and guidelines. Each kit should have the player's name inscribed on it. If the player was active the previous year, he or she may request cards of donors contacted before. Pledge cards have names, addresses, telephone numbers, and titles. Every pledge card has a self-addressed, stamped envelope; both the pledge card and the envelope are numbered. Players are requested to telephone only for an appointment; solicitation should be done in person. All pledge cards and envelopes are to be returned, regardless of final action by the prospect.

April 25   Press luncheon is held. All members of the media are invited. Press kits are prepared and issued; each kit has the person's name inscribed on it. The kit contains all the pertinent information pertaining to the fund-raising campaign. The atmosphere sought is one of mutual understanding and purpose.

May 1   Kick-off event which is usually a luncheon or breakfast. All players receive final information and materials. Present are all campaign workers, coaches, administrators and selected athletes representing all the varsity sports sponsored by the institution.

May 30   Victory dinner is held for all workers, university representatives, and student-athletes representing their sports. At this time the final individual, team, and campaign results are announced; prizes are awarded. Brief messages are presented by the university president, director of athletics, foundation president, and campaign director. A guest speaker may be included; some institutions keep this person's identity a secret. The entire evening should be one of celebration and gaiety.

April 6 Post-campaign meeting of commissioners, owners, secretaries, campaign director, director of the foundation, sports information director, and director of athletics for the purpose of an evaluation and setting recommendations for the future.

SUGGESTED IDEAS, METHODS, TECHNIQUES, AND PRINCIPLES

Some of the random but important acts and responsibilities that should be given full attention include the following.

Pledge cards should show personal information, total pledged, total paid, and method of payment of balance, if any.

Have open meetings on campus for faculty and students in determining goals.

The board of directors of the foundation should be sufficient in numbers but not so large that personal interaction is lost.

Limit the terms of office for officers to two years.

Designate vice-presidents for activities, finances, membership, and public relations.

Establish board meetings on the first Tuesday (Wednesday) of each week.

Pre-planning of campaign financial goal should start in early January and involve the director of athletics and the executive director of the foundation or development office.

Office of the foundation or development office should be in close proximity to that of the director of athletics.

The executive director should be responsible to the director of athletics.

The executive director should keep a daily log of all activities and a file of all materials.

Do not use a commercial fund-raising organization.

Seek "trade-outs" in lieu of money gifts; set a limit of no more than 25 percent of the total fund goal.

Do not give complimentary tickets either for contributions or work; gifts of tickets, blazers, travel, and other items are subject to income tax and are not deductible; the monetary value of gifts must be declared by the recipient. Do not allow fund-drive workers to also sell season tickets; keep these programs separate.

For capital building projects make certain that there is no conflict with university plans and that an Environmental Impact Study is made and approval given.

Solicit largest gifts first.

If a state-wide campaign is used, set up subcommittees in key cities.

"Tradeouts" may include hotels, transportation for coaches and for teams, clothing for awards, advertising space on radio, television, and press, billboard advertising, bus and taxi advertising, medical care, restaurant, printing, photography, housing, and other services or goods.

Limit billing procedure to no more than four or five times annually.

Form a "junior booster" organization; youngsters are future prospective customers and donors; parents must accompany youngsters; provide a special ticket plan for parents; attempt to affiliate the "junior boosters" organization with a commercial enterprise, in order to have the latter underwrite the ticket costs; provide a special clinic and photographer's day for youngsters; youngsters should be provided some form of wearing apparel that has a proper identification on it.

Establish a "Women's Auxiliary" unit, if acceptable to both women and men boosters; this unit may form its own fund-raising teams or it may sponsor its own events to raise money, such as barbeques, fashion shows, and so on. Food for the barbeque may be contributed on a "trade-out" basis.

Prospects as donors may be designated at the local level; outside sources of information include: Contacts Influential (see yellow pages); National Register Publishing Co., Keskogee, Illinois; Sports Illustrated subscriber's list for region or state (exchange on a trade-out of advertising in game programs); Directory of Foundations and Charitable Trusts from the state Department of Justice; lists from Chamber of Commerce; ask each member to suggest at least two prospects for various donor classifications; State Manufacturing Directory; and, the City Directory, which identifys individuals, titles, and addresses.

Invite all graduating athletes to attend a board of directors meeting at which time the organization and purpose of the activity are explained; make all graduating athletes an honorary member for one year following graduation.

CHAPTER TWENTY-ONE
FUND-RAISING
ACTIVITIES BY
COLLEGES AND
UNIVERSITIES

One thing is clear concerning fund-raising activities: each institution and its department of athletics should select, adapt, or develop its own fund-raising programs. There are many factors that influence a decision of this nature. The traditions, loyalty, size of alumni membership, range of income among prospects, level of sports competition, philosophy of the institution and its athletic department, and a host of other considerations help to determine fund-raising programs.

As stated in the previous chapter, nearly all educational institutions of higher education that are sponsoring athletic programs of average or higher caliber have found it necessary to rely upon fund-raising programs. Simply stated, the primary question is no longer whether a fund-raising program should be employed but, rather, what kind of a fund-raising program should be adopted for the specific institution.

Fund-raising has been developed into an art. There are many variations that have proved successful. The director of athletics must acquaint himself or herself with those programs that have been tried successfully and unsuccessfully. After extensive research and study has been conducted in this area, then the director of athletics and those persons charged with the responsibility of raising funds should evaluate all programs for the purpose of selecting the one most appropriate for their institution and athletic program. In some cases, a program used at other institutions may be adopted in full, or, in other instances, the basic idea may be used with variations.

The following are actual examples of fund-raising ideas and programs currently in use by many of the leading colleges and universities in the nation.

The University of Wisconsin at Madison features a combination public relations–fund-raising method in the form of sixteen golf outings held throughout the summer months. This program allows participants to receive something immediately, and it affords them a chance to have personal contact with the coaching staff of all sports. These golf outings are held in various cities throughout the state and usually take place on a date when the local country club is closed to the public or their members; consequently, the university has the use of the entire course and the other facilities. A portion of the entry fee is used to defray expenses and the remainder goes to the student grant-in-aid program. For example, if the cost of playing golf and the dinner held after is about $18, a $50 fee is charged, and $32 per person goes into the fund. During the evening each head coach of at least five sports speak to the group; a question-and-answer session follows. These golf outings are arranged by local groups where the event is held. A coordinator within the athletic department acts as liaison official. The local group is responsible for setting and collecting the fee, arranging all facilities, and then mailing the net proceeds to the athletic department. This program has been the major source of fund-raising the past five years.

The University of Nevada at Reno sponsors one major event. This is a $100 per plate barbecue for men only. It is held at the governor's mansion; the governor is the honorary chairman of the event. A renowned sports figure is the main speaker. This event has attained a prestigious reputation. The net revenue of this single event for the support of the athletic program has reached $55,000.

Drake University at Des Moines, Iowa, formed the "Bulldog" Club in 1970. Honorary Coach memberships are $1000, plus the pledge to render support and time to the program; obtaining at least one new member is included in the pledge. Other classifications are the "Blue and White" membership, which represents a gift of $500 and a pledge to solicit new members; and, the "Century" club member who gives $100 and the pledge to solicit additional members. Members of the Bulldog Club are privileged to travel with teams on chartered flights. Honorary Coaches and Blue and White members are guests of the athletic department at a dinner during the late summer as an expression of appreciation and recognition; the entire athletic department staff attends. A cocktail party is held in late summer, also, for Varsity and Century Club members, at which time emphasis is placed upon inviting guests who may be potential members. Members of the Bulldog Club are given preferred seating, and Honorary Coaches and Blue and White members are provided special parking privileges. All members wear Drake University blue blazers and sweaters to all contests. Names of all members are printed in game programs and other campus publications. During the basketball season members are invited to a private room at the site of the game for refreshments and to check-in their coats. A newsletter is mailed every other month. The Bulldog Club is administered by the athletic director with aid from the assistant to the athletic director and guidance by an Advisory Board.

Kent State University has a "Las Vegas Nite." Tickets are sold to obtain funds for a bank and to rent gambling materials for the temporary casino. The setting is made as realistic as possible. Play is with actual money. A limit is placed on betting to make sure that the "house" can remain solvent. All profits of the evening go to the athletics department. Coaching staff members serve as dealers, cheerleaders are cocktail waitresses (all tips go toward buying their supplies). The athletic department accountant acts as the banker.

At East Carolina University, the "Pirate Club" is the chief fund-raising entity (Figure 6). A full-time executive secretary is employed, along with an office secretary. A Board of Directors meets in early March for the purpose of determining the persons that each director will call upon. A two-week drive is established. The sum of at least $250,000 was committed by the Pirate Club for 1974. Club members receive typical preferential treatment. New members are solicited primarily by the directors.

Wake Forest University's "Deacon Club" raised over $458,000 in

Figure 6.   East Carolina University Booster Membership and Ticket Application.

1974 (Figure 7). Approximately one-half of this amount came from non-alumni. The Atlantic Coast Conference Basketball Tournament Tickets are used to entice memberships. Contributors of $500 receive the right to purchase two basketball tickets; contributors of $1000 may purchase four tickets; and donors of amounts above $1000 are allotted two tickets of each additional $5000. In addition, members receive publications, preferential football seating, decals, and preferential parking privileges.

PURPOSE

To raise funds, through contributions from the alumni, friends, faculty, and staff for the athletic program.

ELIGIBILITY TO JOIN

Anyone who cares about the future fortunes of the intercollegiate athletic program at East Carolina University. The Pirate Club is grateful for the intense pride generated by the membership of the dedicated fans who desire to provide the educational and athletic opportunity for others.

OPERATION

The Pirate Club, Inc. is a division of the E.C.U. Educational Foundation, Inc. Accurate records are maintained and audited annually.

75-76 THEME

"There is a Destiny that makes us brothers
None of us go our way alone
All that we put into the life of others
Comes back into our own."
Edwin Markham

PLEASE READ CAREFULLY

1. This is your 1975-76 East Carolina University **Pirate Club Membership** and **Football Ticket Order Application.**

2. Kindly fill out the application form **completely. Please print** all entries.

3. Detach and return application along with check or indication of pledge. Check should be made out to: **ECU Pirate Club, Inc.**

4. Mail to: **Pirate Club**
P.O. Box 2576 – E.C.U.
Greenville, N.C. 27834

5. All pledges must be paid by June 30, 1975

6. Membership cards, decals and season tickets ordered will be mailed in August.

7. Every effort will be implemented to ensure the location of tickets are in conformance with the desires of our patrons.

8. An early reply will provide more favorable seating assignments for new members.

9. **Membership contributions are tax deductible.**

MORGAN PRINTERS, INC. GREENVILLE N.C.

MEMBERSHIP AND FOOTBALL
TICKET ORDER APPLICATION

Name _____
(First)   (Initial)   (Last)

Address _____
(Number)   (St., Dr., Ln.)

(City)   (State)   (Zip Code)

Phone _____
(Home)   (Office)

Pledge: _____
(Signature)

Month to be billed: _____

Enrolled By: _____

TICKET PRIORITY	CATEGORY		INSERT AMOUNT
1	Plank Owner	$10,000	
2	Admiral	$ 1,000 – $1,999	
3	Commodore	$ 750 – $ 999	
4	Captain	$ 500 – $ 749	
5	Commander	$ 300 – $ 499	
6	Lieutenant	$ 200 – $ 299	
7	Ensign	$ 100 – $ 199	
8	Bo'Sun Mate	$ 25 – $ 99	
No.	Season Tickets–5 Games (each) $30		
	Postage & Handling	$1.00	$1.00
	TOTAL		

········· PLEASE DO NOT WRITE BELOW THIS LINE ······
Paid By: Cash [ ]   Check [ ]
Date Received _____   Date Mailed _____

Figure 6.—(*Continued*)

The University of Utah has a booster club. Minimum membership is $25. Approximately $100,000 was realized in 1974. A "Scholarship Box" was constructed at the top of the football stadium (Figure 8). Seats in this box are sold for $500 each as a contribution to the Utah Development Foundation, which provide funds for grant-in-aids. The box seats 380 people and is equipped with a high-speed elevator, dining area, and restrooms. Special parking, with or without valet, is provided. The "Scholarship Box" accounted for $125,000 the first year of operation that augmented the funds obtained by the booster club.

Boise State University in Idaho has a program somewhat similar to that sponsored by the University of Utah. A "Bronco Athletic Associa-

FRIENDS OF WAKE FOREST

The most vital aspect of any successful college athletic program is the ability to recruit qualified student athletes; and once recruited, to underwrite their grants-in-aid so that the program will not be a burden on the other areas of the University. This is the aim of the Deacon Club Foundation.

The Wake Forest athletic program is supported by many alumni and by many other fans with no direct University ties. We are grateful to each and all. Everything we do is aimed at improving the calibre of our program so that we may justify this expression of confidence and faith in us.

We invite you to contribute any amount that you like through any of our plans. If you are already helping, encourage others to do the same. Through the efforts of the members of the Deacon Club Foundation, Wake Forest athletics can achieve greatness. We invite you to become a part of such a worthwhile program.

Sincerely yours,
BOB BARTHOLOMEW
Director

WHAT IS THE DEACON CLUB?

All funds raised by the Deacon Club are used to pay the educational expenses of worthy student-athletes who are participating in the Wake Forest program. Contributions to this program are tax deductible.

The Foundation has been assisting the athletic program since 1950 and has raised over $1,850,000.00 for worthy student-athletes. At the present level of giving, the Foundation is raising approximately 65 percent of the athletic scholarship budget. Success in recent years has enabled the University to increase the number of scholarships in golf and tennis so that these programs are now competitive with the nation's best.

Since the Foundation has underwritten an increasingly higher percentage of the scholarship budget the University has been able to use funds, previously committed to scholarships, for other areas of the operation. Salaries have been increased recently to a competitive level, enabling the athletic department to hire experienced and established head coaches in football and basketball. Recruiting budgets have been increased. As the Foundation nears its goal of 100 percent of the athletic scholarship budget, additional funds will be released for other needed improvements and Wake Forest will have a similar opportunity for success enjoyed by other Conference schools.

Figure 7.   Wake Forest University Booster Group Application and Information.

tion membership requires a $25 contribution; a "Buckaroo" membership costs $110; and the "President's" Club membership costs at least $500. The President's Club has 254 seats in the stadium at the start of the program four years ago; today it has 362 seats with a waiting list. A current construction project is underway to construct an enclosed "Scholarship Box" that will seat over 200; it will be equipped with an elevator, dining area, and restrooms. This project is being financed by five-year pledges (Figure 9). A $5000 pledge, at $1000 per year, will provide the donor with two seats to any event held in the stadium during the five-year period. An announcement dinner was held, and the entire project was "sold" in one evening.

Purdue University has their "John Purdue Club," named after the

WHO CONTRIBUTES TO THE FOUNDATION

Any person who feels that the Wake Forest athletic program is worthwhile and would like to be a part of it. Originally, the majority of the participants were alumni of the University. In recent years, however, the University has attracted many non-alumni friends, and a large percentage of the current members of the Club did not attend Wake Forest.

MATCHING GIFTS

The Deacon Club Foundation has qualified for every company's matching gift program to which an application has been made. If your company has a matching gift program, you can receive credit for the total contribution; yours plus your company's. Contact the Director of the Deacon Club if you need help with the details.

ACC BASKETBALL TICKET INFORMATION

One of the many outstanding features you receive as a member of the Stadium Club is the right to purchase tickets to the annual ACC Basketball Tournament in Greensboro, one of the top basketball attractions in the nation. The amount of tickets you may purchase varies with your contribution. The allotment for each category is listed under the Stadium Club information.

The Executive Committee of the Deacon Club Foundation makes the decision as to the number each category of the Stadium Club may purchase. The decision is based on the number of tickets alloted to Wake Forest by the conference office and the number of Stadium Club members.

BROCHURES

The Wake Forest football and basketball brochures, which have under gone many changes in the last year, are available to all members of the Deacon Club Foundation at a charge of $2.00 per brochure. The brochures contain many facts and figures, including outlooks, player sketches, information on the opponents and schedules. Space is provided on season ticket orders for your order.

Figure 7.—(Continued)

institution's founder; funds are raised through this club and the alumni association. Purdue University has adopted a low-key approach. No professional fund-raisers are employed, no literature or direct mail is used, and the club has no formal organization. An application form is used by which a current member may recommend a new member. Membership rolls number about 2400 persons, who contribute $100 or more per year, and include about 250 persons who contribute $500 or more each year. All members are on an annual reminder basis and are not solicited by mail. Ticket preferences, parking privileges, and an annual desk calendar are the only rewards, plus an annual John Purdue outing on campus in June which attracts about 800 persons for golf and social activities. Mem-

WHAT ARE THE BENEFITS TO THE MEMBERS?

The University assumes that a donation made to the Deacon Club Foundation is made to help a worthy student-athlete acquire an education at Wake Forest. It is treated as a contribution and we assume that there are no strings attached. The primary benefit a donor receives is the satisfaction of knowing that a young athlete has been aided in this endeavor.

In order to show its appreciation to its members, the Deacon Club Foundation has set up the following ticket priorities and privileges for the various categories:

GENERAL MEMBERSHIP ($25.00 annual contribution)

1. Receive complimentary all copies of "The Demon Deacon" (athletic dept. newsletter), decal, and membership card.

2. Allowed to buy the best available season tickets in football and basketball prior to their being offered to the general public.

GOLDEN C ($100.00 to $499.00 annual contribution)

1. Receive complimentary all copies of "The Demon Deacon," decal, and membership card.

2. Special parking privileges in football and basketball with purchase of season tickets

3. Higher priority season ticket location in football and basketball.

4. Allowed to purchase four tickets to the Big Four Basketball Doubleheader in Greensboro.

STADIUM CLUB

The Stadium Club Room is a beautiful carpeted and air-conditioned facility on the second floor of Bridger Fieldhouse. Golden W, Scholarship Sponsor and Executive Club categories of the Deacon Club Foundation automatically qualify for membership. Club members enjoy special parking privileges in football and basketball. The Club is open one and one-half hours before and after each home football game and on other special occasions. A buffet luncheon is offered members before the home football games.

Golden W ($500.00 annual contribution)

1. Receive complimentary all copies of "The Demon Deacon," decals, membership cards, and an attractive wall plaque.

2. Receive two complimentary tickets in football and basketball and allowed to purchase adjacent seats.

3. Allowed to purchase four tickets to the Big Four Basketball Doubleheader in Greensboro and two tickets to the ACC Basketball Tournament. Members who pay for their season football and basketball tickets and members who do not order season tickets will be given an opportunity to purchase ONE additional ACC Tournament ticket in the event any are left after the original allotments are filled.

4. Automatic Stadium Club member.

Scholarship Sponsor (annual contribution $1,000.00 or more)

1. Receive complimentary all copies of "The Demon Deacon," decal, and membership card.

2. Automatic Stadium Club member. (See Golden W.)

3. Receive four complimentary season tickets in football and basketball and allowed to purchase adjacent seats.

4. Allowed to buy six tickets to the Big Four Basketball Doubleheader in Greensboro and four tickets to the ACC Basketball Tournament. Members who pay for their season football and basketball tickets, or do not order season tickets, will be given an opportunity to purchase TWO additional ACC tickets, if there are any left after the original allotments are filled.

5. Allowed to sponsor a student athlete. The sponsors are recognized in the football and basketball programs (unless omission requested) and receive a beautiful plaque acknowledging the sponsorship.

Executive Club (annual contribution of $2,000.00 or more)

1. Receive complimentary all copies of "The Demon Deacon," decal, and membership card.

2. Automatic Stadium Club member.

3. Receive six complimentary season tickets in football and basketball, if requested, also allowed to purchase adjacent seats.

4. Allowed to buy twelve tickets to the Big Four Basketball Doubleheader in Greensboro and eight tickets to the ACC Basketball Tournament. Members who pay for their season football and basketball tickets, or do not order season tickets, will be given an opportunity to purchase FOUR additional ACC tickets, if any are left after the original allotments are filled.

5. Personalized parking adjacent to the Stadium and Coliseum.

Figure 7.—(Continued)

bers of the Coaches Club are contributors of $500 or more per year; these persons receive special communications and recognitions. This low-key operation derives enough funds to have the university rank third in fund-raising within the Big 10 Conference.

Kansas State University engages in several fund-raising projects. The major activity is the "Wildcat Club"; membership categories range from under $25, $25, $50, $100, $500, and $1000 or more. A "Junior Wildcat Club" is in the process of being formed for youngsters under the age of 16. Club members receive ticket purchase privileges, special parking, newsletters, and publications. The athletic department plans to sponsor

PAT WILLIAMS

LARRY HOPKINS

Perhaps the most pleasing aspect of being a member of the Wake Forest Deacon Club Foundation is the satisfaction you receive in helping worthy student-athletes obtain an education. Such athletes as Pat Williams, Larry Hopkins, Jim Simons and Bob Leonard have also distinguished themselves as outstanding students and have gone on to greater achievements following graduation.

Williams, who played baseball for three years and graduated in 1962, serves as general manager of the Chicago Bulls of the National Basketball Association. Larry Hopkins, who broke Brian Piccolo's rushing records in 1971, will enter the Bowman Gray School of Medicine this fall to complete work for his Ph.D.

As a basketball player, Leonard was a two-time All-ACC performer and now serves as District Court Judge for Forsyth County For two years, Simons was considered one of the top collegiate golfers in the country, but also was a member of the Dean's List during this time. Following graduation in 1972, he turned pro and is considered one of the brightest young stars on the PGA tour.

JIM SIMONS

BOB LEONARD

Deacon Club Foundation Membership Application

We invite you to become a member of the Deacon Club and support the athletic program at Wake Forest University.

Please indicate your membership preference and return this application to: Deacon Club Foundation, Box 7265, Wake Forest University, Winston-Salem, N. C. 27109.

Date:_____

_____General Membership — $25.00 - $99.00   _____Scholarship — $1,000.00

_____Golden "W" — $500 - $999.00   _____Executive — $2,000.00

_____Golden "C" — $100.00 - $499.00

Please bill me as follows: Bank Draft

_____Quarterly   _____Semi-Annually   _____Annually.

(name of Bank)   Alumni Year_____

NAME

ADDRESS

Tax Deductible: please make check payable to Wake Forest Student Aid Fund.

Figure 7.—(*Continued*)

a concert. Also, parking lot stalls with owner identification for donors of $1000 or more are provided.

Duke University organized their "Iron Dukes" club in 1971. The club affairs are administered by an assistant athletic director; no outside employees are paid, nor are volunteer helpers used. Contributions in the amounts of $100, $250, $500, $1000, and $2500 are received. Presently there are no more than 900 members nor fewer than 26 in any one category. No tangible benefits are given to any contributor, regardless of their giving capacity. Membership is solicited on the basis of interest in the university, rather than the win–loss record for any single season.

At the University of Wisconsin at Milwaukee the emphasis is upon receiving gifts of value rather than funds per se. The athletic department

Announcing the University of Utah Scholarship Box

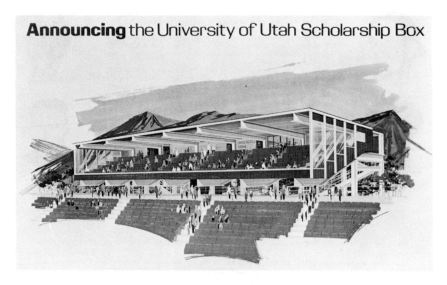

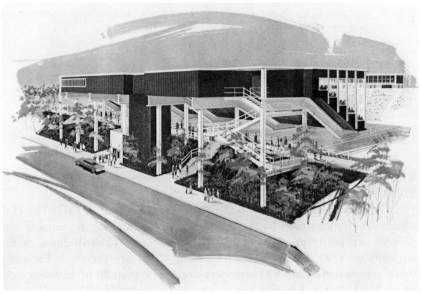

Figure 8.   University of Utah Promotional Plan.

The Bleacher Utes are pleased to announce that Bob Rice's U. of U. Scholarship Box is now under construction, high on the East side of Rice Stadium. And, on Saturday night, September 22, some 320 football fans will experience a new kind of seating comfort for a University football game.

Entry to the Scholarship Box will be by elevator through a new gate at the back of the East stand. Waiting for you at the top is an unexcelled view of the field and the city to the West, the mountains all around.

While clear glass walls protect viewers on the sides, the front will be left open, so that nothing stands between you and the field, the excitement of the crowd, the band and the student sections below. Special infra-red heat will be distributed throughout the box for your comfort.

The seats will all be chair seats, red of course, like the chair seats in the stands, and the entire box will be carpeted. No seat is more than five seats from an aisle.

At the back of the box is a large glass enclosed refreshment area where lunches, snacks, and beverages can be served from the adjoining kitchen. This area also commands a spectacular view of the field and the city.

The Scholarship Box also offers a large coat room and separate restroom facilities. And, because of the height, a seat on the 25 yard line, is as good as one on the 50. Donors will be allowed to select their own season seats, airline style, on a first come/first served basis. So, if a front or back row seat is important to you, we suggest an early reservation, via the enclosed application.

Figure 8—(*Continued*)

Why a Scholarship Box?

When Bob Rice donated a million dollars last year for AstroTurf, new lights and other stadium improvements, he specified that a large portion of the donation be used in a manner that would generate sufficient funds to meet the minimum cost for athletic scholarships. Not just football but scholarships in all 10 sports in which the University competes.

Bob's idea was to build a special seating area, as so many other major universities have done, including Colorado, Oklahoma, Alabama, Nebraska, etc. The University quickly agreed. While some schools have priced their special seats as high as $5,000 a year, the University settled for a much more modest figure. A $500.00 annual donation (fully deductible) to the University Development Fund allows the donor to purchase one season ticket seat (not deductible) at the regular chair seat price.

Based on the experience at Colorado and the other schools which have special seating sections, demand for the seats increases each year. We fully expect that a waiting list situation will develop after the first year.

The University is grateful to Bob Rice for his most generous gift. And we are most pleased that his gift should have carried a means for establishing and perpetuating much needed scholarship funds.

The Scholarship Box, will of course, greatly enhance the physical beauty of the stadium. It will give unexcelled seating and viewing to some 320 donors. More important, those donors will be aiding the University in building competitive excellence in 10 different sports, and enable hundreds of gifted young athletes to have a college education.

University of Utah Scholarship Box Order Form

Return card to —
  Bleacher Ute Scholarship Drive
  University of Utah Development
    Foundation
  306 Park Building
  Salt Lake City, Utah **84112**

Please reserve_____ seats for me in the Scholarship Box. I understand that my donation of $500.00 entitles me to buy one seat in the Scholarship Box for the **1973 Season** at the regular chair **seat season ticket price** of $35.00 per seat. (Additional seats are available on the same basis – $500.00 donation plus $35.00 for each seat desired.)

Enclosed is my donation check for $_____ (fully deductible) made payable to the University of Utah Development Fund, along with my check for $_____ (not deductible) made payable to the University of Utah Athletic Department for the seats.

☐ Please reserve the seats, but bill me separately.

☐ Please reserve the seats, but bill my company.

I understand seats will be assigned on a priority basis upon receipt of reservations.

Name_____

Company_____

Street_____

City_____ State_____ Zip_____

Figure 8—(*Continued*)

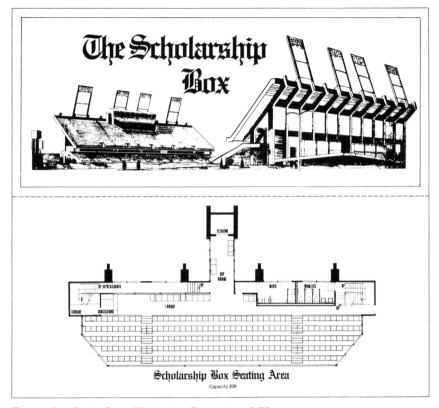

The Scholarship Box

Scholarship Box Seating Area
Capacity 209

Figure 9.   Boise State University Promotional Plan.

has been donated two bus vans for travel purposes, a public address system, a stadium scoreboard, food and refreshments for the media and VIP's at football games, ambulance service at games, and a local reserve unit for security purposes.

South Dakota State University's men's athletic staff engaged in a concentrated fund-raising program throughout the state. Contributions include amounts from $12, $25, $100, $250, to $500. Unique giving programs include "A Steer for State," "Pork for State," "Wheat for State," and other items (Figure 10). Donors of $250 or more in either funds or equivalent are provided special parking privileges at a stall with the donor's name.

Boston College started a "Blue Chip" Club. Solicitation was limited to season ticketholders and Varsity Club members. Some 300 member-

From The President of Boise State University

Boise State University football in recent years has become a matter of state pride and national focus. The outstanding coaching staff, the excellent performance of athletes, and the enthusiastic support of the Bronco Athletic Association and the state of Idaho have all contributed to this important dimension called athletics. We are particularly grateful to the many individuals, companies, clubs, and organizations who stand by the Broncos in the total sports program.

As the University expands its sports program to provide a well-rounded option for both men and women, it is becoming critical that funds be wisely used and soundly developed. The Scholarship Box could make a difference in the long run in terms of pro-viding steady income for the total sports program. The interest in the President's Club has exceeded the ability of the University to provide seats. While retaining the President's Club section, if the Bronco Athletic Association can help fund the Scholarship Box, the University will be assured of the level of income needed to be highly competitive in the Northwest and for that matter in the nation.

Privileges

Exclusive parking for easy access to elevator

Elevator from ground level outside stadium to Scholarship Box

Exclusive use of your seat in heated comfort

Private restrooms and concession facilities for your exclusive use

Charter members' names on a special plaque which will be made and displayed in a prominent location

Figure 9.—(*Continued*)

ships at $100 each were sold, generating more than $40,000. Modifications in the club operation now accounts for about $25,000 a year to be used to improve facilities and about $25,000 a year for grant-in-aid purposes.

University of Northern Iowa has their "Athletic Club" with memberships from $25, $100, $250, $500, and $1000 or more. Each category

---

Scholarship Pledge

(I) (We) the undersigned do hereby pledge and promise to pay to the order of the Bronco Athletic Association, a non-profit corporation, the sum of $5,000.00 to be paid in five equal $1,000.00 annual installments. The first annual payment shall be paid on or before July 1, 1975, and continue thereafter on the first day of July of each year thereafter until the pledge is paid in full.

In making this pledge it is understood that each person who makes a scholarship pledge shall receive from the Bronco Athletic Association two season tickets in the Scholarship Box to be constructed at the Boise State Football Stadium. This pledge is limited to the payment of the amount specified herein and the undersigned shall in no way be responsible to pay any more than the amount specified herein.

Dated at Boise, Idaho this _____ day of _____, 1974.

_____

_____

Figure 9.—(*Continued*)

of membership receives some benefits, while those in the higher brackets receive more. The club has a board of directors. Each year this group with a partner for every director solicits new membership. The club sponsors a Valentine Dinner Dance and a Summer Stag Golf Tournament each year; club members are allowed to purchase seats on chartered flights with the team.

Utah State University has their "Big Blue" club, conducted along traditional lines. Additionally, they have their "Training Table" Club. An animal worth $300 or more entitles the donor to the same privileges as an equivalent member of the "Big Blue" club. Also, commodities such as wheat, potatoes, and the like are accepted and turned into cash. These animals and commodities are sold to the university cafeteria at going rates. The athletic director makes most of the contacts for these items, and an assistant follows with the necessary accounting and recording. In the first year of operation, 91 animals were obtained.

The University of Illinois divides the state into ten districts for its fund-raising projects. Within each large city a Grant-in-Aid Golf Day is held. Members of the booster club are invited, and, in turn, encouraged to invite a prospective joiner. After the costs of golf, dinner, prizes, and miscellany are deducted, the net proceeds are presented to the athletic department. The program has been in operation seven years, and each year the participation has increased.

PORK
for
STATE

South Dakota
State University • Brookings

PORK FOR STATE

HPER Cente

Pork Plaque

Figure 10.   South Dakota "Pork for State" Donor Mailer.

Vanderbilt University has a full-time executive director for the "National Commodore Club" who reports directly to the athletic director. The executive director's duties include the preparation and mailing of all publications, coordination of club membership drives, maintenance of liaison with major donors, and assistance in general public relations.

Clemson University organized its "IPTAY" Club in 1934. Each year some 400 or more club members engaged in a membership drive. Prizes are awarded for new memberships, total amounts of funds obtained, and for new $2500 or more memberships. Prizes are special blazers, wrist watches, or stadium blankets. Club members are recipient of traditional privileges.

Rice University at Houston, Texas has its "Owl" Club for fund-raising activities. The athletic director is also the executive officer of the

South Dakota State University Jackrabbit

PORK for STATE

A project designed to support the intercollegiate athletic program at South Dakota State University

COVER PHOTO: First "Pork for State" donor, Russell Wirt, Parker, shown on the cover with his daughter, is a purebred pork producer and former SDSU track letterman.

PURPOSE
The purpose of "Pork for State" is to encourage pork producers and the Pork Industry to donate "pork" in support of the athletic grant-in-aid program at State University.

ORIGIN
Grants in-aid have been financed for several years by donations from State University faculty, business and professional people, alumni and friends in Brookings and throughout South Dakota, the nation and, the past several years by the Steer for State Program."

The "Pork for State" idea has been employed successfully at the University of Nebraska, Kansas State University, Iowa State University and Oklahoma State University. The program provides a fine opportunity for a co-operative effort by the pork industry and the State University to improve the sports program.

HELPS WHOM?
"Pork for State" helps scholastically deserving young men representing all the colleges that comprise South Dakota State University who participate in any of the ten intercollegiate sports. Intercollegiate competition at State University includes baseball, basketball, cross country, football, golf, indoor and outdoor track, field, tennis, wrestling, swimming and gymnastics.

BENEFITS
The "Satisfaction" of assisting in a worthy project is the main benefit offered. Other fringe benefits to contributors:
● Contributors name carried in the Greater State Fund Honor Roll.
● An invitation to be our guests at a designated "Pork for State" basketball game.
● Opportunity to purchase reserve season or single game reserved tickets early for home basketball and football games.
● A membership plaque for participating in the "Pork for State" program.

INFORMATION
Persons interested in becoming a part of the "Pork for State" effort may contact Warren E. Williamson, Coordinator "Pork for State," the South Dakota State University Athletic Department or a staff member in the College of Agriculture. Details of the project will be explained during a visit to you by a State University staff member.

Figure 10.—(Continued)

club; the university director of promotions is the executive secretary. A board of directors is used; there are 18 directors plus six board members. Each director serves four years, with six new members elected each year. Board members represent the administration, trustees, staff, students, and alumni as well as community groups. Membership drives are held twice a year, in January and August. Department staff members and the athletic director are the primary membership solicitors. The club has paid for a $330,000 club room, as well as contributed substantially to the athletics program. Membership levels range from $100 to $4000 or more. Typical privileges and benefits accrue to the various levels of contribution.

Mississippi State University started their "Bulldog Booster" Club in 1968. Initially memberships were $25; two years later $100 and $1000 categories were added. In 1974, the executive director of the club was relieved of the coordination of recruiting and assigned full-time to the club activities. A new approach is to allow a donor to contribute in whatever way he or she wishes to do so. For example, donors may give bank drafts, post-dated checks, bonds, stocks, or other items of monetary worth. Membership extends for one year from the date of receipt. Each board member will be involved in fund-raising. A monthly statement is mailed to him, showing the status of each of his members. A competitive angle has been included to award board members for their efforts. Club members receive typical accommodations, privileges, and publications. A somewhat different incentive is the addition of an Honor Roll inside the stadium, listing all members.

Texas Christian University has its "Athletic Scholarship Program." This is administered by the athletic department. It is a soft-sell approach, soliciting memberships from those persons genuinely interested in the athletic fortunes of the university.

The University of Pacific "Tiger Boosters" has combined all of its athletic department fund-raising activities into one organization. A full-time executive director is employed. The team concept is used to stimulate fund-raising. The team concept involves the appointment of owners and coaches of teams; teams are selected by means of a "draft." Goals are established for each team. Awards are given to the highest team score, individual score, and rookie. First prizes include an all-paid trip with the football team; other prizes are wrist watches, decanters, jackets, and plaques. The drive begins on May 2 and ends June 7. "Trade-outs" count as one-half value for drive and prize purposes. All members receive typical privileges and articles, according to the amounts contributed.

The University of Houston started its "Cougar" Club 15 years ago. In 1973, the "National Cougar" Club was started. Membership is limited to contributors of $100 or more. Various categories of contributions are established, and appropriate souvenirs and certificates are given to donors (Figure 11). Memberships are solicited by correspondence to graduate lettermen, alumni, and other interested representatives of the university, including small and large business operations and industry.

Indiana University has its "Varsity Club." Within the club there are three separate divisions, depending upon amounts contributed. "Varsity" Club members give from $10 to $100; "Loyalty" Club members give from $100 to $500, and the "Hoosier Hundred" give $500 or more. Varsity

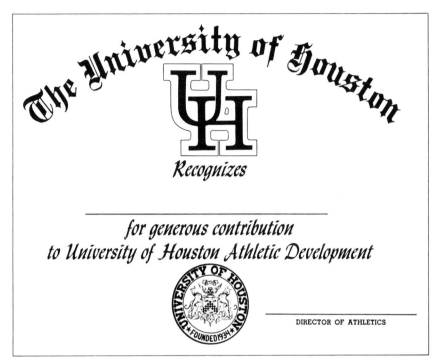

The University of Houston

Recognizes

*for generous contribution
to University of Houston Athletic Development*

DIRECTOR OF ATHLETICS

Figure 11.   University of Houston Certificate for Donors to National Cougar Club.

Club members receive 15 copies of the athletics newsletter during the year; Loyalty Club members receive the newsletter and the priority to purchase football and basketball tickets accompanied by parking privileges; Hoosier Hundred members receive four complimentary football tickets and two complimentary basketball tickets with the priority to purchase more. During the past ten years, this operation has raised approximately two million dollars. In 1974–1975, donations exceeded $400,000. New directions will incorporate the development of insurance policies on the part of donors.

The University of Oklahoma operates the "Athletic Scholarship Donor Program." Its primary purpose is to raise funds for grant-in-aids. Members are solicited by mail. The only incentive is the privilege of purchasing football seats. A $250 donation or more entitles one to purchase one seat in any area of the stadium; a $150 donation allows the donor the second choice of a seat in the stadium; and, a $100 donation allows the third choice of location in any area of the stadium. In addition

UNIVERSITY OF OKLAHOMA • SOONER BEEF CLUB

SOONER BEEF CLUB

Figure 12.   University of Oklahoma Sooner Beef Club Mailer.

to this program, the university also sponsors a "Sooner Beef Club (Figure 12). The donation of a live steer, or its equivalent in money, entitles
one to club membership. These animals are used for the training table
at the university. Members receive a parking pass, a brochure, and a
weekly newsletter from the head football coach each week. Names of
donors are posted in the dining hall.

The University of Alabama endorses two programs. The first is the
"Educational and Athletic Scholarships." Each scholarship cost is $1500 a
year. Donors have their names appear in the football program along with
the picture of the recipients. The other program is a format that allows
any donor of $300 to purchase four tickets for football games with a pri-

The Sooner Beef Club is an organization of loyal University of Oklahoma supporters who are interested in assisting our athletic program by donating a beef either "on the hoof" or an equivalent amount of money to purchase a beef in their name.

It is most important that our athletes be well fed, and you can have a part in seeing that this is done by your donation of beef.

Our athletic food costs have increased 22.5% in the past five years. This program will help to alleviate the expense of feeding our athletes, will assure them of a "good table," and will be a tremendous help in our recruiting program. All donations of beef will go directly to the athletes' dining table.

Benefits to the contributor are that the gift is tax deductible under the present applicable laws; you will receive a special parking permit for our home football games, an O. U. Press & TV Guide each fall, and the Chuck Fairbanks Football Letter during the football season. Most of all you will share in the knowledge that you are, in a special way, helping deserving young men in their quest for an education.

In our dining hall, we will display a large plaque bearing the name of our association and the names of donors. Your name will also be listed in the programs of all home football games as a member of the Sooner Beef Club.

We invite you to become a member of the Sooner Beef Club.

Figure 12.—(*Continued*)

ority. The two programs account for an income of approximately $400,000 per year. The university does not have a fund-raising club or drive.

The University of Arkansas sponsors the "Razorback" Club. Donations are $10, $100, $500, and $1600. Each level of contribution entitles the member to certain benefits. The $1600 member receives top ticket priority, reserved parking, a display plaque, name listed on a permanent plaque in fieldhouse, sneak preview with the football staff, special pre-game buffets and other social functions, top ticket priorities for away games and for bowl games, recognition in the football program, top basketball ticket priority, basketball game parking, admission to spring football games, admission to closed practices, admission to all spring sports events, football brochure, a monthly newsletter from the head coach of football, spring sports brochure, decal, membership card, and football schedule. Other levels of donors receive appropriate benefits. A special program allows the acceptance of $25,000 for one full scholarship perpetually, $20,000 for a three-fourths of a scholarship perpetually, $15,000 for one-half of a scholarship perpetually, and $10,000 for a one-fourth scholarship perpetually (Figure 13). These gifts may be paid by installments over a five-year period.

The University of Minnesota operates the "Williams Fund." Categories of donations range from $25 to $1000 or more. Donors receive typical benefits and souvenirs. Special attention is directed to having members assign some part of their last will and testament to the Williams Fund. Two special fund-raising activities are held annually. One is the basketball tournament at the city sports center. This is a two-day tournament that nets about $30,000 annually. The other is the stag golf tournaments, held in nearly a dozen cities throughout the state. This format uses celebrities who are professional athletics as an added attraction. Entry fees are $100. This program nets between $20,000 to $30,000 each year.

The University of Miami at Miami, Florida, has a fund-raising club with categories of contributions ranging from $100 to $1000 or more. The latter members are seated in the VIP section at home football games, and participate as guests at pre-game social functions. All members receive certain benefits and tokens, depending upon the amount contributed.

Ohio University at Athens, Ohio, started a fund-raising program in 1973. One letter was written by the athletic director and mailed to all former university athletes. A second letter was addressed by the alumni director to all former athletes. The various amounts listed were translated into actual expenses. For example, a gift of $25 will pay the expenses of a coach for a one-day trip to a neighboring city for recruiting purposes.

The University of California at Irvine holds a men's round robin tennis tournament on the second Saturday of each month. Local citizens are invited to join the club for $120. This fee entitles them to one tournament each month for ten months, a special tennis shirt, and use of facilities. The first year there were 30 members; a women's division will be opened this year.

The University of Virginia uses its "Virginia Student Aid Foundation" as its athletics fund-raising organization. An executive secretary and field secretary are responsible to the director of athletics. The former heads the activities in or near the location of the university; the latter heads the activities throughout the remainder of the state. The state is divided into sixteen districts. Each distrist has a volunteer chairperson and a volunteer executive committee. A six to eight week fund drive is held during the spring each year. A "smoker" is held in each district at the start; the head coach of a revenue sport, the head coach of a non-revenue sport, and the field director speak. At times, other representatives of the athletics department also speak. The major incentives for membership is a desire to sponsor or be part of a successful athletics program and to receive priority for the purchase of Atlantic Coast Conference basketball tournament tickets.

...have You Considered the University of Arkansas
RAZORBACK EDUCATIONAL TRUST FUND
IN YOUR WILL, FOUNDATION, TRUST or as A DIRECT GIFT?

"A Permanent Scholarship Based on Perpetual Interest"

Now you can provide a college education for a deserving Razorback athlete through a sound program administered under the direction of the University of Arkansas Board of Trustees.

The Razorback Educational Trust Fund was established to perpetuate scholarships as tributes or memorials to friends of the Athletic Department or University. It has become an integral part of the University's overall development program for educational support. Only the interest is used in the permanent program of education support.

Scholarship, character, need, and athletic participation will be the factors considered by the U of A Athletic Scholarship Committee in making Razorback Educational Trust Fund scholarship awards.

The common concept of a state-supported university is that of a totally tax-financed institution. State appropriations do cover a major portion of the annual cost for the university to educate each student. But the fact is that every public university needs funds in addition to those appropriated by the state, in order to achieve academic excellence and to provide for certain areas and activities, such as Athletics, which state funds do not, or will not, cover.

For More Information Contact   Wilson Matthews, Asst. Director of Athletics, University of Arkansas, Fayetteville, Ark. 72701

Figure 13.   **University of Arkansas Mailer for Bequest or Major Gift.**

Arizona State University at Tempe sponsors a multifaceted program. One organization is the "Sun Angel Booster" Club. This is a "senior" group and for the most part consists of business firms. The club has a permanent executive secretary and it generates funds through donations. Another group is the "Sun Devil" Club, of which there are some 6000 members. A third approach is personal solicitation of individuals and groups to provide facilities. The athletic director is the main contact for this activity. To date $250,000 was obtained from one contributor to help construct a baseball field. Another large donation built the tennis center. New electronic scoreboards have been obtained for the stadium and fieldhouse from local banks and automobile agencies. A fourth program is calling attention to the various athletic department functions and clubs by printing information on milk cartons, schedule cards, and so on. A special follow-up program is used to contact the purchaser of tickets who is not a member of a booster group.

Washington State University has successfully adapted the team concept for fund-raising activities. This program is spearheaded by an assistant athletic director. Owners and coaches of teams draft players. Teams are assigned to divisions: national, metropolitan, and central. Quotas are determined for each team and for each division. An executive director supervises the fund-raising campaign. Worthwhile gifts and privileges are used as incentives for teams, divisions, and individuals. Approximately $300,000 is realized annually.

Rutgers University at New Brunswick has its "Scarlet R" Club for athletic fund-raising. An executive secretary coordinates and plans the activities. Membership categories range from $25 to $1000 or more. The annual campaign is held each August. The most successful tactic has been to hold a cocktail party at the home of an alumnus. Invitations are extended to prospective new donors and current members. The evening's format includes a welcome from the host, an explanation of the purpose of the evening, introduction of university personnel, and general comments; this is followed by responses from representatives of the university and a question-and-answer session; a very short highlight football film is shown; and the final phase includes a summary of the evening and expression of the readiness to accept pledges or contributions at the moment. The entire scheduled program requires one hour.

Floissant Valley Community College at St. Louis raises funds by the sale of promotional T-shirts. Another activity involves the members of the swimming team that participates in the equivalent of the better known "walkathon." For each lap that is completed, the school receives

```
┌─────────────────────────────────────────────────┐
│                                                   │
│   HERE IS WHAT YOUR GIFT CAN DO                    │
│                                                   │
│   $25,000    Will provide ONE FULL                │
│              Scholarship Perpetually              │
│                                                   │
│   $20,000    Will provide a THREE-QUARTER         │
│              Scholarship Perpetually              │
│                                                   │
│   $15,000    Will provide a ONE-HALF              │
│              Scholarship Perpetually              │
│                                                   │
│   $10,000    Will provide a ONE-QUARTER           │
│              Scholarship Perpetually              │
│                                                   │
│                                                   │
│   YOUR GIFT AS SELECTED FROM THE                  │
│                                                   │
│   ABOVE LIST MAY BE PAID IN ONE                   │
│                                                   │
│   INSTALLMENT OR SPREAD OVER A                    │
│                                                   │
│   5-YEAR PERIOD . . . . . .                       │
│                                                   │
│   WHICHEVER BEST FITS YOUR                        │
│                                                   │
│   INDIVIDUAL TAX SCHEDULE . . . . .               │
│                                                   │
└─────────────────────────────────────────────────┘
```

Figure 13.—(*Continued*)

a certain percentage of the lap-fee; the remainder goes to the National Hall of Fame Swim-a-thon.

Hutchinson Community Junior College at Hutchinson, Kansas, sponsors a ticket sales program whereby purchasers are charged $100 for football and basketball seats. In 1974 there were 112 members in the club that made over $12,000 available to the athletics department.

APPENDIX A
CHECKLIST FOR STAGING A SPORTS CLINIC

	Yes	No	NC*
1 Approval obtained from proper authorities	____	____	____
2 Date selected is free from serious conflicts	____	____	____
3 Reservations for date, site and facilities approved	____	____	____
4 Preliminary meeting of steering committee (comprised of all chairpersons of subcommittees) for purposes of determining objectives, content, and procedures	____	____	____
5 Committee members appointed	____	____	____
6 Committee for "facilities and equipment" convened and arranged for:	____	____	____

____ specific facilities

____ keys to all facility needs, including equipment storage

____ seating

____ lighting

____ air-conditioning

____ public address system (and standby system)

____ emergency action if inclement weather (if outside activity)

____ dressing accommodations for student participants

* NC—Not Certain.

	Yes	No	NC

_____ dressing accommodations for leaders and officials

_____ security measures for all dressing areas

_____ restrooms for participants and spectators

_____ all equipment (balls, goals, watches, etc.)

_____ responsibility for security of equipment

7   Committee for "food and refreshments" convened and arranged for:

_____ drinks: storage and serving

_____ food: storage and serving

_____ collection of money or tickets

_____ cash

_____ cash boxes

_____ complimentary refreshments

8   Committee for "emergencies and first-aid" convened and arranged for:

_____ physician to be present or on call

_____ ambulance to be present or on call

_____ athletic trainer in attendance

_____ emergency supplies on hand

9   Committee for "clean-up" convened and arranged for:

_____ time and place to meet after event

_____ removal and storage of equipment

_____ supervisor

10   Committee for "parking" convened and arranged for:

_____ reserved parking area

_____ time and place for crew to meet for instructions

_____ directional signs

_____ flashlights (if night event)

	Yes	No	NC

_____ security for parking area throughout the event

_____ reserved parking for VIP's, guests, and
media members

11 Committee for "hosts and ushers" convened and
arranged for: _____ _____ _____

_____ time and place for hosts and ushers to
meet for briefing

_____ identification of hosts and ushers

_____ instructions in case of emergencies

12 Committee for "program content, supervision and
control" convened and arranged for: _____ _____ _____

_____ develop master plan

_____ develop master time schedule

_____ selection of public address announcer

_____ guidelines for public address announcer

_____ notification of each performer, instructor, or
participant of the exact time allotted to each

_____ notify persons involved of exact topic or
content of their portion of program

_____ obtain brief biography of each participant

_____ limit introductions of each participant to
specific time

_____ arrange to have as much pertinent information
regarding each participant in the printed
program as possible in order to conserve time
in introductions

_____ arrange for any preparation and distribution
of hand-outs

13 Committee for "promotion and public relations"
convened and arranged for: _____ _____ _____

_____ determine if fees will be charged

_____ prepare all pre-event news releases regarding
event and persons involved

	Yes	No	NC

_____ obtain biographies and pictures of all
persons involved

_____ arrange for press photographer to attend

_____ arrange for television cameraman to attend

_____ send special invitations to members of
the media

_____ prepare and disseminate post-event
news releases

14 Committee for "evaluation" convened and
arranged for:

_____ set time and place for all chairpersons of
each subcommittee to meet to evaluate event

_____ prepare written critique of the event

_____ file critique for future reference

15 Letters of appreciation prepared and mailed as
soon as feasible after the event to all workers and
participants

APPENDIX B
CHECKLIST FOR
STAGING A BANQUET

	Yes	No	NC*
1 Has approval been obtained from proper authorities?	___	___	___
2 Has date been cleared of any serious conflicts?	___	___	___
3 Have reservations been completed for date, site, and facilities?	___	___	___
4 Has chairperson of each subcommittee been appointed?	___	___	___
5 Has initial organizational meeting of steering committee, comprised of all chairpersons of sub-committees, been conducted to discuss objectives, general program, and procedures?	___	___	___
6 Has committee for "facilities and equipment" convened and arranged for:	___	___	___

_____ actual visitation of site, if off campus

_____ has diagram of table and seating arrangements been given to proper persons

_____ has diagram of head table arrangements been given to proper persons

_____ have tables been numbered or otherwise identified

_____ has necessary general lighting been approved

_____ have instructions been received on how to regulate general and special lighting

* NC—Not Certain.

Yes   No   NC

_____ have arrangements been made for special
lighting, e.g., spotlights, etc.

_____ have arrangements been made to control
air-conditioning

_____ has seating and performance area for
entertainment been arranged

_____ has an area been designated for convening
all VIP's and guests before the event

_____ have arrangements been made how and
where to locate the proper person in
case of need

7   Has committee for "food, refreshments, and
serving" convened and arranged for: _____ _____ _____

_____ has the menu been approved as to exact
dishes, quality, quantity, and temperature
at serving

_____ have the exact items for table settings to be
pre-set been determined

_____ have the exact food and drinks to be
pre-set been determined

_____ have arrangements been made as to when
entrees will be served and in what order

_____ have arrangements been made as to when
desserts and drinks will be served and
in what order

_____ have arrangements been made concerning what
should be done to meet requests for
milk, coffee, tea, etc.

_____ have precise instructions been approved as
to when table settings will be cleared,
in what order, and noiselessly as possible

_____ have precise instructions been given about
the policy on serving additional orders,
servings, special requests

	Yes	No	NC

_____ has a written agreement been co-signed by the chairperson of the committee and the manager as to the exact menu, including the quality and quantity, number of dinners guaranteed, and the exact cost per person, including taxes and gratuities

_____ have arrangements been agreed about the manner of billing and payment

8   Has committee for "content, supervision and control" of the program convened and arranged for: _____ _____ _____

_____ has the master of ceremonies been selected

_____ has the master of ceremonies been informed about the specific guests who will be in attendance and provided with a brief biographical sketch of each

_____ has the master of ceremonies been advised of the ages and sex of those who will be present

_____ has a brief biography of the master of ceremonies been obtained

_____ have seating arrangements at the head table been arranged

_____ have placecards been prepared for the head table

_____ has it been decided who will introduce persons seated at the head table, other than speakers, and when

_____ has a brief biography of each person at the head table been provided the person who will make the introductions (other than the main speaker)

_____ has special entertainment been arranged

_____ has the director of the entertainment been advised of when and how much time is allowed for each segment

_____ have the musical selections and other forms of entertainment been approved

Yes   No   NC

_____ has the appropriate person been provided with information pertaining to the director of entertainment and the performers

_____ have arrangements been made to have as much information printed on the banquet program as possible regarding every person who is involved in the program in any way

_____ has the entire program been planned as to content, sequence, and allotted time

_____ has each person who is assigned a segment of the program been advised in writing beforehand as to the exact number of minutes allotted, the precise topic, and the makeup of the audience

_____ has the invocator been selected

_____ will the national anthem be played

_____ will there be a salute to the flag and who will lead it

_____ has each coach been advised that all relevant individual and team information and data will appear on the printed program; that his or her remarks should avoid duplication; and, the total number of minutes allotted is made clear

_____ has it been determined that each student-athlete will stand at his or her chair upon being introduced by name, position, and academic standing

_____ has it been determined if student-athletes will be seated separately or assigned to specific tables

_____ has it been determined if all persons will be issued lapel nametags at the reception desk

_____ has it been determined if student-athletes only will be issued nametags with name, position, and academic year

| | Yes | No | NC |

_____ will all banquet tickets be collected
at the reception desk

_____ will guests be seated at random or will
they be assigned seats; if the latter,
has a plan been devised how they will
be informed of this location

_____ if special awards are to be presented,
have these been ordered, received, and
properly engraved

_____ has it been determined who will present
special awards and what the limits are
on comments regarding the recipient

_____ have arrangements been made to include
as much as possible concerning the
recipients and the award in the printed
program

_____ have special seating arrangements been
made for members of the media

_____ if films will be shown, has it been
determined when this will occur, how
much time is allotted, and who will take
care of technical requirements

9   Has the committee for "promotion and public
relations" convened and arranged for: _____ _____ _____

_____ is the sale of tickets to be conducted

_____ has a master plan been devised for
promotions and public relations

_____ have pre-event news releases been prepared
concerning the general program, specific
segments, and personalities

_____ have pictures of participants been made
available beforehand for use in the
media and printed program

_____ have special invitations been mailed to
members of the media

	Yes	No	NC

_____ have arrangements been made for printing
the program

_____ will pictures be used in the printed
program

_____ if pictures are to be used in the printed
program, who will this include

_____ have arrangements been made for a press
photographer

_____ have arrangements been made to film for
television

_____ have arrangements been made to tape for radio

_____ have supplemental information kits been
prepared for the media representatives

_____ have complimentary tickets, parking passes,
and directions been mailed to members
of the media

_____ have special arrangements been made for
members of the media and guest speakers
and recipients of special awards to
meet at the conclusion of the banquet

10   Has the committee for "parking" convened and
arranged for: _____ _____ _____

_____ have arrangements been made to reserve
parking areas

_____ have arrangements been made to have a
working crew meet at a specific time and
place before the event for briefing purposes

_____ have arrangements been made to properly
identify the crew

_____ have arrangements been made to provide
flashlights to crew if the event is held
after dark

_____ have arrangements been made for necessary
directional signs

                                                    Yes   No   NC

_____ have arrangements been made to reserve a
        special parking area for VIP's and guest
        speakers

_____ have arrangements been made to secure the
        parking area throughout the entire event

_____ have arrangements been made to assist
        automobiles in departing

_____ have arrangements been made in case of
        emergencies

11   Has the committee on "hosts and ushers" con-
vened and arranged for: _____ _____ _____

_____ have specific persons been designated as
        official "hosts"

_____ have "hosts" been provided with proper
        identification

_____ have ushers and usherettes been appointed

_____ have ushers and usherettes been advised
        to meet at a certain time and place prior
        to the event for briefing purposes

_____ have ushers and usherettes been advised
        of action to take in case of an emergency

12   Has the committee for "clean-up" convened and
arranged for their assignments (providing the
event is held on-campus):   _____ _____ _____

_____ has a supervisor been appointed

_____ have members of the crew been appointed

_____ have members of the crew been advised
        where and when to meet after the event

13   Has the committee for "evaluation" convened
and arranged for: _____ _____ _____

_____ has a time and place been determined for
        all chairpersons of the subcommittees to
        meet as soon as feasible after the event for
        purposes of evaluating the event and to make
        recommendations for similar future events

                                          Yes   No   NC

_____ has a record of all information and
       recommendations related to the event
       been filed for future use

14   Have arrangements been made to send letters
of appreciation and commendation to participants
and their superiors:

APPENDIX C
CHECKLIST FOR
STAGING A
CONFERENCE

The following items are typical for staging of a conference, symposium, or other major activity. Use of this check list as a prototype can be helpful in staging events involving many persons or more than one institution.

PRESIDENT OR CHIEF OFFICER

1 Site Selection

_____ Approved by representatives of participating units

_____ Physical appraisal of facilities

2 Financial Arrangements

_____ Conference manager has sufficient working funds

_____ Policy articulated for accounting, expenditures, and other fiscal matters

_____ All income sources have been explored

3 Invitations

_____ Letters of invitation mailed early to special guests

4 Follow-Up

_____ Evaluation meeting scheduled; written reports to be submitted

_____ Letters of appreciation to guests and participants

_____ Letters of commendation to superiors of contributing personnel with copies to those people concerned

_____ Evaluation reports to be made accessible to successors

GENERAL SESSION (President)

1 Program

_____ With Conference Planning Committee determine theme

_____ Seek suggestions for speaker from all concerned

_____ Obtain firm commitment from speaker(s) six months in advance

_____ Obtain minister to give invocation

_____ Obtain key administrative officer to extend welcome

_____ Arrange to have brief remarks from past officer to present official

_____ Prepare introduction of guests, exhibitors en masse, or others

_____ Acknowledge persons responsible for event who will not be introduced for other reasons

_____ Arrange details for any special presentation of award, and so on

2 Invitations

_____ Invitations (accompanied by parking pass and instructions) mailed at least six weeks in advance

_____ Invitations (or accompanying letter) give explicit instructions to guests where to park, entrance to area, obtaining badge, program, dinner ticket, and so on.

_____ Guests are informed of nature of event, makeup of audience, whether or not they will be introduced, and where they are to convene before and after the formal event

3 Physical Arrangements

_____ Mail instructions to Operations Chairperson at least four weeks in advance of event

_____ Arrange to have a "Guest" and "VIP" registration table set up removed from table for general registration

_____ Identify each table; have place card for each guest; upon registration notify each guest of table assignment

_____ Arrange to have corsage for each lady and boutonniere for each man

_____ Ascertain that podium, reading light, public address system, operator of public address system, and other special needs are provided

_____ Approve decorations of head table

4 Follow-Up
_____ Send letters of appreciation to each participant in program

PROGRAM CHAIRPERSON

1 Advance Preparations (four to six months)
_____ Obtain evaluation reports of preceding events

_____ Meet with president to clarify areas of responsibility

_____ Obtain funds for operating expenses

_____ Prepare memoranda for sub-chairpersons; specify responsibilities and procedures for fiscal obligations

2 Other Preparations
_____ Develop an equipment, supply, and facility checklist for each major segment of program

_____ Personally visit site of event, along with sub-chairpersons involved

_____ Meet with Chief Custodian or Facilities Supervisor; review all details; issue written request of equipment, supplies, facilities, and other needs

_____ Assign one person to serve as supervisor of each facility; arrange to have at least one or more persons to serve as messengers for supervisor

_____ Arrange to have directional and informational signs painted in advance and plan for their display

_____ Arrange details so that you are completely free of specific obligations and can direct your efforts as needed

_____ Arrange to have a standby crew (3 to 6 persons) ready to move equipment, furniture, etc.

_____ Prepare an evaluation of the event; submit recommendations for future use

GENERAL SERVICES
_____ Solicit school, university, or community organization to aid

_____ Duties:
   a. Guides:
      To direct persons to proper location
      To monitor entrances and exits

b. Hostesses:
   Be on hand for each session or meeting
   Distribute materials
   Collect materials
   Usher persons to seats or tables
c. Refreshments:
   Serve refreshments at time and manner designated

2 Organization

_____ Several weeks or months before event appoint leader

_____ Several weeks or months before event specify duties, procedures, etc.

_____ Identify persons who will serve as hosts and hostesses

_____ About two weeks before event, hold meeting of all persons to:
   a. Outline duties
   b. Explain the purpose of event
   c. Explain necessity for good public relations
   d. Determine dress or uniform to be worn
   e. Assign specific duties
   f. Identify time and place to convene
   g. Specify emergency procedures

3 Ushers and Usherettes

_____ Specify mode of dress

_____ Set time and place to meet

_____ Assign specific duties

_____ Stress importance of good public relations

_____ Describe emergency procedures

REGISTRATION

1 Registration Area

_____ Exact location of registration tables

_____ Determine number of registration stations; divide for efficiency

_____ Use separate tables for guests, nonpaying attendees, and purchase of special tickets

_____ Operate an "Information Desk" aside from registration tables; provide attendants with adequate factual materials, directories, maps, and programs

_____ Operate a "Message Board"; provide materials to be used; identify board by use of adequate sign

_____ Provide attendants and other knowledgeable persons with "Ask Me" badges or ribbons

_____ Provide adequate signs to denote various registration stations and procedures to be followed

_____ Divide registration process into logical and separate operations; arrange flow of persons to avoid congestion and confusion

_____ Assign only one person to handle financial transactions; if it is necessary to relieve the person charged with financial affairs, plan to have a substitute available who has a separate change box, tickets, etc.

_____ Predetermine the methods of closing registration, selling of tickets, and other activities in this area; plan to convene all persons involved for purposes of submitting final tallies, money, refunds, thumbtacks, pins, Scotch tape, masking tape, etc.

2 Equipment and Supplies

_____ Itemize all equipment and supplies at least four weeks in advance; place reservations where needed. Materials may include: tables, chairs, typewriters, sign holders, blackboard and chalk, public address system, stationery, envelopes, badges, ribbons, pencils, counter checks, receipt books, cash boxes, filing trays, rubber stamps, change, etc.

_____ Place all hand-out materials in large envelope or special container for ease of distribution and convenience to attendee

_____ If possible, prepare nametags in advance; arrange in sequential order

_____ Prepare nametags for guests, speakers, participants, workers, and other predetermined personnel in advance; distribution of these nametags (and hand-out materails) should take place from separate stations

PROMOTIONS

1 Newspaper Coverage

_____ Take pictures of main committee, leaders, and personalities several months ahead of event

_____ Schedule news releases; usually preliminary or initial announcement should occur fuor to six weeks in advance of event

_____ As event approaches, news releases should be more frequent and they should progressively contain more detailed information

2   Radio and Television Coverage

_____ Provide radio and television with special news releases

_____ Provide television with visual materials, including photographs

_____ Arrange to have "live" or "taped" interviews for use by radio and television

3   Publicity

_____ Prepare publicity flyers, posters, pamphlets, and other materials several weeks in advance

_____ Plan the date and method of distribution of various materials

4   Photography

_____ Arrange for taking of photographs or television film several weeks beforehand; plan exact method and procedures to make these results available to media

5   Follow-Up

_____ Prepare materials for media to be used to tell what occurred

_____ Send messages of appreciation to media representatives

MEALS

1   Facility

_____ Obtain written agreement for use of facility

_____ Obtain written agreement, with forfeiture clause, relating to any cause for nonperformance

_____ Provide diagram of table and chair arrangements

_____ Check on lighting, air-conditioning, heating, etc.

_____ Check on interference from external sources, such as machinery noise, traffic, kitchen, etc.

2 Menu and Service

_____ Obtain written agreement pertaining to specific items to be served, size or quantity of portions, quality, etc.

_____ Predetermine table settings, including pre-set salad, butter, rolls, water, etc.

_____ Predetermine serving order; predetermine removal of dishes as to time in program

_____ In addition to primary waiters or waitresses, assign sufficient number of persons to serve liquids, replenish bread and butter, and clear tables

3 Controls

_____ Predetermine time, place, and method of collecting tickets

_____ Predetermine procedure to be followed in case of missing ticket

_____ Predetermine procedures for completing report of tickets sales and disposition of funds

_____ Obtain numbered tickets in advance

_____ Have adequate signs prepared in advance pertaining to location of ticket sales, time of sales, costs, etc.

_____ Have a cash box with adequate change beforehand

BIBLIOGRAPHY

The following is a list of books and periodicals dealing with public relations and fund-raising.

GENERAL

Adams, A. B. *Handbook of Practical Public Relations*. Crowell, 1970.

Bernays, Edward L. *Public Relations*. Rev. ed. University of Oklahoma Press, 1970. Origins and development of public relations. Applications of principles.

Blumenthal, L. R. *The Practice of Public Relations*. Macmillan, 1972.

Budd, J. F. Jr. *Executive's Primer on Public Relations*. Chilton, 1969.

Canfield, B. and F. Moore. *Public Relations: Principles, Cases, Problems*. 6th ed. Irwin, 1973.

Cutlip, Scott M. and Allen H. Center. *Effective Public Relations*. 4th ed. Prentice-Hall, 1971. The most widely used classroom text.

Darrow, R. W., D. J., Forrestal and A. O. Cookman, *Dartnell Public Relations Handbook*. Dartnell Corp., 1968. Practical, comprehensive corporate manual.

Hall, Babette. *Public Relations, Publicity, Promotion*. Washburn, 1970.

Lesly, Philip. *Lesly's Public Relations Handbook*. Prentice-Hall, 1971.

Marston, John E. *The Nature of Public Relations*. McGraw-Hill, 1963. Case studies are included in this text.

Nolte, L. W. *Fundamentals of Public Relations*. Pergamon, 1974.

Roalman, A. R. *Profitable Public Relations*. Dow Jones-Irwin, 1968.

Simon, Raymond, ed. *Perspectives in Public Relations*. University of Oklahoma Press, 1966. Writings of 35 leading public relations practioners.

Stephenson, Howard. *Handbook of Public Relations*. 2nd ed. McGraw-Hill, 1971.

SPECIAL INTEREST

Anderson, Walter G. *Handbook of Business Communications*. Box 243 Lenox Hill Station, New York NY 10021. 1975.

Ayer Public Relations and Publicity Style Book. Ayer Press, West Washington Square, Philadelphia PA 19106. 1974.

Berelson, B. and G. A. Steiner. *Human Behavior: An Inventory of Scientific Findings,* Harcourt, 1967.

Bernays, Edward L. *Biography of an Idea: Memoirs of Public Relations Counsel.* Simon & Schuster, 1965.

Bloomenthal, H. *Promoting Your Cause.* Crowell, 1971.

Boetting, H. M. *Moving Mountains: The Art and Craft of Letting Others See Things Your Way.* Macmillan, 1969.

Drucker, Peter. *Management: Tasks, Responsibilities, Practices.* Harper & Row, 1974.

Donahue, Jody. *Your Career in Public Relations.* Messner, 1967.

Fairman, Milton. *The Practice of Public Relations.* Foundation for Public Relations Research and Education, 845 Third Avenue, New York NY 10002. 1973.

Finkel, C. *How to Plan Meetings.* Bill Communications, 633 Third Avenue, New York NY 10017. 1973.

Golden, H. and K. Hanson. *How to Plan, Produce and Publicize Special Events.* Oceana, 1960.

Gordon, G. N. *Persuasion: Theory and Practice of Manipulative Communication.* Hastings, 1971.

Hayakawa, S. I. *The Use and Misuse of Language.* Premier.

Hill, John W. *The Making of a Public Relations Man.* McKay, 1963.

Jacobs, Herbert. *Practical Publicity: A Handbook for Public and Private Workers.* McGraw-Hill, 1964.

Jones, Gerre L. *How to Market Professional Design Services.* McGraw-Hill, 1974.

Klein, Ted and Fred Danzig. *How to Be Heard: Making the Media Work for You.* Macmillan, 1974.

Kobre, S. *Successful Public Relations for Colleges and Universities.* Hastings, 1974.

Lesly, Philip. *The People Factor: Managing the Human Climate.* Dow Jones-Irwin, 1974.

Liebert, E. and B. Sheldon. *Handbook of Special Events for Nonprofit Organizations.* Association Press, 1972.

Lerbinger, Otto. *Designs for Persuasive Communications.* Prentice-Hall, 1972.

PRSA. *Careers in Public Relations.* 1974.

Robinson, Edward J. *Communications and Public Relations.* Merrill, 1966.

Robinson, Edward J. *Public Relations and Survey Research.* Irvington, 1969.

Samstag, N. *Persuasion for Profit.* University of Oklahoma Press, 1958.

Seymour, H. J. *Designs for Fund Raising.* McGraw-Hill, 1966.

Simon, Morton J. *Public Relations Law.* 1969. Available from PRSA.

Stahr, John. *Write to the Point: A Byoir Style for Press Releases.* Macmillan, 1969.

Strunk, William Jr. and E. B. White. *Elements of Style.* Macmillan.

Unruh, A. and R. Willier. *Public Relations for Schools.* Fearon, 1974.

Weiner, Richard. *Professional's Guide to Publicity.* Richard Weiner Inc. 888 Seventh Avenue, New York NY 10019. 1975.

DIRECTORIES/BIBLIOGRAPHIES

Anderson, Walter. *The Complete Editor from A to Z.* Box 243 Lenox Hill Station, New York NY 10021. 1974. Bibliography of articles appearing in company publications (house organs), indexed under 150 subject headings; articles summarized.

Ayer Directory of Newspapers, Magazines, Trade Publications. Ayer Press, West Washington Square, Philadelphia PA 19106. Annual.

Bacon's International Publicity Checker. Bacon's Publishing Co. 14 E. Jackson Blvd. Chicago IL 60604. 1975; also *Bacon's Publicity Checker: Magazines/Newspapers.* Annual.

California Publicity Outlets. 3807 Wilshire Blvd. Los Angeles CA 90010.

Editor & Publisher International Yearbook. 850 Third Avenue, New York NY 10022.

Fortune Double 500 Directory. Fortune Directories, 541 N. Fairbanks Court, Chicago IL 60611.

Gebbie House Magazine Directory. National Research Bureau, 424 N. Third Street, Burlington IA 52601. 1974.

Gebbie Press All-In-One Directory. Box 1000, New Paltz NY 12561.

Hudson's Washington News Media Contacts Directory. Hudson's Directory, 2814 Pennsylvania Avenue NW, Washington DC 20007.

Midwest Media Directory. 176 W. Adams Street, Chicago IL 60690

New York Publicity Outlets. Washington Depot, CT 06794.

News Bureaus of the U.S. Richard Weiner Inc. 888 Seventh Avenue, New York NY 10019.

Norton, Alice. *Public Relations: Guide to Information Sources.* Gale Research, Book Tower, Detroit MI 48226. 1970.

Northwest Handbook. Box 9304 Seattle WA 98109.

O'Dwyer's Directory of Public Relations Firms. J. R. O'Dwyer Co. 271 Madison Avenue, New York NY 10016.

PR Blue Book, 4th ed. PR Publishing Co., Meriden NH 03770. 1973. Directory of public relations firms edited by Robert L. Barbour.

Public Relations: A Comprehensive Bibliography 1964–72. Compiled by
   Robert L. Bishop. Foundation for Public Relations Research and Educa-
   tion, 845 Third Avenue, New York NY 10022.
A Public Relations Bibliography (1900s–1963). Compiled by Scott M. Cutlip.
   2nd ed. 1965. Available from Public Relations Society of America.
Public Relations Register. Public Relations Society of America membership
   directory.
Weiner, Richard. *Professional's Guide to Public Relations Services.* Prentice-
   Hall, 1971.

PERIODICALS
Channels. National Public Relations Council of Health & Welfare Services,
   815 Second Avenue, New York NY 10017. Twenty issues yearly.
*Editor's Newsletter: News of Trends and Techniques in Business Communica-
   tions.* Box 243, Lenox Hill Station, New York NY 10021. Monthly.
International Public Relations Review. Box 4304, Honolulu HI 98612.
   Monthly.
Jack O'Dwyer's Newsletter. 271 Madison Avenue, New York NY 10016.
   Weekly.
PR Aids' Party Line: Placement Opportunities in All Media. 221 Park
   Avenue South, New York NY 10003. Weekly.
PR Reporter. PR Publishing Co., Meriden NH 03770. Weekly.
Practical Public Relations. 31 Gibbs Street, Rochester NY 14607. Twice
   monthly.
Public Relations Journal. PRSA, 845 Third Avenue, New York NY 10022.
   Monthly.
Public Relations News. 127 East 80th Street, New York NY 10021. Weekly.
Public Relations Quarterly. 221 Park Avenue South, New York NY 10003.

Index

Associated Press (AP), 107
Athletic relations, 73–79
    athletic director:
        responsibilities of, 77–78
        role of, 76
    authorization of, 74
    community college, programs for, 78–79
    director of sports information, 74–75
    handbook, staff, 76–77
    objectives, public relations, 77
    practitioner:
        public relations, 75–76
        selection of, 75
    public relations, reliance on, 73
    uniqueness of, 74–75

Barnun, Phineas T., 9

Cantril, Hadley, 21
Center, Allen H., 22, 23, 43, 100
Central Press Association, 108
Checklists (selected), 240–258
    staging a banquet, 244–251
    staging a conference, 252–258
    staging a sports clinic, 240–243

Communications:
    education institutions, 64–72
        alumni, 72
        assessment, of, 68–69
        citizen groups, 65–66
        external, 65
        higher education, 70–71
        information, importance of dissemination,
            of, 70
        ingredients of, 64–65
        internal, 65
        methods of receiving, 67
        opinion leaders, 65
        school board, 69
        school publications, 67–68
        students, 69–70, 71–72
    tools of, 109–118
        alumni groups, 115–116
        banquets, 115
        board of athletics, 116
        campus publications, 111
        campus tours and visitations, 114
        communications center, public relations
            office as a, 110
        community affairs, 116

controlled tools, 110–118
club awards, 117
displays and exhibits, 114
essay contests, 115
faculty affairs, 117
faculty-student sports contests, 116–117
grapevine, 113
handbooks and manuals, 111
information racks, 112
institutional advertising, 112
invitations to parents, 117
letters and bulletins, 111–112
letter writing, 117–118
motion pictures and slide films, 113
nature of, 109
open house, 116
publications, distribution of, 117
photographer's day, 115
posters, 112
pioneer's day, 116
public address system, 113
public meetings, 112–113
senior citizens, 116
speaker's bureau, 113
staged events, 114–115
student liason, 115
television clips, 113–114
tributes to support staff, 117
Communications process:
evaluation of, 68–69
academic profile, maintenance of, 68
advisory board or committee, use of, 69
affiliated groups, promote discussions by, 69
exit interviews, use of, 69
face-to-face relationships, use of, 69
formal instruments, use of, 68
interviews, use of, 68
major publics, reach all, 69
media, analysis of, 68
school board candidates, evaluate platforms of, 68
school bonds, evaluate cause for success or
failure of, 68
telephone calls and letters, record of, 68
Cultip, Scott M., 22, 23, 43, 100

Data, sources and needs, 28
instruments, use of approved, 28

Editor and Publisher Yearbook, 108

Education, 58–71
analysis of voting, 58–59
citizen groups, 65–67
opposition to, 61–62
public apathy, 58–59
public relations, 71
Engstrom, Yvonne, 92

Fund-raising, 171–182
appeals, psychological, 183
athletic programs, 172
attitude, importance of proper, 184
bequests, matching of, 209–210
cause, importance of a good, 176
collections, differences from fund-drives,
181–182
corporation, accounting requirements of a,
207–208
operating as a, 204–205
starting a, 205–207
director:
responsibilities of a, 202–203
selecting of a, 202
failures, causes of, 185–187
finances, choices of athletic program, 172–
173
financial plan, need for a, 184
funds, sources of, 177
gift table, preparation of a, 185
giving:
need to ask for, 182–183
patterns of, 183
grants, matching, 209–210
ideas of, 213–214
interrelationships of public relations,
promotions and fund-raising, 173
institutions, educational, 171–172
leaders, selection and development of, 203
news releases, typical events for, 180–181
principles of, 174, 213–214
principles and practices, 187–201
accounting fund, 198
agenda, 190
alibis, 195
attendance, successful, 193
failures, 199
fund-drive, period of, 199
gifts, solicitation of large, 195
leadership, 189
literature, 195–196

mailing, mass, 196–198
materials, campaign, 188
meetings, 189–190
  atmosphere of, 195
  conduct of, 192
  follow-up of a, 192
  schedule of, 191
  visual aids for, 192
office, campaign, 187
panacea substitutions, 198–199
personal contact, 194
post-campaign:
  actions during, 200–201
  planning during, 198
prospects, 187–188
publicity, 195
solicitations, methods of, 193–194
solicitors, assignment of, 194
visual aids, 188–189
workers, 189
  briefing of, 193
professional, 173–174
prospects:
  cataloguing of, 184–185
  identification of, 182
psychological involvement, 177–179
publicity, 179–180
regulations, government, 208–209
strategies of, 173–174
students, preparing for membership of,
  210–211
tactics of, 173–174
tax deductions, use of, 184
tax exemptions, 181
team concept, 211–213
techniques of, 173–174
time length, campaign, 179
United States, fund-raising in the, 171
workers, productive, 177
Fund-raising activities:
by colleges and universities, 215–240
  examples of successful programs, 215–
    240
    Arizona State University, 238
    Boise State University, 219–220
    Boston College, 227–228
    Clemson University, 230
    Drake University, 217
    Duke University, 223
    East Carolina University, 217

Floissant Valley Community College,
  238–239
Hutchinson Community Junior College,
  239
Indiana University, 232–233
Kansas State University, 222
Kent State University, 217
Mississippi State University, 232
Ohio University, 236
Purdue University, 220
Rice University, 230–231
Rutgers University, 238
South Dakota State University, 227
Texas Christian University, 232
University of Alabama, 234–235
University of Arkansas, 235
University of California at Irvine, 236
University of Houston, 232
University of Illinois, 229
University of Miami, 236
University of Minnesota, 235–236
University of Nevada at Reno, 216
University of Northern Iowa, 228–229
University of Oklahoma, 233–234
University of Utah, 219
University of Virginia, 236
University of Wisconsin at Milwaukee,
  223–224
Utah State University, 229
Vanderbilt University, 230
Wake Forest University, 217–218
Washington State University, 238
uniqueness, recognition of need for,
  215–216

King's Feature Services, 108
Kovalick, Jerome G., 67

McNaught's, 108

National Collegiate Athletic Association, 74
News, 91–97
  competition, 91
  mass media, use of, 92
  media, needs of the, 94
  news, sources of, 95–97
  Newspapers, 92
  radio, 92–93
  radio and television, use of, 94
  television, 92–93

schools, interest in, 95
Newsom, Earl, 23
Newspaper Enterprise Association (NEA),
    108

Opinion research, 29–33
  evaluation, opinion, 29
  interviews, in-depth, 33
  media, analysis of, 33
  opinion, forces shaping, 29
  panel, use of a, 33
  questionnaire, use of a mailed, 33
  situation, assessment of current, 29
  survey, use of cross-section, 33
  testing, before and after, 29

Physical education public relations, 80–82
  methods of conducting, 81–82
  needs, 80–81
  strategy for developing a program of,
    81–82
Promotional activities for athletics:
  by colleges and universities, 153
    Arizona State University, 166
    Bellevue Community College, 166
    Boise State University, 160
    Boston College, 166
    Clemson University, 162
    Drake University, 156
    East Carolina University, 157–158
    Kansas State University, 161
    Kent State University, 157
    Lehigh University, 161
    McNeese State University, 160
    Mt. Hood Community College, 166
    Northeast Louisiana State University, 154
    Ohio University, 165
    Princeton University, 160–161
    Rice University, 163
    Rutgers University, 166
    South Dakota State University, 162
    Temple University, 161
    Texas Christian University, 163
    University of Arkansas, 164
    University of California at Irvine, 154
    University of Illinois, 154
    University of Iowa, 164
    University of Miami, 164–165
    University of Minnesota, 164
    University of Pacific, 164

    University of Utah, 159–160
    University of Virginia, 165
    University of Wisconsin at Milwaukee, 161
    Utah State University, 162
    Vanderbilt University, 162
    Wake Forest University, 158–159
    Washington State University, 166
Publicity, 98–108
  complaints, media, 101
  effect, 99
  ethnic publications, 100
  news outlets, references of, 100
  newspapers, 99–100
  news releases:
    causes for rejection of, 107
    procedures for, 103–105
    remedies for rejected, 107
  national and international coverage, 107–108
  objectives of, 98–99
  press conferences, 105–106
  principles, publicity and media relations,
    101–103
  practitioner, public relations, 101
  publicity, a tool of public relations, 108
  radio, requirements for, 106–107
  syndicates, uses of news, 108
Public opinion, 19–25
  attitude change, 19–20
  attitudes and opinions, 19
  communications, 20–21
  laws, 21–22
  opinion change, principles of, 23–24
  persuasion, principles of, 22–23
  publics, 19
  public relations, role of, 24–25
Public relations:
  for coach and teacher, 124–134
    game officials, 127
    guidelines, 125
    home contests, 126 ·
    on-campus, public relations, 130–131
    parents, 127–128
    parent conferences, 132–134
    parent relationships, 132–134
    personal gain, avoid seeking of, 126
    personal assets, 129–130
    practices, desirable personal, 125–126
    promotional activities, 129
    promotions, club and group, 130
    publications, 131–132

public relations, importance of personal,
   124–125
radio, 126–127
team banquets, 129
telephone, use of, 131
conduct of, 26–50
   advisory boards or panels, use of, 31–32
   communications, 38–44
      barriers, 41
      evaluation, 43–44
      importance, 38–39
      media, 40–41
      mental processes, 39–40
      leaders, 39
      publicity, 42
      semantics, 43
      symbols, 41–42
   planning, public relations depends upon,
      33–38
      crises, planning for, 37–38
      criteria, good planning, 36
      responsibilities, planning requires
         assignment of, 36
      timing, planning entails, 37
      written plan, essential to have a, 35
   power structure, identify the, 31
   process, analysis of the public relations,
      27
   public leaders, identification of, 30–31
   public opinion, assessment of, 32–33
   research, public relations and publicity
      uses of, 27
external, 51–55
   college publics:
      attitudes of, 52
      typical structure of, 53
      typical sub-groups of, 53–54
   external public relations, nature of, 51–
      52
   publics, attitudes of, 52
general, 3–5
   definition:
      commonly accepted, 4–5
      confusion with, 3–4
   need, justification of, 5–6
history of, 7–23
   Catholic Church, 8
   Greek philosophers, 7
   Roman leaders, 8
   United States, 8–17

applications, modern public relations,
   12–13
American Medical Association, 11
athletics, 15
attainment as a profession, 13–14
big business, 11
corporations, 10
Civil War, 9–10
education, 15
physical education, 15
politics, 8–10
press-agentry, 9
publicity bureaus, development of,
   12–13
public relations, coining of the term,
   11–12
society, meeting demands of, 16–17
internal, 47–50
   college publics, 50
   communications, need for two-way, 48–49
   foundation, internal public relations as a,
      48
   internal public relations, importance of,
      of, 49
   needs, internal public relations
      acknowledges, 47–48
and today's society, 16–17
   acceptance, 16
   dependency, 16
   management function, 16
   molding of public opinion, 17
   societal changes, 16
Public relations activities:
   for athletics by colleges, 135–143
      Arizona State University, 142
      Boise State University, 137
      Clemson University, 140
      Drake University, 136
      East Carolina University, 136
      Kansas State University, 138–139
      Kent State University, 136
      McNeese State University, 138
      Montana State University, 137
      Mt. Hood Community College, 143
      Ohio University, 141
      Purdue University, 137–138
      Rice University, 140
      Rutgers University, 142–143
      South Dakota State University, 139
      University of California at Irvine, 135

University of Houston, 140
University of Illinois, 139
University of Iowa, 141
University of Miami, 141
University of Minnesota, 141
University of Nebraska, 140–141
University of North Carolina, 139
University of Utah, 137
University of Virginia, 141–142
Utah State University, 139
Vanderbilt University, 139–140
Wake Forest University, 136–137
Washington State University, 142
for athletics by high schools, 143–144
for physical education in colleges and
    schools, 145–150
needs, 145–146
programs, typical successful, 147–150
public relations, assignment of responsi-
    bilities for, 146
trends, physical education requirement,
    146
Public Relations News, 4
Public relations practitioner, 83–90
administrator's support, 84
athletic director, 89
budget, public relations, 87–88
internal relations, importance of, 83
obligations, 85–86
office location, 89
past, importance of knowing the, 89–90
personal attitude, 88
research, importance of, 86–87
responsibilities, 87
staff, relationships with, 84–85
staff, understanding of, 88–89
Public relations process, 27
Publics, special, 50–55
college internal, 50
college, external, 54–55
college sub-groups, 53

Public speaking, 119–123
cliches, use of, 120
content, importance of, 120
importance, 119–120
information file, use of a, 121
opportunities, seeking of, 122–123
preparation, importance of, 120
presentation, importance of, 121–122

Radio, 92–95, 106–107

School bonds, 56–63
athletic programs, 56, 62–63
campaign strategy, 59–60
competition, 60
failures, 57
opposition, 60–61
overreaction to failures, 57–58
physical education, 62–63
public relations, 62
supporters, 58–59
voting patterns, 56
Senior citizens, 59
Sports information director, 74–75
Sumption, Merle R., 94

Television, 92–94

United Features, 108
United Press International (UPI), 107
United States intercollegiate and inter-
    scholastic athletic programs, iii-iv
entertainment, competition for, iv
needs, public relations, promotions and
    fund-raising, iv
philosophical justifications, iv
uniqueness, v
Unruh, Adolph, 58–59

Willier, Robert A. ,58–59